A Life for Mankind

The Biography of Hugh Joseph Schonfield

Stephen A. Engelking

Published by the Hugh & Hélène Schonfield World Service Trust
27 Delancey Street London NW1 7RX
Johannesstrasse 12 D-78609 Tuningen Germany
www.schonfield.org
Copyright © 2015 Stephen A. Engelking
ISBN 9781999869106

Table of Contents

Acknowledgements	7
Introduction	9
Roots	13
The Early Years	19
Christian times	41
The Servant-Nation Movement	69
The Work of the War Years Continues	77
The Commonwealth	85
Fame Starts to Spread	101
The Passover Plot Era	105
Popular Culture	109
Increasing Affluence	115
The Politics of God	121
Travels	129
The Delights of Hollywood	133
Tragedy Strikes	141
Life Must Go On	147
The Travels Continue	149
Of Jews and Christians	153
Jesus: The Evidence	159
The Final Break?	163
Not for Want of Trying	173
Time is Running Out	177
And My Eyes Shall See Jerusalem Once More	187
Life Beyond Death	193
Some Last Thoughts	201
Postscript	205
Appendix	209
INDEX	221

List of Illustrations

Wedding Invitation..16
Maj. William Schonfield..21
The Schonfield Brothers (Hugh on the right)..24
Linton House Certificate...26
Hugh Aged 16...32
Front page of tract which included the text below..................................35
Fiat Lux—A Postcard by Hugh J. Schonfield...39
Bessie..43
Certificate from Glasgow University...46
Sir Leon Levison...48
IHCA Certificate...49
Abstract Drawing by Hugh J. Schonfield...53
The 1928 IHCA Conference..54
Cigarettes..57
Hadleigh Castle Essex—Water Painting by Hugh Schonfield...............58
Design for a Palestine Stamp by Hugh J. Schonfield............................63
A View of Goose Green Farm—Hugh J. Schonfield............................67
A Service Nation Movement Demonstration...69
Goose Green Farm by Hugh J. Schonfield..70
Invitation to the Play "Hadassah"...72
Inscription written in the front of the Bible given to Hugh by his colleagues.81
Hugh signs the constitution of the Republic..91
"Lyons" A Design Study by Hugh J. Schonfield...................................93
Prospect Cottage...99
Hugh and Hélène..111
Willi Haller..112
A Design by Hugh J. Schonfield..116
House Salvatore in Malta..117
Abstract Design by Hugh J. Schonfield...122
Mondcivitan Community School..123
Group Picture...125
Hélène in a serious moment...143
Card for Parcels to Germany..145
Sir Anthony Brooke..181
CND Peace Symbol..196

Acknowledgements

It is not possible to reconstruct a life without the help and understanding of others. This book has been no exception. My thanks go particularly to Hugh Schonfield's daughter Audrey who gave me encouragement and snippets of information from her own and her mother's memories of her father. Hugh's grandson Barry has also been a great support and encouragement.

My wife and life companion Sandra Engelking has given me the time and space to do this work and provided tips and jogged my memory from time to time.

Charlyne Valensin has also helped by sorting archive material and pointing out things of importance in Hugh's thinking.

Stephen A. Engelking, January 2015.

Introduction

This book is about one of the most fascinating and amazing personalities of the 20th Century. He became a source of inspiration of the thinking of such celebrities as John Lennon. For some, the ideas he proposed were challenging and revealing, whilst others found them to be preposterous or even ridiculous. For certain groups they were even blasphemous and apparently worthy of death.

Apart from this obviously popular side to his work, it may be less known that he was also historian of the Suez Canal and was instrumental behind the scenes in a number of high level negotiations in the Middle East. So apart from being one of the most erudite historians of New Testament times, he was politically active in a most novel way. His official work in the Republic which he had caused to come to fruition would lead him to make proposals to governments, many of which would be integrated into final agreements. It has been suggested, for example, that his ideas played a role in the passing of the Test Ban Treaty.

He was a prodigious and skilled writer and researcher and was always on the look out for uncovering the truth and discovering novel interpretations.

It was these efforts and particularly his work for world peace which in fact caused him to be nominated for the Nobel Peace Prize. He fought inexhaustibly for this cause to his last dying breath, convinced that there was an eternal plan for a servant people to arise as the only lasting way of saving man from seemingly inevitable disaster..

He was also the first (and I think) only Jew to have translated the New Testament into English. I might add that this rendering is also one of the most informative, beautiful and understandable versions.

Thus in writing this biography, I was dealing with a personality so multifarious that it was necessary to try to reconstruct both Schonfield's life and character and how he was driven by a strong mission and destiny if I was going to enable the reader to gain an understanding of the life work of this great visionary.

I met Hugh Schonfield by a series of coincidences which finally led me to pick up a book in the Surrey University Library in Guildford in 1972 entitled *The Politics of God*. I was studying to become a teacher majoring in Religious Studies at the Surrey outpost of the London University at the time. The title of the book gripped me and I felt compelled to read it.

That evening, when I got home, I opened the book and started to read. I could not put it down. The theme and the writing style were so compelling and felt so relevant for me that I stayed up the whole night until I had finished it. It seemed that all my experiences through Christianity, the disillusionment with the churches and the feeling of wanting to belong to God's people were summed up in this book.

The next morning I described my feelings resulting from reading the book to my wife and we both determined to drive to London to seek out this "Nation" at its headquarters in Delancey Street, Camden Town.

I guess what met our eyes would have discouraged most people—a small office, manned by a casually dressed young man, heaps of papers and nothing of what one would expect to find in the consulate of a nation. But the vision as expressed in Hugh Schonfield's book seemed of such import that we felt compelled to get involved so we signed up and became citizens on the spot.

It did not take long and we became heartily involved. Shortly afterwards the secretary resigned and we encouraged my step-brother Peter Deed to take up the vacant position. Soon the three of us were re-organising and printing magazines, running shops, building a school and generally trying to bring life into the thing.

Soon we met with Hugh and a friendship developed between us. It was invigorating for me to be able to discuss biblical themes with such a scholar and I finally wrote my thesis on the Jewish understandings of Jesus.

My wife and I felt a considerable parallel to Hugh and Hélène—we too had been bound to each other since teenagers and both Hugh and I had found supportive and loving life partners. I also share Hugh's appreciation and respect for women which has come out of our common personal experience.

Hugh had once intimated that he felt that I was one of the few persons who really understood his ideas but it was in my retirement years, long after Hugh and Hélène had passed away, that I was able and decided to try and do what was within my power for the Schonfield legacy. In his lifetime, Hugh had appointed me and Peter as trustees of the Hugh and Hélène Schonfield World Service Trust and under this banner I started work on re-publishing Hugh Schonfield's books and essays which had gone out of print so that they could be made available to interested readers.

As this work progressed, I increasingly became aware of the need to investigate the reasons behind why such a scholar as Schonfield should come up with the idea of establishing a biblical Servant-Nation with an interpretation for modern times. Thus the idea of writing a biography was born.

The Trust was in possession of considerable archive material from the Mondcivitan Republic but this would not be sufficient to create the whole picture of a life. It was then that after making contact with Hugh's grandson Barry, that I was kindly given access to the archives in family possession which were about to be transported to Boston University for safe keeping. Whilst reading a draft copy of this book, Barry reminded me of Hugh's humorous side. I affectionately remember him cracking a joke and then laughing about it himself in such a way that those listening could not be sure they were laughing at the joke or at his infectious laughter! Such moments of a personality are difficult to reproduce in such a book but, despite his serious view of life, Hugh was a jovial, lively and dynamic character.

Although Hugh Schonfield did not actually write an autobiography, some material is to be found in the archives which show that he made an attempt to start one and which I have been able to make use of. We are also fortunate in having a number of autobiographical snippets from notes and from the introductory passages in his books and I have included such autobiographical texts in their original wherever possible. He had a particular style of writing which anyway would be hard to improve on!

Thus this massive amount of material needed to be sifted through, pertinent biographical material extracted and all put into some logical order. It soon became apparent what a multifarious life I was about to investigate. I was also fortunate to receive the support of Hugh's one living daughter Audrey who kindly relayed to me lots of family anecdotes and pieces of information. I am very grateful to the Schonfield family for all the support they have given and the critical and helpful feedback they have provided during the years spent preparing this work.

I made several false starts to the book but I finally decided that, in order for it to be of interest to the general reader, I would refrain from including an exhausting analysis of the Schonfield literature, which would be better handled specifically by others but, keeping it concise, rather to try and trace the development of his thinking as a child of his times in the context of history. I realised that this was Hugh's approach to Jesus and history in general. I think it is not unfair to say that hardly any scholar has done more to make the Jesus of history understandable and come alive in the context of his times than our subject person.

Therefore the reader will find reports of events in history, which I feel would have been of interest to Schonfield at the time or which I feel were relevant to his work, interwoven into the narrative. These items should not be considered as being of particular academic value in their own right but are purely an attempt to put the story into a timeline. The main source for this has been the online encyclopedia Wikipedia and the interested reader will be able to verify and deepen any interest in those events himself.

Thus this book attempts to be a brief account of the very full life of a man who was not only an accomplished biblical scholar and historian but also a philosopher in the truest meaning of the word; a man with a mission and the founder of a nation. It is rewarding to know that, making use of modern media, the search for an expression of this dream still continues to this day. May it one day come to pass that humankind finds the way to peace.

Roots

Hugh Joseph Schonfield was born on the 17th May 1901 in 52 Ladbroke Grove as the second child of Major William Schonfield, listed as an Iron Merchant on Hugh's birth certificate, and wife Florence May née Joseph. Father William was actually born as William Schoenfeld (Schönfeld). Hugh's parents had married on the 28th September 1898 in the New West End Synagogue in St. Petersburgh Place, Bayswater, London which had only been completed in 1879 at a time when the Jewish community in London's West End were beginning to feel more secure[1]. At that time William Schonfield was a captain in the British Army. The duties of Best Man were carried out by his brother Gustav. His mother attended the wedding but his father had died in the meantime. A newspaper article reporting the wedding paid a lot of detailed attention to the attire of those partaking. The report of William's wedding later reports that their page, William's nephew Leo Michaelis, was dressed in Highland costume which demonstrates a close integration into Scottish culture. William and his wife spent their honeymoon at the Italian Lakes which altogether gives a picture of a somewhat affluent family.

To allow the reader to gain the impression of the society affair this was, this article in the *Jewish Chronicle* (date unknown) should be of assistance:

> Wedding at the New West End Synagogue.— A very charming and picturesque wedding took place at the New West End Synagogue, St. Petersburgh Place, on Wednesday the 28th ult., when Captain William Schoenfeld, B.S.O., second son of Mrs. Charlotte Schoenfeld, and the late Herrman Schoenfeld of Glasgow, was married to Miss Florence May Joseph, eldest daughter of Mr. and Mrs. Lionel B. Joseph of "Brightlands," Pembridge Villas, W. The officiating clergy were the Revs. S. Singer and J. L. Geffen.
>
> There was a full choral service, and the synagogue was exquisitely decorated with flowers. Mr. L. B. Joseph gave his daughter away, and Mr. Gustav Schoenfeld. brother of the bridegroom, fulfilled the duties of "best man." The bride was charmingly attired in a rich white brocaded satin with full Court train of satin duchesse and trimmed with orange blossom, and veil. Her bouquet was of choice white exotics, and she wore a diamond heart-shaped locket and chain, the gifts of the bridegroom. There were four bridesmaids, the Misses Cecile Joseph, sister of the bride, Dora Davis, Effie Joseph, and Dora Sommerfeld.
>
> They were most tastefully dressed in white poplin silk, trimmed with Valenciennes lace and fichus, and wore picture hats with ostrich feathers. They carried shower trail bouquets, and wore, as gifts of the bridegroom, pretty lover's knot brooches of gold and pearls. The little page. Master Leo Michaelis, nephew of the bridegroom, was dressed in Highland costume. Mrs. Joseph, mother, of the bride, was exquisitely gowned in a rich silver-grey brocade, trimmed in embroidered velvet and turquoise blue. After the ceremony, a numerously attended reception was held at "Bright-

---

[1] "Most official forms of anti-Jewish discrimination had been lifted. There were about 46,000 Jews in the UK, before the huge influx started by the anti-Semitic riots in Russia in the 1880s. It was 20 years since the law began allowing practising Jews to become MPs, an anglicised Jew, Benjamin Disraeli, was Prime Minister, and most of London's congregations were joined under the United Synagogue." (McSmith) in *The New West End Synagogue* http://www.victorianweb.org/art/architecture/audsley/1.html. Accessed 9.11.2013.

lands," and later in the afternoon Captain and Mrs. William Schoenfeld left for the Italian lakes.

The year of Hugh Schonfield's birth was an auspicious one. In fact, on the very day some parts of the world had experienced a total solar eclipse. We have to imagine a world which had just broken into a new century and there was a storm of technical and industrial innovation breaking upon the world. It was the year the famous Queen Victoria died at the age of 81 after reigning for some 63 years over the biggest empire the world had ever known. Her death would mark the beginning of changes in society and open the doors to what may be called 'the Modern Age'. She was succeeded by her son Edward VII. In the same year there was a census in the United Kingdom which showed the all-time highest number of people employed in manufacturing. The agricultural society was becoming history. At the same time there were student riots in St. Petersburg and Moscow and the first Australian Parliament opened in Melbourne. It also became public knowledge that in 45 Boer concentration camps genocide had been committed and over 26,000 men, women and children had died.

That year Theodore Roosevelt became president of the USA and the first Nobel Prize ceremony was held. Hugh would later be nominated for the Nobel Peace Prize but who could have imagined that at his birth? The technology which Hugh would later use was also making big leaps with Marconi transmitting the first trans-Atlantic radio signal.

Hugh's father William was born in 1869 in Dirschau (Tczew) Prussia, a town on the Vistual River in Eastern Pomerania, now in Poland, as the second son of Hermann and Charlotte (née Henschel) Schoenfeld of Posen, which was then part of Prussia and today is in Poland. They had married three weeks after the 6th June 1853 in a marriage contract drawn up in Nackel, Germany, thereafter moving to Schubin (today Szubin, Poland). Charlotte was 21 and Hermann was 30. Her father was the local master baker Henschel Arndt in Nackel. Her mother was Hannchen née David. Hermann was the Cantor, lived in Schubin and was the son of Wolf Schoenfeld and Ester née Ettig-Schoenfeldchen from Grätz (today Grodzisk Wielkopolski in Poland). The documentation states that "those present were of the Mosaic Religion and this implies minority of Charlotte Henschel with the therefore ensuing restriction of ability to negotiate". It was thus necessary, at that time, for the father to sign the required marriage documents. Hermann was described as "the son of the still-living man of private means". In those days it was expected that the wife would bring a dowry into the marriage, which in this case was some five hundred Thaler as well as gold and silver objects, furniture (including "one servant's bedstead, kitchen utensils, bedding, clothing, two wall pictures and a violin"). Hermann later moved to Glasgow in Scotland, presumably with his son and daughter-in-law.

It is hard for us to imagine the world into which William was born. There had been serious restrictions imposed on Jews living in that part of Prussia but after the establishment of the North German Confederation with the law of July 3, 1869, all remaining statutory restrictions were abolished. Some of the restrictions applied to marriage whereby only a certain number of marriages were allowed each year and the family would have to demonstrate that it had sufficient wealth etc. By 1871, Dirschau had been fully incorporated into the German Empire. The town had been occupied by Polish troops in the Napoleonic invasion at the beginning of the 19th century and became part of Prussia in 1815. In 1742, it was part of Silesia which had been seized by King Frederick the Great of Prussia in the War of the Austrian Succession, becoming the Prussian Province of

Silesia[2]. I find it fascinating to think that it was in fact an ancestor of mine, Frederick the Great's Privy Councillor Simon Heinrich Sack, who had been responsible for clarifying property ownership in Silesia after the Prussian annexation and who would certainly have had many dealings with such Jewish families and who knows, perhaps even the ancestors of the Schonfields!

At this time, we find that the whole world was in a process of change and turmoil, marked by such events as the first law giving women the right to vote being passed in Wyoming in that year and Leo Tolstoy's novel War and Peace being published. Tolstoy's work was to influence the thinking of such peace leaders as Mohandas Gandhi. This was to become relevant for William's son Hugh in his later life.

William's wife Florence was the eldest daughter of Mr. and Mrs. Lionel B. Joseph. Lionel (1826-1905). She was also the great-great-grand-daughter of Barnet Levy, whose daughter Judith married Lyon Joseph. The writer conjectures that they may have been related to Nathan Solomon Joseph who lived from 1834-1909 and who was a philanthropist, social reformer, architect and Jewish communal leader. It is worth noting in this context that he collaborated in the design of the New West End Synagogue. In any case, the family, as Hugh describes himself, were very much part of the Jewish aristocracy and known for being somewhat unconventional[3].

William was probably the first Jew to join the London Scottish Regiment in 1892[4] and he became Lance-Corporal in his second year of service. He was promoted to Major in 1909 and gained high commendation for his training scheme for specialists. He retired from the army in 1911 and joined the Territorial Force Reserve. He was appointed to command a Battalion Headquarters Depot at the beginning of the First World War and continued to work in administration and training until 1919 when he was demobilized. He became Vice-President of the Jewish Ex-Servicemen's Legion and travelled to Palestine on their behalf. He also acted in his lifetime as the Honorary Treasurer of the Princess Elizabeth Hospital for Children and "Knew Her Majesty personally when she was the Princess of Wales"[5]. As mentioned later, he was also responsible for recruiting for the Jewish Battalion.

William was also a member of the committee of the Jewish Religious Union and honorary president of the Southend and Westcliff Zionist Association, whose meetings he would attend with his son Hugh[6].

It is difficult to exactly reconstruct Hugh's relationship to his father but it was undoubtedly a strictly run regime at home and there would be considerable emphasis put on education, something for which Hugh was later thankful even if his scholastic performance must often have been a disappointment to his father. He writes:

2 cf. http://en.wikipedia.org/wiki/Silesia for more information.
3 More information on the Jews of Falmouth can be found at
    http://www.jhse.org/book/export/article/15939.
4 The Jewish Ex-Serviceman, (date unknown) p.17.
5 According to a note "about my history in a British national context", written by Hugh to Ambrose Appelbe (no date).
6 cf. Jewish Chronicle December 1919. Report of a meeting where Hugh presided: *A pleasant evening was spent by the members of the Zionist Association on Tuesday week in celebration of Chanucah. Mr. Hugh Schonfield presided. The lights were kindled by Mr. D. Scheinman, and addresses were delivered by the Rev. M. Gollop, B.A., Major W. Schonfield, T.D., Mr. Teff, and the Chairman. Mr C. J. Phillips exhibited his interesting collections of old coins and read a brief paper on the subject. Mr. D. Scheinman contributed items on the violin.*

At this juncture it is needful to make some reference to my equipment. I could be said to have been fortunate in that I was a Classics scholar, a student of Greek and

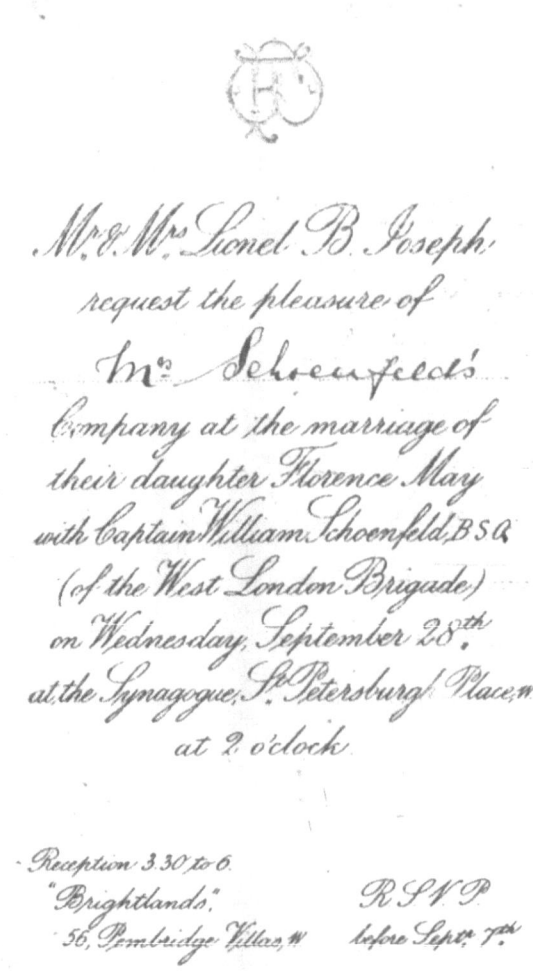

Picture 1: Wedding Invitation

Latin, as well as through my religion familiar with Hebrew. My father used to make me and my elder brother translate from Hebrew into English three verses of the Bible before we went to school in the morning[7].

Florence later inherited property in San Francisco from her parents who sold building materials to the gold prospectors in the Californian gold rush. Florence took her baby daughter with her to San Francisco to sell the property probably around 1903. Sadly the baby died on the ship going over. This baby was the third child out of six and was survived by 5 brothers. The two brothers born after her were dressed as girls until they were five, without any obvious ill effects! Hugh was the second child. All the boys atten-

7   Schonfield, Hugh J. (2004) *Jesus Man-Mystic-Messiah*, The Open Gate Press, London, p.3.

ded St. Paul's School and were very close. The three youngest all married non-Jewish girls without any parental disapproval as far as the writer has been able to ascertain. So all in all, there were five surviving sons born to William and Florence.

The Early Years

Hugh's grandmother on his mother's side was Katie Joseph who lived at Pembridge Villas in Paddington. It was obviously a matter of great joy to congratulate Hugh on his first birthday as is documented in a letter to him in 1902. It would also seem that the Joseph side of the family always played an important role in the family and it was probably no coincidence that this had been chosen as his second name. Hugh undoubtedly identified himself very much with the character of Joseph in later life and the significance of the name and the biblical character of Joseph as the example of a servant leader would not have escaped him.

Only three years after Hugh's birth, Hélène, who was to become his future wife and life companion, came into the world in 1904. Hélène was to play a vital role in the thinking and work of Hugh. Her birth year was undoubtedly significant when the first Labour Party in Australia became the first such party to gain control in the world and Theodore Roosevelt announced with the Monroe Doctrine that the USA would intervene in the West when governments were incompetent. The landscape of the world was changing and new powers were beginning to undermine the power of the British Empire.

It was at the age of six when Hugh "frankly and unreservedly gave himself to God" and began to be aware of God's guidance and preparation "for a task that would one day be revealed."[1]

The Second Hague Peace Conference was opened in that same year, a matter which would later be of some importance to our subject.

Initially there were few signs of how his spiritual experience would later move him and chart his career. An involvement with Christianity was not evident at this stage of his life. In his book *Jesus Man-Mystic-Messiah* we read:

> In my childhood Jesus was almost a total stranger to me. I knew virtually nothing about him beyond that he figured prominently in the Christian Religion[2].

Fortunately, we have some autobiographical notes, mentioned in the introduction to this book, which Hugh composed around this time and we let him speak for himself:

> For convenience in charting the course of terrestrial events we have devised various divisions of time, ages and eras, decades, centuries and millennia. Some of them have a rough justification in trends or mark a significant point of origin. But they are not related to any natural laws, neither do they record precisely a rhythm of ebb and flow. In the more exact sense of changes affected by outstanding occurrences these rarely coincide with our orderly artificial divisions, yet we attach a certain mystique to these intervals as if they had a meaning and comprehended a clear-cut phase. There is nothing that specially distinguishes any decade as a decade or any century as a century; but the ancient conviction of a magical power residing in numbers induces us to follow our fortunes in numerical terms, indulge in prognostical mathematical calculations, and see virtues or vital climaxes in the rounding off of periods like the termination of the nineteenth century and the commencement of the twentieth of the Christian Era. Many are already beginning to look towards

---

1 Harvey, Richard (2002) *Passing over the Plot? The Life and Work of Hugh Schonfield (1901-1988)* in Mishknan, Issue No. 37, 2002, p. 38.
2 Schonfield, Hugh J. (2004) *Jesus Man-Mystic Messiah*, Open Gate Press, London, p.8.

the twenty-first century as if its very arrival offered a hope for humanity which could not be realised before that date line was achieved.

This numerology goes hand in hand with astrology, the government of our lives by the zodiacal signs and planetary conjunctions. It is very easy to have a superstitious feeling about such matters and to give them some credence. We have an inherited sense that our affairs to an extent are controlled by fate. Knowledge of destiny is sought in the heavens, in the numerical value of names, the combination and permutation of figures, and the recognition of certain numerals as more worthy than others. I have been myself intrigued by the fact that the number 8 has cropped up again and again in my life. I was born under the sign of Taurus, the symbol for which resembles this figure, on May 17 (1+7 = 8) in the first year of the twentieth century, and I married at the age of 26 (2+6 = 8). My name Hugh has the numerical value of 8 (8+21+7+8 = 44 = 8). I could offer several other instances of this recurrence, but they would only be of interest to the cabalist[3]. In my youth, as will later appear, the conviction was so strong upon me that I was being trained for some special employment that I included occultism among my studies. They had their value, but only a contributory and subordinate one: it would have been foolish to have become obsessed by them, and would only have detracted from the efficacy of work which had to be done at a different level by other ways and means. Inevitably they faded into the background, and while granting that they have a relevance to the overall picture, I have long ceased to make a fetish of dates and times and seasons.

I see a fitness and an objective purpose in certain things happening when there is need; but it is insulting to a higher intelligence to harness these operations to any man-made chronology like those who predict the day on which the world is to end.

Historically, the year in which I was born had marked a change which was widely felt in Europe as well as throughout the British Empire. There was nothing psychic about this: it was simply the fact that the long and remarkable reign of the Great White Queen was ended. I had just missed being a Victorian, and was thus at my entry into the world linked with the future rather than the past.

My family was middle-class, and I was a Londoner born and bred. But my background was of two worlds, because we were Jews as well as being British. My parents proudly united these worlds in many respects as if it were a single allegiance of a special kind, a spiritual alliance between the land where the sun once stood still and the empire on which the sun never set. The affinity was seen to be even closer by some non-Jews who were convinced that the British were the Lost Ten Tribes of Israel.

In another source, Hugh relates:

> Our domestic staff, nurse, cook and parlour-maid, was presumably Christian; but I do not recall that any of them ever mentioned Jesus to me. Neither do I remember that they ever went to church, though one or other of them may have done so.[4]

---

3   Audrey née Schonfield pointed out to the author that he said he was to die at the age of 88 or in 1988. He actually died in 1988. He became engaged to Hélène when she was 18 who is quoted as saying that "my eyes first met those of 8 year old Hugh and I was a captive for life. The two older boys and I were the only ones to taken to Richmond Park. I tried to run after them through the nettles.".
4   Schonfield, Hugh J. (2004) *Jesus Man-Mystic Messiah*, Open Gate Press, London, p.8.

The Early Years

And continuing with his biographical notes:

My father's people had migrated from Europe to Scotland, and he grew up a

Picture 2: Maj. William Schonfield

Glaswegian with its characteristic accent which he retained to the end of his days, together with a love of the songs and ballads of the highlands and an aptitude for dancing the native reels. Yet he was devoted to his religion and its ritual, and my paternal grandfather had been a noted talmudist, accorded the meritorious title of Morenu[5], 'Our Teacher.' Unexpectedly, as it might appear for a Jew, my father when he came to London as a young man joined the London Scottish Regiment, and before he married was already gazetted Captain in the Middlesex Volunteers. He was a sort of Maccabean, who was not in the very least militant, a pious patriot who served Moses and Queen Victoria with almost equal fervour. I was his second son, born during the Boer War, and thus it came about that I was cradled in the midst of the panoplies of war, and the pictures at which my infant eyes gazed were of military commanders, Kitchener, Roberts, Redvers Buller, and George White, with illustrations of their exploits. The nursery walls were adorned with portraits of members of the Royal Family.

My mother was of older Anglo-Jewish stock. Her ancestors had reached England in the reign of Good Queen Anne, and settled at first at Falmouth in Cornwall. In due course the Josephs came to rank in their own regard among the Jewish aristocracy, and my mother was accustomed to moving in titled circles. There was a strong streak of unconventionality in this family, which manifested itself in some of the members in unusual interests and pioneering pursuits. They were inventive, in cer-

---

5   Term used since the middle of the fourteenth century as a title for rabbis and Talmudists. cf. http://www.jewishencyclopedia.com/articles/11012-morenu

tain respects far-sighted, and ready to take calculated risks. My maternal grandfather Lionel and his brother Josephus had participated in the Californian Gold Rush, not as prospectors but in supplying doors and windows for their shacks. Lionel had also invented a tram which travelled on sunken rails. My mother's brother Leonard was the black sheep of the family, because he married out of the faith and was a rationalist. He was a very colourful character, who wrote a book entitled *What Are We?*[6], a copy of which was accepted by King Edward VII, and he was a great authority on the Gypsies. My mother's character was the very opposite of that of my father, who was unambitious, cautious and fatalistic. In her faith she was much less orthodox, and her religious thinking was tinged with mysticism like that of my grandmother. Both my parents, however, had a strong sense of humour.

I inherited qualities from both sides fairly evenly, but rather inclining towards the Joseph family. Like my father I had a concern for what was fair and just. I was somewhat diffident socially, tending to undervalue my abilities and competence. I was studious, not at all personally ambitious, with little interest in commerce or money-making. I had my father's retentive memory and attention to detail, but fought shy of things mechanical. When I had made up my mind on a matter, I gave out my conclusions, whether justified or not, with enormous assurance. From the Josephs I had a love of adventure, imagination, a willingness to embark on quests and strange enterprises, a philosophical speculativeness and a wide-ranging attraction to out-of-the-way subjects. From this side also I received some artistic and literary aptitude, powers of self-expression and determination. I had my mother's less rigid and formal faith, and a sense of the other-worldly which imposed itself on the practical affairs of life. Just as if the maternal family name went back lineally to that of the Biblical Patriarch, as in my childhood's fancy it did, so it seemed to explain itself how I was a visionary and a dreamer. In the same respect I came to feel an affinity with the land and people of Egypt.

Decidedly I derived comfort from the fact that Joseph was my Hebrew name, especially when I was teased by my brothers about my dreams.

All Jewish children have two sets of nomenclature, the one according to the law of the state and the other as members of the house of Israel, as offspring of their father. Thus outwardly I was Hugh, with Joseph as my second name, while inwardly I was Joseph, Joseph son of David, the name I answered to in the synagogue.

Being alive was for me something very exciting and wonderful. I took to life as a duck to water. Its potentialities seemed infinite. I was blessed with the liveliest curiosity, and as I developed became ever more eager to discover for myself the kind of world I was in. My thoughts ranged far beyond my immediate surroundings, and I was quickly aware that there was so much more to existence than appeared on the surface.

Almost as soon as I could walk and talk I entered the animistic phase of human experience, readily crediting that there were mysterious powers and properties in plants and stones, in storm and tempest. Everything had a magic. My mentor at this time was a local German youth called Hugo Hahn, who used to walk me round the garden-square at the back of our house on St. John's Hill, Ladbroke Grove, Holland Park, filling my mind with primitive legends and fairytales. I was entranced by

---

6 Jospeph, Leonard (1906) *What Are We? An Attempt at an Intelligible Exposition of The Universe and the Place we Take Therein*, London, Kegan Paul, Trench, Trubner & Co. Ltd.

The Early Years

colour and design. I never minded going to bed because of the certainty sleep offered of marvellous explorations and adventures.

Of course it was quite another world in those days at the beginning of the twentieth century, with so much more to be personally observed and engage attention because there was no cinema or television to take charge of the imagination and relieve it of creative responsibility. To borrow the language of Robert Louis Stevenson, we could be as happy as kings simply because the world was so full of a number of things, around each of which our fancy could play freely. There were the crossing-sweepers, the bare-footed urchins, the German bands, the street-criers, the muffin man, the man with the dancing bear, the people in the carriages, the different coloured horse-buses which went who knew where, the wedding awnings and the streets covered with straw to muffle the sound of traffic when someone was seriously ill, the big balloons which sometimes floated across the sky, and so much else beside to be scrutinised and fitted into one's own pattern. People and things meant so much more because there was a more visible difference between them. Through their varied uniforms men and women were less uniform and more stimulating.

Then there was Kensington Gardens in which I spent so much of my childhood like Peter Pan, who was created by Barrie[7] out of the very atmosphere I breathed. There was the Palace there, and the Round Pond with its model yachts, the little well over the hump of the Broad Walk, the glorious Flower Walk and the Golden King of the Albert Memorial, the bird island in the Serpentine, the riders in Rotten Row, and always at the gate of the Gardens its stalwart sentinel, the stout red-faced lady with the black straw boater with an enormous collection of toy balloons for sale. There were twisting tree roots to negotiate, low railings to walk on like a tightrope, and the broad steps of the Orangery to jump off until the great day when one could leap the whole flight and land safely on one's feet. In the Gardens I could indeed hold my head high among the other children, for they did not have what I had a nurse who was married to one of the Keepers, the tall bearded Mr. Bass.

They were blessed years, savoured to the full with that acuteness of enjoyment I derived from the inspection of everything that went on.

Looking back now, I can well understand how my family found me a rather baffling little boy who made great demands upon their patience. I was healthy and good at games, and could run like the wind, winning a prize for sprinting when I was seven. But I was elusive in a spiritual sense, wanting to talk too much about God, and reporting my dreams, one of which was recurrent for a great many years. In this dream I visited a seaside town. I came to know it intimately, travelling there by land and through the air, so that I could and did describe it in detail and draw pictures of it. No one ever recognised the place.

When I grew up and married, my wife and I spent a holiday at Folkestone in Kent. To my astonishment this was the town of my dreams, and I was able to conduct her round telling her what she was going to see, even to a particular tea-house near the harbour. Nothing of consequence happened while we were there to make it intelligible why I had often gone in my sleep to a resort with which I was otherwise unfamiliar, and after our holiday I never dreamt about it again. But there was one connection of which I was not aware at the time. At the Sandgate end of Folkestone there was a house which had been designed and lived in by a man whose books and

---

7 Sir James Matthew Barrie, (9 May 1860 – 19 June 1937) was the creator of Peter Pan.

ideas were a great stimulus to me. The man was H. G. Wells, whom ultimately I came to know personally. Not long ago, when I was Chairman of the H. G. Wells Society[8], a party of us made an excursion to inspect the house, and were welcomed by the Mayor of Folkestone.

It seemed quite natural to me to have such experiences, and I shall mention one or two others in the course of my story.

The things I came out with as a child did not greatly please my parents. I was start-

Picture 3: *The Schonfield Brothers (Hugh on the right)*

ing far too young to express myself about religion and the universe, not so much asking questions as stating my views in a positive manner as if I already had the answers. I was sharply told by my father not to talk chokmahs[9], a Hebraism implying that I was being too clever by half. But I was not trying anything on: I really felt that I did know what I was talking about. Occasionally at night I got out of bed to stand at the window when there was a clear sky, gazing up at the stars, with all that was within me reaching out to penetrate the depths of space as if it were the home to which I belonged and from which I had been parted.

I loved God, and never thought of Him as a Being or in any physical guise. He seemed to me an intensely living all-pervading Presence with which I could commune. Because I was Jewish, God was never depicted for me as an old man in the heavens with a long white beard, and my mind was quite uncomplicated by having to entertain such a notion as incarnation. To worship and praise God was a continual joy and delight. In our synagogue the wardens used to smile kindly at me from their seats which were close to ours as I lifted up my voice clearly and fervently in the Hebrew hymns. Of this synagogue, the New West End, my grandfather had

---

8 In fact Hugh Schonfield was also a founding member of the society. Archive material of the society is deposited with the London Metropolitan University. See http://www.aim25.ac.uk/cgi-bin/vcdf/detail?coll_id=5393&inst_id=49&nv1=search&nv2=basic.

9 Lit. 'wisdoms'.

been one of the founders. The Chief Rabbi himself worshipped there, and had given me his blessing.

As a small boy I was acutely conscious of unexplained contrasts in my circumstances, which tended to encourage in me the building up of an imaginary world of my own without in the least losing interest in the one I inhabited. We were, to begin with, an old-fashioned household living according to fairly strict rules both Jewish and British at our social level. My elder brother and I occupied the top floor of the house with our nurse, while my parents were in entirely different and more luxurious surroundings on the first floor. There was a minimum of communication. My mother came sometimes to the nursery before bedtime, and we descended to our parents' bedroom to say good morning.

The reception rooms on the ground floor were largely denied to us except for Sabbath meals and prayers, and when we were brought down briefly for inspection dressed in velvet suits and silk blouses with lace collars like Little Lord Fauntleroy on At Home days and other occasions when relations and friends had called. It seemed a wonderful act of revolt on my brother's part when on a memorable day he slid down the banisters from the top of the house to the bottom and landed with a clang but relatively unscathed on the great gong in the hall.

My parents in those days seemed much more severe and disciplinarian than they really were, and I must often have made them uncomfortable with the kind of things I said. I was advised that 'mysteries belong to God' and were not for us to probe. The important thing was to be clean and decent, putting everything, including religion, in its proper place in the same way as clothes and toys. So I was more at home with the non-Jewish staff, especially my nurse whom I adored, and consequently became quickly acquainted with the existence of a difference by no means clear to me between Jews and Gentiles. The world around me was apparently largely Gentile. I moved about in it, but was not of it. It Intrigued me with its unknown qualities and possibilities, and I wished I had complete access to it. I listened with pleasure to the pealing of church bells, and looked at all the people coming out of St. John's Church on Sundays. I wondered what they had been doing inside. But it was indicated to me that this was forbidden and indeed hostile territory, since Christians disliked and persecuted Jews. They worshipped a man on a cross. I saw this extraordinary effigy which was the symbol of their idolatry, and marvelled that intelligent people had not risen above such ignorance of the nature of God. I found it hard to believe that there was not more to this religion than I was told; but I could not penetrate the barrier to find out.

So life began for me in a state of puzzlement about myself and about the world. There were exciting things to discover if one had the courage and determination not to be put off by what anybody said.

I felt strongly that I was being wilfully prevented from learning the truth. To these circumstances I attribute in no small measure the eager curiosity that grew in me, the desire to overcome all obstacles so that I could make living contact with everyone everywhere.

I admired my elder brother because he was much braver than I was, and much more willing to do as he pleased. At least once in boyhood he dared to run away from home, though he did not get very far. We quarrelled sometimes because we had a different outlook and different interests, but we had in common an attitude of protest against the way in which we were hemmed in and circumscribed. He was blond, while I was dark, and my three younger brothers as they came along were also fair. This too contributed to making it seem to me that I was the odd man out, not fully belonging to the family of which I was a member, more like an adopted child.

The atmosphere of our home was rather military and puritanical. The important thing was obedience. We were treated as little men, and experienced very little of physical affection. We were not fondled or hugged, and were kissed only perfunctorily. A sister was born when I was two years old, but she died in infancy. It might have changed many things if she had survived. I remember that my mother was deeply grieved at the time, and it was always her regret that she had no daughter. My father's leisure was largely occupied in studying signalling and military tactics, and was rewarded by achieving equestrian rank and being gazetted Major. There was an annual dinner for brother officers at the house after the shooting competitions at Bisley. Of course we were proud that Dad had a horse on which occasion-

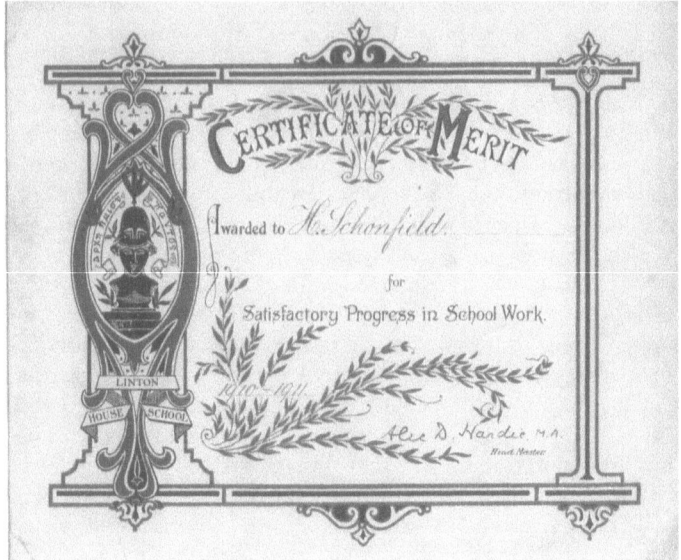

Picture 4: Linton House Certificate

ally we were given a ride, and we greatly admired his appearance when he donned full dress uniform.

But my brother and I were very much driven to create our own games and entertainment, since we were not permitted to associate with children who were not Jewish and did not know any Jewish children in the neighbourhood. Among my own inventions was a clan which bore my name, and of which I was the leader. I believe that such an imagination is not uncommon among small boys; but I could not guess that this invisible land which I captained, and which served as a substitute for more companions of my own age, was faintly foreshadowing ultimate events.

At the age of seven Hugh was found attending the Kensington Park High School and his report states that "Hugh is a very bright boy and equally keen in work and play. He has made satisfactory progress in every subject". He then moved to the Linton House

Preparatory School in Holland Park[10] and his report from the Christmas term states that "Has made a very good start. Most earnest and industrious".

Hugh attended the Linton House School until 1911 and according to the report from the Summer term he was "Top in his form. Works very well and very accurately. Writing is very poor". By Christmas term 1910 he was "third in form". Maybe his progress would have had to do with the fact and his fascination that Haley's Comet was visible from Earth in that year. It was certainly a portentous year with George V becoming King of the United Kingdom. Certainly life had changed since the year he was born with some 6.7 million passengers being transported in the electric street cars of the cities of Europe.

In 1911, as already mentioned, Hugh's father retired from the army in a year when Italy declared war on the Ottoman Empire and the World's first combat aerial bombing took place in Libya in the Italo-Turkish War.

It was an eventful time for the family and in 1912 Hugh moved to the St. Paul's Preparatory School under the headmaster J. Bewsher. His Michaelmas term report states that he is "an intelligent boy but a very untidy worker. He has made good progress". This year was the year in which Woodrow Wilson was elected President of the USA. Woodrow Wilson became an example of good statesmanship for Hugh, especially his idea that he saw America's role as a Servant-Nation. Hugh was so impressed with him that he later wrote a book about the president entitled *This Man Was Right*.

Come 1913, things are brewing for a World War. There was a major industrial strike in the North of England which threatened military production and the first Balkan War took place. Violence was rampant and in Dublin was 'Bloody Sunday' where many demonstrators were injured. Mahatma Gandhi was arrested whilst leading a march of Indian miners in South Africa. But Hugh's school report stated "Conduct good" and by the summer term 1913, "His work has much improved especially in Mathematics. Conduct good". His Michaelmas term report states that "He has made very fair progress especially in French and Classics. Conduct good."

According to Hélène, around this time his imagination was stimulated by a 14 year old German boy and he was teaching himself hieroglyphics and apparently seemed very sure of himself and felt he was in preparation for some special destiny. His friend would talk to him of fairies and the magical properties of some plants, teaching him to recognise wild flowers. Hélène pointed out that Hugh's gifts however, remained unappreciated by his grandmother Katie whose son Leonard was similar in looks and interested in philosophy. Hugh made his first attempt at public speaking whilst at St. Paul's and the subject was 'Potatoes'! She mentioned that their talks would always continue from where they left off last time and that there was a strange bond which remained even when we were away from each other. She stated. "I think we both knew already that our lives would be intertwined although he was to form a deep relationship with a country girl [Bessie, mentioned later] who died tragically young, he always denied his intention

10 "Nos. 11-27 (odd) Holland Park Avenue. The site on which No. 11 Holland Park Avenue (Linton House) stands was at the eastern edge of the property Hanson purchased from the Lloyds. In 1830 he sold the plot to the Reverend Hibbert Binney of Paddington, (ref. 48) who built a detached house on it known as Mound House. In 1877 a preparatory school called Linton House School was established there, the house itself being used as the headmaster's residence and new school buildings erected in the garden at the rear. The present Linton House, a block of flats designed by T. P. Bennett and Son, replaced the school in c. 1936." http://www.british-history.ac.uk/report.aspx?compid=49869 (29th January 2013)

of marrying her as told me by members of his family after we became engaged. Hugh's need for female companionship was very great and he was going through a turmoil of spirit that he could not confide to his parents or even to me. However, every human emotion does not have to be divulged to one's nearest and dearest. His parents also told me that Hugh had got into bad company and had left home and was in Scotland and his name was not to be mentioned". She goes on to say, "Looking back as I now see over a period of sixty years I see only too clearly that Hugh has been continually hemmed in and frustrated. As a boy, surrounded by family with a remarkable lack of understanding and complete incomprehension of the norm set during the Victorian epoch, and it would seem at St. Paul's school at that time, this strange boy made little or no impression on his instructors, the successors of the pedagogues. Today such a boy would probably have joined the hippies or similar group, but then the authority of parents and school was too strong. The bottled-up emotions and enthusiasms almost produced a teenage breakdown and he was obliged to leave home at 16."

In 1914 he moved on to St Paul's School under A.E. Hillard as headmaster. It was then in this year that the great catastrophe of World War One made its debut set off by the assassination of Archduke Franz Ferdinand of Austria on 28th June. The German Empire declared war on the Russian Empire and France mobilised with Germany marching into Belgium, a neutral country. Thus Britain became involved. Gandhi was in the English Channel when he heard the news that war had been declared, arriving later that day in London. I could imagine that all these events must have had a considerable impact upon the young thinking boy's mind at the time.

His school report here in December 1914 states "He has made good progress in Classics and English. He works well and takes an interest in his work. His Mathematical work also is satisfactory".

St Paul's School was an influence on many and it is worth noting that Victor Gollancz also attended the school and also developed thinking which has parallels to Hugh's:

> During the fighting that marked the creation of the state of Israel, Gollancz became concerned for the plight of the Arabs and in October 1948 he founded the Jewish Society for Human Service (JSHS), with Rabbi Leo Baeck as its president. This body was based on "the universalist ethic of Judaism" and aimed to work in the newly formed state of Israel "to relieve the suffering of Jews and Arabs indifferently."[11]

The School declares its historically founded intercultural approach as:

> In 1509 John Colet founded St Paul's School to educate 153[12] boys "from all nations and countries indifferently". Our history is the kind that inspires bold ideals for the future. These are our aims:
>
> To provide an outstanding intellectual, spiritual and physical education, combining tradition with the best of the present, which prepares gifted boys for their future.
>
> To foster a culture of scholarship, and to develop a spirit of enquiry and curiosity, through inspirational and responsive teaching.
>
> To honour John Colet's founding commitment that St Paul's is open to all academically eligible boys, regardless of their economic or social circumstance.

11 http://en.wikipedia.org/wiki/Victor_Gollancz accessed 8th July 2014.
12 This number significantly links to the miraculous catch of fish in John 21:1-14. The school still has 153 foundation scholars who may use a silver fish emblem..

> To treat the welfare of pupils as the highest priority, and to provide individual pastoral care that promotes a boy's independence, whilst fostering respect, tolerance, kindness and service.
>
> To develop and maintain the school's facilities to ensure that the physical environment of St Paul's sustains the excellence of its education.
>
> To build substantive links with the local community through Pauline voluntary service, outreach programmes and the sharing of our facilities.[13]

Amongst the list of notable Old Paulines[14], as they are called, we find the name of Leonard Woolf (1880-1969) which explains the later book connection with the Woolfs. The list of renowned persons of course is endless and of course includes the subject person of this book.

Hugh celebrated his Bar-Mitzvah on July 11th at 64 Ladbroke Road, Holland Park, where the Schonfields were now living. The celebration included an eight course menu served in their home.

Hugh writes about this time in the following words:

> The growth of our family by the addition of two more brothers necessitated removal to a larger house in Ladbroke Road, Holland Park, which was only just round the corner from the Private School where my elder brother and I were now pupils. At the age of seven I heartily welcomed these developments because they offered new contacts and interests. The elementary school lessons were easy to master and in the first year I was top of my class. But what I specially enjoyed was having companions, and those to whom I was particularly drawn were boys of other nationalities. I particularly remember Portuguese twins and an Indian. They represented the enlargement of comprehension I was eagerly seeking.
>
> What meant most to me, however, was ability to read. I devoured books, notably historical novels and adventure stories. I worked through Scott, Dickens, Ainsworth and Kipling, Stevenson, Henty, Fenimore Cooper, Ballantyne and Rider Haggard. Then of course we had the Boy's Own Paper and Chums. Wherever the scene of the tale was laid, and in whatever period, I soaked myself in the atmosphere.
>
> The doors of time and distance were thrown wide open. Now there were most wonderful day dreams to supplement those on which I embarked at night.
>
> I was always rather naive and unassuming. I liked people and accepted them readily as I found them, young and old, and having a bright face and a cheerful smile I got on happily with most of them, even with my crusty octogenarian great-uncle Josephus Joseph, who used to imprint a limp parting kiss on my forehead when we visited him on Sabbaths after the synagogue service. My one faux pas was with a deceased relation whom I had never met. My father showed me one day a portrait of his mother wearing a lace cap, and asked me who it was. To his evident distress, I said, "Cook".
>
> We were never spoilt, and received few gifts and sweets. I suppose I have always wanted sweets because I had so few of them as a child. Treats were infrequent, a rare drive in my maternal grandmother's carriage, birthday parties, and an occasional outing. A memorable day was a trip to Richmond Park where we were to pic-

---

13 http://www.stpaulsschool.org.uk/ accessed 8th July 2014.
    See also: http://en.wikipedia.org/wiki/St_Paul's_School,_London
14 http://en.wikipedia.org/wiki/List_of_Old_Paulines, accessed 8th July 2014.

nic with the Cohn family. Hans Cohn had been a bachelor friend of my father, and had been introduced to his future wife Ethel through my father's younger brother. They had two daughters, Hélène and Ena. Hélène was then about five and she and I got on famously. We seemed to have an affinity from the beginning and the eventual happy outcome was our marriage some eighteen years later.

This period during the First World War must have been very formative for the ideas which were to become apparent later in life and which would determine his career. This is certainly a matter which he felt himself for he states:

> …as a Jewish boy I was myself strongly drawn towards the messianic, influenced by the apocalyptic atmosphere of the First World War. It was thus inevitable that I should encounter Jesus, and desire to get to know him and what he represented[15].

It would have been around this time when he was to be seriously confronted with the ideas of Christianity. He writes:

> I was now thirteen, a very impressionable age, and the war was one increasingly to stir the imagination. From the beginning it seemed something awesome, not wholly of this world. There was talk of Armageddon, of the Four Horsemen of the Apocalypse, of the Angels of Mons[16]. The sense of participating in the climax of the Ages seized upon many, more especially with the start of the campaign to liberate the Holy Land from the Turks.
>
> At this time the Jewish community became more corporately involved. My father was called upon for the recruitment and organization of the Jewish battalions which fought in Palestine under General Allenby. The very name of this general, in sympathy with the spiritual concept of the hostilities, was arabized as Allah-Nebi (Prophet of God). My elder brother, who had joined up under age, was wounded on the road to Jerusalem.
>
> It was at the West London headquarters for Jewish enlistment in Chenies Street (jokingly dubbed Sheeny [Cockney for Jew] Street) that I met Zionist volunteers, some of whom had travelled from the United States. I was now sixteen. Among those who visited us was an ardent Jewish warrior Vladimir Jabotinsky[17], then a British sergeant, who impressed upon me that I must learn to speak Hebrew.
>
> I caught the fire of revived Jewish nationhood, and decided to take up land work both to help Britain and to gain experience of farming with the object of settling in Palestine after the war. At the time I actually had a job as a junior clerk in a merchant's office in the City of London.
>
> It so happened that I encountered a gentleman who belonged to the Christadelphians[18], a Christian sect very sympathetic to the Jews and enthusiastic on the subject of prophecy. We got talking, and he gave me some literature. So far as the war was concerned the Christadelphians were conscientious objectors, and many of their

---

15 Schonfield, Hugh J. (2004) *Jesus Man-Mystic-Messiah*, The Open Gate Press, London, p.3.
16 The Angels of Mons was a legend about a group of angels who supposedly protected members of the British Army in the Battle of Mons at the outset of World War I.
17 Vladimir Yevgenyevich Zhabotinsky was a co-founder of the Jewish Legion of the British army according to Wikipedia which would explain the connection to the family. He was awarded the MBE in 1920. Cf. http://en.wikipedia.org/wiki/Ze%27ev_Jabotinsky.
18 Christadelphians also reject the idea of the Trinity and are conscientious objectors and helped save Jewish children from Nazi terror in the Second World War. These ideas would certainly have influenced Hugh's thinking.

young men were on land work as an alternative to military service. Learning that I wished to take up farming, my acquaintance found me a job in a market garden at Feltham near London, where some of his sect had been taken on as labourers.[19]

It should not be underestimated how formative this experience was as others have observed:

> No reader of this book [Jesus: Man-Mystic-Messiah] can fail to notice the remarkable parallel between Hugh Schonfield's own religious explorations and those he hypothesizes for Jesus. Schonfield recalls how his interest in the historical Jesus was kindled by his early acquaintance with Christians (first Christadelphian sectarians, then evangelical revivalists) during the apocalyptic days of World War One. The world was exploding around him, pregnant with both new and unimagined dangers and possibilities. These factors pushed him into studying the apocalyptic inheritance of his native Judaism as well as an inquiry into a Man whom Christians but not Jews venerated as the Jewish Messiah. We have a sense of deja vue when Schonfield describes Jesus as a youth soaking up the influences of the apocalyptic movement and earth-shaking events of his own century. Has Schonfield, like so many historical Jesus questers, merely remade Jesus in his own image? Or has he rather followed the principle of analogy so absolutely central to historical research: understanding the past on analogy with present experience? Do we end up with a Jesus modelled after Schonfield, or a Schonfield modelled after Jesus? There is much to learn either way.[20]

From now on it would seem that Hugh was not to be spared the usual problems of puberty and his school reports began to include not only purely positive comments such as the one from July 1915: "He needs pressure to make him put forth his best but there has been improvement. His French is satisfactory and he shows much interest in his drawing. It is unfortunate that so much of his work is untidy". And in December: "He works hard with results that are moderate in Classics, very fair in Mathematics. His Spelling and punctuation are unfortunately poor but he has a capacity for getting up facts in connection with his English work". We can already see the qualifications for his future life's work coming to the surface in this report.

It was around this time, on August 26th 1915, that something occurred which has been of such a coincidental nature that it moved the author to some emotion when this discovery was made whilst researching amongst the Schonfield archives (which are now housed in Boston). Hugh had perhaps been attending one of the meetings of the Zionist movement in Southend-on-Sea where there was an extensive Jewish community. Probably, on a sightseeing outing, or perhaps they were spending a holiday there, he went to the nearby Hadleigh (misspelt on picture) Castle where he made a water painting depicting his brother Douglas. It is to be remembered that these were war years which has also been noted on the painting. It was some decades later when the author found that he himself had in fact, at around the same age yet over forty years later, unwittingly and coincidentally been living literally just around the corner from this spot, which was a common place for his childhood recreation. It was during this time in Hadleigh that he

---

19 Schonfield, Hugh J. (2004) *Jesus Man-Mystic Messiah*, The Open Gate Press, London, p.11.
20 Robert M. Price:
    http://www.robertmprice.mindvendor.com/reviews/schonfield_jesus_mmm.htm, accessed 24th July 2014.

was to discover an interest in politics and the just society – and also to meet his future wife without which this book would never have been written. As the well worn adage goes, "it's a small world".

Picture 5: Hugh Aged 16

In the world at large of 1915, we find the Ottoman Army beginning raids on the Suez Canal of which Hugh Schonfield was later to become the official historian. The British were hard pressed at the Battle of Loos in France where the first use of poison gas in World War I was made.

Even if Hugh's school work was not always at the level of enthusiasm which his teachers would have liked, it would seem that this aptitude for art and drawing was something which would always continue with him. Thus we find this comment on his July 1916 St. Paul's school report: "He has ability which he sometimes uses but not always. His Greek has improved a good deal. Mathematics weak. Drawing good" and again in December: "Classics weak – perhaps he is losing heart in the subject. French and Mathematics fair. Drawing good".

The Early Years

In 1916 Germans blew up a munitions factory in Kingsland (now Lyndhurst, New Jersey) which was a main driver for involvement of the USA in WWI.

In another document about his qualifications as a translator written later, Hugh writes of himself:

> As a child I would spend time with my father (who also studied the Hebrew Scriptures) to go over with him the translation of a few verses every morning before school. I was a keen student of history and archaeology, and as a boy at St. Paul's School I commenced on my own account the mastery of Egyptian hieroglyphics at the age of fourteen. I enjoyed the friendship and assistance of the famous Egyptologist the late Sir Flinders Petrie[21]. Being possessed of a vivid imagination, and learning all I could of past civilisations, I delighted to travel back in time and move about the cities of the ancient world. Their streets and temples and peoples became almost as familiar to me as my own London.

Hugh's school leaving report dated 13th October 1926 confirms his attendance at St. Paul's from September 1914 until April 1917 and states: "He was on the classical side and showed very fair ability in all the usual subjects of that side. His conduct was always satisfactory and he bore a good character in all respects". One can assume that he required this report for his entrance application to Glasgow University.

In 1917, Woodrow Wilson called for "peace without victory" in Germany and in March entered his second term of office. The Russian Empire came to an end, becoming a Republic, and Woodrow Wilson declared war on Germany. In October the revolution broke out in Russia where the Bolsheviks under Lenin overthrew the provisional government being the first rebuttal of capitalism in history. These things would certainly not have gone unnoticed by our subject person. More directly relevant to the young man's interest would have been the Balfour Declaration where Britain proclaimed support for the "establishment in Palestine of a national home for the Jewish people" with the clear understanding "that nothing shall be done which may prejudice the civil and religious rights of existing non-Jewish communities".

As we have mentioned previously, without a doubt, the vision of St. Paul's School's founder was a considerable influence in the development of Hugh's thinking on internationalism and discrimination. Needless to say, term fees made attendance at the school prohibitive except for the more wealthy members of society unless fortunate to receive a bursary. It is noteworthy that the school chosen by Hugh's parents is actually one which is Christian based, demonstrating that the Schonfield family were probably more culturally than religiously Jewish.

It is also interesting to note that Hugh took voluntary courses on public speaking whilst at school because he must have had a sense that he was going to need this in his future life.

From 1917 Hugh attended King's College London and started to write and draw spiritual ideas. One of these was a poem entitled *The God of our Fathers*:

> *Give ear, O Israel, hearken now*
> *The Lord is One, a Unity*
> *For Him alone your humble bow*

---

21 Sir William Matthew Flinders Petrie 3rd June 1853-28th July 1942.

For Him alone your bended knee.

He is your Father, Saviour, King
To him alone is right to pray
Obey Him then in everything
Take heed to what you do or say.

His the mighty arm that wrought
Vengeance on proud Pharaoh's and
His the outstretched hand that brought
Israel to the Promised Land.

His the judgement stern and true
His the mercy, His the care
His the love that bears us through
Many an hour of dark despair.

It was at this time that he designed a tract which gives an indication of his thinking at the time.

The text on the back states:

BE PREPARED NOW AND ENROL YOURSELVES UNDER OUR BANNER

Children of Israel

The Promises God made to our fathers are about to be fulfilled in our days.

God has not deluded us with vain hopes of the restoration of his people under the kingship of his anointed. But are we ready to receive him, are we united in our preparation for the setting up of David's throne?

In the fear that this is not so this Society has been formed having for its objects, the education of the Jewish masses to the reception of these great facts, by means of teachers and lecturers and to assist colonists in Palestine that they be ready to serve the king when he comes.

We can see that the idea embodied here was already messianic (but not yet Jesuanic) in its fundamental concept, whilst concentrating on the 'Children of Israel'. Inside are a number of Bible quotations referring to the messianic promise and headed 'Read and Doubt No Longer but Trust in the Lord'. It will no doubt have been influenced by the aforementioned Balfour Declaration made that year. He was seeing a fulfilment of prophecy in the event which was undoubtedly shared by many.

In May 1917 Hugh found a job working for Woodhead Plant Ltd. In the City of London. He probably did clerical work here but it did not last long and he left this employment in August 1918. This work he may not have found particularly fulfilling and he found time to ponder and write down his emerging ideas. Remembering that he was still only seventeen years old, the reader can consider what depth of thinking was already becoming apparent in the following piece:

Power

Pile Peelion on Orsa, Mont Blanc on Everest.

Picture 6: Front page of tract which included the text below

Let me scale the dizzy height and stand supreme upon the summit.
For a time, I'll be mighty Jove, wielding almighty power.
"Tell me, am I alone?"
"How can I be alone, when every vibrant sound, every motion of minute, molecule, proclaims the life that throngs around me.
But all this life is my life, every stir the echo of my spirit.
Alone! What mockery."
Would you strive to confine me?
Know then that I am Creation, the vastness of space and as immeasurable as Eternity.
Now then, I command you go!

Drag every human action from town and tower, country cottage, hut or hovel, and bring them here: yes! Even bid the grave revive its dead.

What glory! I am full of vital force.

That's right place them there, in the valley, body to body, flesh to flesh.

I raise aloft my thunderbolts.

They quiver, not as so many human creatures, but as one cast grey, leprous mass.

They fear me!

Is that the moan of a wounded breast or the sobbing sorrow of the wind?

"Tis the cry of many voices" say you.

Wrong, wrong, I prove you wrong.

What I have here is a brute, senseless, fearful timid, with voice indeed, and power to move, eat, smell and see. When spread abroad they may be men; but here and now this is a brute.

Kill them! Kill them! And bring me their souls.

What's this, you bring me again, a part of myself.

Have I then part in these? How awful is the thought.

Do they claim my image, not the beauty of one unit amongst them all, but the features of this beast humanity?

It can not be.

And is all creation like this?

Let me destroy.

Space, Time everything, must perish.

Cause the utmost darkness to reign!

Who says I may not do this?

A voice soft, sibilant, whispers in my heart.

You are the Universe, you can not destroy yourself.

No 'tis true!

The voice speaks on.

Can there be darkness when you are light?

Can there be hatred against Creation when you are Love?

Voice! You are answered!

Bitterly I exclaim.

Can the glow worm call itself the sun?

Can a mortal love a grain of sand?

What have I done I have answered like a man speaking to his God; or say like God in man would humbly declare himself.

God alone then, is Love, Light, and Life.

He alone has infinite Power and infinite Mercy.

Man can not take his Maker's place a single moment, for man's first word is destruction. Even silence would not save him. This I have learnt.

The Early Years

> *Let me go down in shame and mingle with the mournful multitude and seek His Face in sorrow.*
>
> *O Omnipotent one thou art Good!*
>
> *Man, thou art mad.*
>
> *Let thy loving Creator save thee, thyself thou canst not save.*

Again in the following prayer, we are able to observe a deep spirituality which belies later accusations that he was atheistic:

Prayer

> *Lord of the Universe, was ever a prayer of a tired and trusting heart, that Thou didst not answer?*
>
> *Was ever a cry of worn and weary, that did not bring forth thy Spirit to comfort and heal?*
>
> *Because of this and for all Thy Blessings on the head of man: I will pour out my heart, and cause my mouth to declare, to all the World, Thy Love.*
>
> *I have never sought thee in vain.*
>
> *I know that hidden in my being is a spark of Thy Spirit. Will not flame leap towards flame?*
>
> *Water run to water?*
>
> *Thy Spirit in me, hath but sought thee again, the Loved One, who sent it in to the World, and my body hath been drawn after it with Thy Presence.*
>
> *I stood on the threshold; I made my prayer unto the Most High. I was bowed down with sorrow when I entered the gate.*
>
> *I was bidden to the feast. I devoured Thy Words of comfort, and drank Thy Light as water.*
>
> *I came forth, a sob in my voice, and a song in my heart.*
>
> *My brow glowed with glory.*
>
> *This is the reward of them that hear Thy Voice.*
>
> *Art Thou my Father and I Thy son?*
>
> *Behold, only half would then be told.*
>
> *Thou art above me, in me and around me.*
>
> *I can give Thee no name. Thou art what Thou art.*
>
> *Am I a drop in the sea of Thy Creation? The whole greater than the part.*
>
> *Not so, my King: for the whole without the part is incomplete. But the part alone, is but a smaller whole and in itself lacks nothing.*
>
> *Though I were the least of all Thy Works, yet am I great as any, within Thy all embracing Spirit.*
>
> *Thou art all, and I in Thee can share Thy all.*

In the Introduction to *Gospel Untruth: A Disclosure of Christian Fraud,* an unfinished work, Hugh relates:

I left school to go on Land Work, and was recommended to a farm by a gentleman who believed that we were living in the Last Times and they had all been mapped out in the passages of the Great Pyramid of Egypt[22].

On the farm were conscientious objectors to military service, members of the sect of Christadelphians.

Inevitably there were discussions about the Messiahship of Jesus, and as a consequence I borrowed an English Bible from my landlady and read the New Testament for the first time. It made a deep impression on me, convincing me that Jesus had believed himself to be the ultimate king of the Jews his people were awaiting. What was unacceptable was the Christian doctrine of his deity, and I felt sure that it had been the conversion of pagan Gentiles which had been responsible for this development. I wanted to know what had been the convictions of his Jewish followers, not fully represented in the New Testament. There had once been a Hebrew Gospel, of which only significant fragments had survived in quotations. I was given an incentive in my quest when a second-hand bookseller opposite the British Museum notified me of an ancient Hebrew version of the Gospel of Matthew, which I acquired and translated into English[23].

The path was set for me to become deeply involved in Christian Beginnings, and the significance of the Messiahship for Jesus himself.

And so by 1918 the Jews in Europe were gaining more and more recognition. Finland granted civil rights to Jews for the first time. There were also hopes of peace as Germany signed the armistice agreement with the Allies on the 11th November of that year thus marking the end of WWI. However, these were dark days also with the Spanish Flu becoming pandemic, which in its course killed up to 100 million people in the world—up to 5 percent of the world's population!

In 1919 he gave a talk at the Zionist Association in Southend at which his father was present. It would seem that they often visited the area and were quite involved in the association. Obviously, this Zionist thinking had been inspired very much by his father who had been involved in the politics of Palestine from an early date, as mentioned earlier. It is tragically ironic to note that Adolf Hitler gave his first speech on October 16th of that very same year. In the USA, prohibition was introduced against the veto of Woodrow Wilson yet they never managed to ever ratify the Treaty of Versailles! At least countries like Germany and Luxembourg were now allowing women to vote.

In fact, in March 1920, a play entitled *Hadassah, A Purim Play* and written by Hugh was performed at an association meeting. The play was preceded by a concert performed by a quintet. The Jewish Chronicle reported that "the play proved to be an unqualified success"[24]. Subsequently, the English Zionist Federation[25] wrote to Hugh congratulating him on the success and asking if it had been successful in raising Zionist funds.

Hugh's involvement with the movement was considerable at the time and he was asked by the Rev. Gollop, Minister, to propose a motion to be discussed in a debate at the

---

22 This could be referring to Sir Flinders Petrie mentioned previously. Petrie had discovered the first mention of the word "Israel" in an Egyptian text during excavations.
23 Schonfield, Hugh J. (2014) An Old Hebrew Text of St. Matthew's Gospel. London, The Hugh & Hélène Schonfield World Service Trust.
24 The Jewish Chronicle, March 7th 1920.
25 The Zionist Federation, was established in 1899 to campaign for a permanent homeland for the Jewish people.

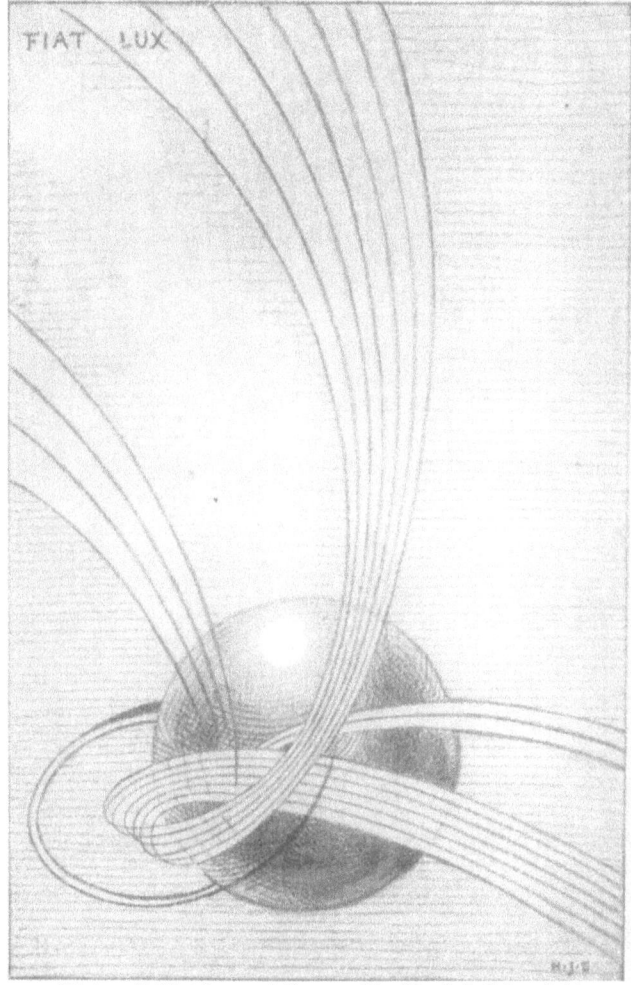
Picture 7: Fiat Lux – A Postcard by Hugh J. Schonfield

Southend and Westcliff Hebrew Congregation[26]: "That the establishment of a Jewish state in Palestine is detrimental to the best interests of Jewry at large.". Rev. Gollop wanted Hugh to oppose the motion, stating,

> The opener will be in favour of it and you will open against. I have done that as you preferred to oppose, so that you may have the opponent's speech to pull to pieces.
>
> It is obvious that, if you so wish it, you could finish your criticism with positive pleadings in favour of Zionism in general.
>
> I am convinced that your contribution will be worth listening to.
>
> I naturally expect Father [William Schonfield] to preside, as he is the Hon. President".

---

26 http://www.swhc.org.uk/ It is interesting to note that when I accessed this site on 25th November 2014, I noticed that they were displaying a photo of that same Hadleigh Castle which Hugh painted and which I previously commented on.

Christian times

Hélène mentioned that it was around this time that Hugh became a regular visitor to her home and the family learned that he had actually been compelled to leave home owing to religious difficulties with his father who apparently came from a very rigidly orthodox background. She stated "I still have preserved the first present he gave me after we became engaged – a copy of the revised version of the New Testament. By then I knew that he was a follower of Jesus as Messiah and by the standards of the time he had committed the unforgivable sin".

She goes on to say, "It was while he was working on the farm that he found himself in contact with evangelical Christians and that he found the courage to read the forbidden book and found to his surprise and wonder that it contained the answers to all his questions. He found it was no alien writing but that it dealt with Jews and Jewish expectations. It may be imagined that it lead to prolonged heart searchings and very nearly a breakdown, but he had introductions to friends in Glasgow where he also had a cousin married to a medical professor and with their help and understanding kept in contact with his family while he enrolled at the Bible training institute the director of which was a saintly character with a dear motherly wife who had great regard for their only Jewish student. In the meantime he was collecting books and reading that would widen his knowledge of Jesus' time".

In the Introduction to *Gospel Untruth: A Disclosure of Christian Fraud*, an unfinished work, we find another autobiographical snippet where Hugh relates:

> It is, to say the least, unusual for a Jew to be so involved in the beginnings of Christianity as I have been in my writings and researches throughout a long life. There has seemed to be in this a kind of fate which there was no evading, and it began to manifest itself in my childhood.
>
> I am a Londoner. My father was an orthodox British Jew who had come south from Glasgow in the late nineteenth century to seek his fortune, and married my mother, who came from an Anglo-Jewish family which had settled in Cornwall in the reign of Queen Anne. I was their second son, born at the opening of the twentieth century, in May 1901.
>
> Christianity was on our doorstep, since there was a church at the corner of our road, and as a child I wondered about what were the beliefs of those who attended. But indeed it was even closer, because, strange as it may seem, in our dining room there was a very large oil painting, and its theme was Peter denying Christ after his arrest. How we acquired it I have no idea. While the picture did not raise a problem, something else did, the question of my elder brother and myself attending synagogue wearing our school caps which bore the emblem of a cross. We were then at Colet Court, preparatory school for St. Paul's Public School. Actual contact with Christianity only began when I entered the senior school on the Classical side shortly after the outbreak of the First World War. I had a master who was also an Anglican clergyman, and who spoke to me of Jesus as "our Saviour and your Messiah". I had not previously thought about the messianic, and my interest was aroused.
>
> The Great War, as we called it, the First World War, was now in progress, on land and sea and in the air, creating an apocalyptic atmosphere, so that many believed it

heralded the Second Advent of Christ. There was the Vision of the Angels of Mons, and the rescue of the Holy Land from the Turks. The British General concerned, General Allenby, had his name interpreted in Arabic as *Allah-nebi* (Prophet of God). His forces included Jewish battalions. My father, Major William Schonfield, was in charge of recruiting them, and my elder brother was one of those who joined, and was wounded on the road to Jerusalem. There was the amazing Balfour Declaration, declaring that the British Government favoured the restoration of Palestine as the National Home of the Jewish People. I was present at the great Jewish Meeting in London to mark the event.

Hugh's interests and activities now started to widen as he gradually gained an idea of the knowledge he needed to acquire. With this in view, a visit to Palestine was called for and a letter of introduction was duly sent by a supporter to Dr. Albright[1] in October 1920 in which Hugh's general interest in archaeology was explained and the fact that he was anxious to see some excavation whilst there. The letter asks if he could come to Gezer with Dr. Albright's party.

By 1922, Hugh had got involved with a Christian missionary group called the British Society for the Propagation of the Gospel amongst the Jews[2] in Waltham New Town in Hertfordshire. He had some sort of close friendship with a young lady called Bessie in the house he was living in at that time—he had moved out of home and his parents did not approve of what he was doing. This was prior to his marriage to Hélène who had been his friend since early childhood (4-5 years old). His parents were rigidly against him marrying outside of Judaism and as the girl was non-Jewish, they put pressure on Hugh to break up the relationship, it would seem. Hugh worked as a missionary for this society and as a lay preacher and was responsible for a number of conversions to Christianity. Apparently Hugh's brother and his parents tried to persuade Hugh to go back home but Hugh would not be budged. Eventually, Hugh gave in to the pressure and resigned from the society. According to the records of the minutes, from 14th October 1922, Hugh's resignation from the society was discussed and accepted on October 10th 1922 with the words:

> Resignation of Mr. Schonfield. The Secretary expressed his profound regret at having to announce the entirely unexpected resignation of Mr. Hugh Schonfield, recently appointed for work in Bow. The young man had become reconciled to his family and had accepted the condition laid down by them that he should not be connected with any missionary society for at least three years. A letter was read from him conveying his decision, thanking the committee for what had been done for him, and expressing the hope that he might be able to lead his family to Christ.

---

1   I imagine this must have been the American archaeologist and biblical scholar William Foxwell Albright (May 24, 1891– September 19, 1971who became well known for his work in authenticating the Dead Sea Scrolls in 1948.
2   The British Society for Propagating the Gospel Among the Jews founded London 1842, was the Presbyterian and dissenting churches' counterpart to the Anglican London Society for Promoting Christianity Among the Jews (founded 1809, today CMJ).[1] The two societies were in large part identical, but representing high-church and low-church traditions in British Christianity.[2] Among the founders of the low-church body in 1846 was Ridley Haim Herschell who founded Trinity Chapel on the Edgeware Road.
    (http://en.wikipedia.org/wiki/British_Society_for_the_Propagation_of_the_Gospel_Among _the_Jews accessed 11.6.2012)

An officer described an interview at which Mr Schonfield had told him of the step he was taking, and expressed his disappointment at this termination of a promising missionary career. The disappointment was shared by the committee generally. It was decided that his salary for the month of September should be paid to Mr. Schonfield and that the Secretary should convey to him in an interview the committee's acceptance of his resignation. It was also agreed that the Principal of the Glasgow Bible Training Institute be informed of what had taken place.

Picture 8: Bessie

Sadly the young lady died shortly afterwards in November 1922 at the age of 18 as the result of a bout of the Spanish Flu pandemic mentioned above. A recent correspondent with the family recollected:

> Bessie seems to have left Tottenham Girls High school to be a secretary at the American Express Company in London. She had the notorious Spanish flu, and went back to work too soon and had some kind of seizure, which left her paralysed down one side. She eventually died of "malignant endocarditis" in November 1922. Her birthday was in April.

Apparently this H1N1 virus particularly hit healthy young adults. It was nicknamed 'Spanish Flu' because wartime censors played down the effects it was having at home, concentrating on reporting on the epidemic in Spain which was neutral. My first thought was that the symptoms of the relapse and the seizure seemed to point to Aspirin poisoning. At the time overdoses of Aspirin were sometimes administered to patients suffering from the virus and this could have been the reason that Bessie died after she had apparently recovered from the flu. However, upon asking my son, who is an experienced surgeon and medical practitioner, he replied that he did not think that this was the case:

> As it is stated that she died of malignant endocarditis it is more probable that the flu weakened her immune system that she got a bacterial superinfection, a common complication in or after viral flu (= relapse, but actually a different infective agent).

> The seizure could have been caused by very high fever (common in either) then leading to paralysis.
>
> Of course a paralysis can be caused by Aspirin. It does not even need to be an overdose, just permanent intake of 2-3g/day for a longer time thins the blood and could lead to haemorrhage, but except the paralysis there is nothing else indicative in this direction.
>
> The remark of returning back to work too early would be quite typical for bacterial endocarditis, you have a phase of recovery, in between there can be high spikes of fever and the heart valves are slowly destroyed finally leading to death.
>
> I would say the thing was common bacteria as cause, sure, Aspirin is possible, but not so likely I would say.

It can only be speculated what their relationship actually was but it seems to have been framed by the particularly evangelical emotions which were driving Hugh in his search for truth at that time. The family's concerns seem to have been more with Hugh's involvement with evangelical Christianity than with any personal relationship with the young lady and it does not seem to be fruitful to read too much into that affair whilst there is no reason to expect that a young man of his age should not have an emotional experience. The love of his life was however to become Hélène whom he had known since he was five years old. Whether the young lady mentioned here had greater expectations than Hugh was able to return we shall never know.

Commenting on the situation in Waltham, our correspondent states:

> Hugh came and went fairly freely. My father says that he remembers on occasions waking up to find that Hugh had arrived the previous night and been put in his bed with him because there was no where else for him to sleep. He remembers listening at the top of the stairs after being sent to bed while Hugh and other people in the kitchen argued about whether the Jews would still be Jews when Jesus came back at the Second Coming. He says Hugh was "one on his own", meaning that he was unique, and impressed everyone at Bible studies with his knowledge of Hebrew.
>
> At some point Hugh's uncle visited the house and may have had a meal with my grandmother. He tried to persuade Hugh to come back home but Hugh would not. Someone with a title, a knight, gave Hugh and Bessie an award, a "statuette"? as the most promising young missionary couple. I wondered if this had been Sir Leon Levison as I have seen the biography by Frederick Levison. They were definitely regarded as a couple, and my cousin has a silver hairbrush-set Hugh gave to Bessie.

Hugh apparently had no further contact with the family or the group, and the family was upset that he did not attend Bessie's funeral.

Hugh was presented with a bible by his society colleagues and the King James' Bible was inscribed with the text "Presented to H. Schonfield as a token of esteem and appreciation. From his fellow workers June 8 1922". Jane McIntyre (the third daughter of David McIntyre) sent a copy of her father's book and an invitation to tea.

The world at large was still in turmoil and Mohandas Gandhi was sentenced to six years imprisonment in India for sedition. Joseph Stalin became General Secretary of the Soviet Communist Party and the Soviet Union, which lasted until 1991, came into being. The process of hyperinflation in Germany led eventually to the collapse of the currency. The International Parliamentary Union which was co-founded by Sir William

Randal Cremer was established. Hugh was later to become very much involved with the work of Cremer.

According to one of his daughters, Audrey, interviewed in the process of researching for this book, Hugh does not seem to have finished his studies at Glasgow University. However we do see mention in the above affair that the Principle of the Glasgow Bible Training Institute was informed of Hugh's resignation from the Society so he must already have been involved with them in 1922.

His actual studies at the Bible Training Institute in Glasgow, which later became the Glasgow Bible College, lasted two years and he graduated with a diploma. According to the Institute's report, he studied "Bible, Christian Doctrine, Elements of Mental Science, Elements of Medicine, Hebrew, etc. He took a good place in his classes."[3]. David McIntyre, evangelical and principal of the Institute from 1913 to 1938, pointed out that "I believe him to be a sincere Christian and trust that, with the blessing of God, he may be useful in the service of our Lord"[4]. The Bible Training Institute, located in Bothwell Street, Glasgow, was started under the influence of Dwight Lyman Moody and Ira D. Sankey, and even today ICC has close links to the Moody Bible Institute in Chicago, USA. The college offers Certificate, Diploma, Degree and Postgraduate level qualifications in Theology, Youth Work, Urban Theology and Children's Ministry[5]. In a letter written in 1988, Fred Levison says that he remembers Hugh from these days in the early 20's when he was studying in Glasgow and Hugh visited him in his home in Edinburgh. It is worth pointing out that there were close links between the Institute and the University of Glasgow which awarded David McIntyre an honorary doctorate of divinity in 1924[6]. It is reported of Hugh that "he attended some courses at King's College, London, and in 1926 went to Glasgow University to study Semitic and Oriental Languages"[7]. A footnote in this quoted text states that "This is stated by Frederick Levison (1989:279) but the archives at Glasgow University show only that he was present for the 1926/1927 session and attended classes in Logic and English, giving no evidence of graduation or a degree award [as discussed below]. On his record it states that he opted to take Hebrew but he was not listed on class lists for this session."[8] The author of that article goes on to say "This lack of information may reflect the concern of the times not to record detailed information about Jewish students, and the question of the precise nature of Schonfield's academic qualifications, including the doctorate [see below] that is referred to in later publications, awaits further research"[9].

Another researcher remarks that

> Schonfield never states that he worked towards a degree or that he was a graduate and it should not be implied that he was dishonest or some kind of 'failure' for not entering for any examinations as we do not know the circumstances. Schonfield

3   This is documented in a letter from the Glasgow Bible Training Institute dated 22nd April 1926 and signed by D.M. McIntyre, principle of the Institute. He was the author of a number of Christian books, the most well known being *The Hidden Life of Prayer.*
4   Ibid.
5   http://en.wikipedia.org/wiki/International_Christian_College
6   Oxford Dictionary of National Biography
    http://www.oxforddnb.com/view/printable/101334. (10.11.2013)
7   Harvey, Richard (2002) *Passing over the Plot? The Life and Work of Hugh Schonfield (1901-1988)* in Mishknan, Issue No. 37, 2002, p. 38.
8   Ibid.
9   Ibid

does mention that after he left college he got married, worked during the day for Michael (sic.) [Herbert] Joseph the publisher and carried out his studies in the evenings; so financial considerations may have precluded an academic career[10]. On the other hand, as we will see, Schonfield was very much a 'man on a mission' and not likely to have the inclination or the patience to complete a degree programme. He had a thirst for knowledge and probably viewed a degree as unnecessarily bureaucratic[11]".

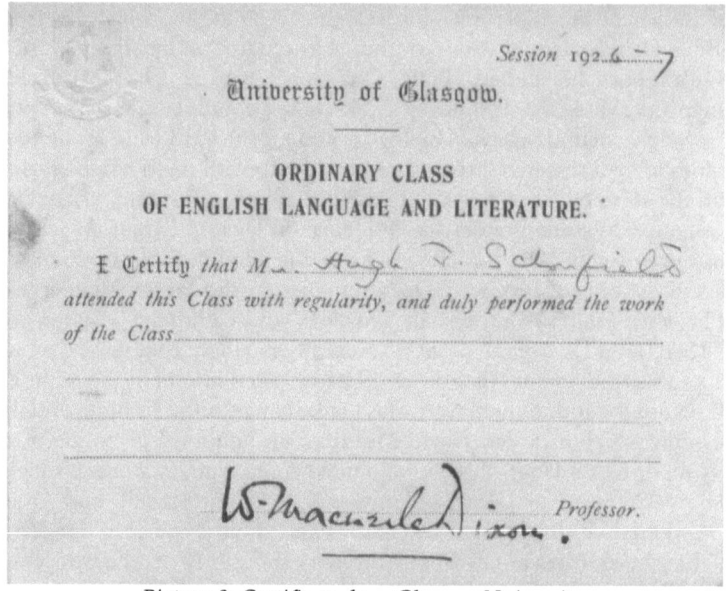

Picture 9: Certificate from Glasgow University

Since this was written, other information has come to light which would tend to detract from that author's last hypothesis. There were obviously personal and family issues involved in Glasgow which would have made the move essential.

It is clear from the above that during these years Hugh underwent an evangelical conversion to Christianity and became a committed Christian. However, it seems that the pull of his Jewish roots were still exerting a considerable influence on his thinking.

Once again, as we can observe, there has been some controversy about Hugh's academic qualifications and inadvertently, it was understood by some that he received his doctorate from Glasgow University. There have also been those who have been at pains to discredit his academic achievements in some way, especially when these ideas conflicted with cherished concepts of Jesus and Christianity. There may be a confusion with the honorary doctorate received by David McIntyre at this time as Hugh's doctorate was in fact an honorary doctorate awarded to him by an Indian University much later, based on published works. St. Paul's School believed that he received his doctorate from Glasgow – a DS Litt. – but, as has been stated elsewhere, the University has no record

10 Schonfield, Hugh J. (1970) *The Politics of God,* Chicago: Henry Regency Company. Cited in Power, Owen M. (2011), p. xv. – see reference below.
11 Power, Owen M. (2011) *Hugh Schonfield: A Case Study of Complex Jewish Identities.* A thesis submitted to the University of Manchester for the degree of Master of Philosophy in the Faculty of Humanities, p. 16f.

of his graduating and neither did Hugh make any claim to this himself. He attended 'ordinary Class of English Language and Literature' at the University of Glasgow between 1926 and 1927 and we have written confirmation of this.[12]

On the other hand, we have a letter of recommendation for admission into Glasgow University dated 23rd April 1926 from an Alex Hay, Joppa Portobello, Senior Minister of a church with the following text:

> I have much pleasure in giving testimony on behalf of Mr. Hugh Schonfield. I have known him for some years and have also known something of his decision and his Christian Work.
>
> I believe him to be an ernest and sincere believer – one who is keenly anxious to do his utmost for the cause – who will make an eager and successful student.
>
> He has already learnt to survive some sadness which has formed the reality of patience of his faith.
>
> I am glad to know that he is seeking admission to your College and I therefore most cordially commend him.

It seems rather strange that a minister would recommend someone for an English literature course and make a special point of dedication to Christian work. I think it probable that the mention of 'survive some sadness' in this letter refers to the affair with the young lady mentioned previously. Undoubtedly, Hugh, who was, in my experience, a highly sensitive person, would have been very emotionally hurt by all that transpired at that time.

Again, we have a letter of recommendation written by a Robert McLean of Buchanan Memorial U.F. Church in Caledonia Road dated April 23rd 1926 which reads as follows:

> This is to certify that Mr. H. Schonfield is well known to me having acted as missionary at the above church, also having supplied the pulpit with great acceptance during the vacancy. The Kirk Session recorded in their minutes at the time their high estimate of his character and ability. I have the greatest pleasure in recommending him to the College Committee. His early training is of great value in the exposition of the Scriptures.

Michael R. Derby also wrote about Hugh as a scholar in the following terms:

> He studied Semitic and Oriental languages at the University of Glasgow and attended courses at the Bible Training Institute, a conservative college in the city, and, although he received no academic training in theology, he was an accomplished writer on religious themes. he was general secretary of the International Hebrew Christian Alliance for a short period, contributed frequently to the Hebrew Christian Quarterly, its periodical, and as literary editor most of the reviews were from his pen. An important essay in serial form in this journal was the Short History of Jewish Christianity, published in 1936 as The History of Jewish Christianity. As an advocate of the inclusion of Jewish cultural traditions within Christian worship — he was a first generation Hebrew Christian —and of the foundation of a Jewish

---

12 Email from Glasgow University dated 14th February 2013: *Thank you for your enquiry about Hugh Joseph Schonfield. I can confirm that he studied at the University of Glasgow in 1926, aged 25 years old (Source: matriculation album, our reference R8/5/47/9). This is the only information that I have been able to find on him as it seems he did not graduate and there is no record of him abandoning his studies. This is the only record we have for him in our archive.*

Christian synagogue, Schonfield's emphasis in this work is on the revival of an independent Jewish Christian community which will re-establish its original apostolic position of authority[13].

Picture 10: Sir Leon Levison

All of this is rather confusing and we have not been able to come to a final conclusion of exactly what and how long he studied at Glasgow University which seems to have lost its records of that time. Maybe he decided to study English literature after not being able to get a place in the theology department or just that he obtained recommendations from those he knew and they just happened to be in the theological area. However according to his own recollections later, his studies in Glasgow either included or allowed him to study a number of foreign languages and to research the sacred literature. It would also seem that the studies at the Bible Training Institute were connected with the University. Hugh Schonfield's learning and qualifications were sourced much more in his own research and lifelong study but undoubtedly the experience with Christianity which he received at the hands of the Glasgow Bible Institute and his own conversion will have stood him in good stead in understanding the Christian perspective.

After this intensive brush with Christianity, Hugh started to consider how this all tied into Judaism. Jesus may have been the expected Messiah but somehow the Christian in-

---

13 Darby, Michael R. (2010) The Emergence of the Hebrew Christian Movement in Nineteenth-Century Britain, p.14-15.

terpretation was missing something and yet there had to be a message for Judaism in all of this. So he became involved with the International Hebrew Christian Alliance, be-

Picture 11: IHCA Certificate

coming a life member in September of 1925. At that time Leon Levison was the president and J.E. Davidson was secretary. This was to be the beginning of a very moving time for Hugh and later also Hélène. Hugh put an enormous effort into the organisation and felt strongly that it was important for the Jewish people to accept Jesus as Messiah. There may have been a dawning awareness of the Christian attempt to intrude into Judaism and a realisation that Jews would have difficulty with some of the Christian doctrines, particularly the idea of a divine Jesus.

It would seem with hindsight that the world was rapidly heading towards the next catastrophe as Mussolini became dictator in Italy and Adolf Hitler published *Mein Kampf*. The world was still very much oppressed by conservatism and bigotry and a biology teacher in the USA was even arrested for teaching Darwin's Theory of Evolution. In technology great advances were being made and one, which Hugh would later make use of, found its roots at this time when Charles Jenkins achieved the first transmission of moving pictures with sound with a mechanical device. Charles Logie Baird managed to transmit the first TV greyscale images.

Of course he needed to start thinking about how to earn a living as he was planning his marriage to Hélène Cohn, his close friend since childhood. Apparently, he had fallen in love with her at a certain picnic in Richmond Park[14]. Later, Hélène was to relate to Charlyne Valensin that this was "holy ground". He retired from Holford Bottomley Advertising Service Ltd (the company was founded in 1900 and was wound up in 1965) to take up an appointment as promotions manager for the Northcliffe Newspapers Group, which he held from 1926-1936[15]. Holford Bottomley's father Hans was a dealer in wireless accessories.

Britain was not without troubles in 1926 as martial law was declared because of the General Strike.

In 1927, on 27th July, the marriage to Hélène, which was to be such a key factor in Hugh's life, took place in London. Out of this marriage there would be three daughters, Marion, Joyce Wendy and Audrey. In the ensuing years, life would very much be an uphill struggle in these years of economic depression. With a family to support, it meant that the early books were written after a day in the office. He yearned for the day when he would be able to give himself completely to writing and research but for a period of six months he was out of work. This enabled him to write his first important book. This task required great determination as they were living on a small amount of savings and some insignificant borrowings from his mother. Audrey feels that he always believed that he had not used his gifts to the full, that far from interruptions and trivial domestic disturbances, the perfect book could be written but that he did not expect he would ever write it. She believes that book, however, was *Man, Mystic and Messiah*.

Interestingly, as an aside, it would seem that in the early days before their marriage, Hélène went regularly to synagogue and that she would meet him there.

Thus in this eventful year Hugh's first book was published by T & T Clark, entitled *An Old Hebrew Text of Matthew's Gospel*. According to the Hornsey Journal of April 15th 1955, he carried out the work for this book whilst 'at Glasgow University' which again would suggest that he studied more than English literature there and which I think puts it in a nutshell. The book was published on a shared profit agreement.

The publishing of this book was a very important milestone in Hugh's career as a scholar as is demonstrated in an article in *The Expository Times* January 1928 Vol. XXXIX No. 4:

> Mr. Hugh J. Schonfield, in *An Old Hebrew Text of St. Matthew's Gospel*, makes the startling claim that the du Tillet MS. of St. Matthew's Gospel, published in 1555, and hitherto considered to be a Hebrew version of the Vulgate, may be a descendant of a lost Hebrew original of St. Matthew's Gospel, and that at any rate it contains within itself evidences of the existence of a Hebrew original underlying St. Matthew's text.
>
> A comparison of Mr. Schonfield's translation of the Hebrew Matthew—for which we owe him a debt of gratitude—with our English Version reveals many interesting variants, and a careful consideration of them would help us to form a judgment on his thesis.

14 According to Rabi Rayner in his memorial address on 15th March 1979. We have not been able to ascertain when this took place but it would suggest that whilst Hélène was his childhood friend, he actually fell in love with her much later – and possibly even after the affair with Bessie.
15 Information furnished by St. Paul's School.

A very interesting reading in the Hebrew Matthew is to be found in 8:20: 'And Jesus saith unto him, Foxes have holes, and the birds of the heavens nests; but the Son of man hath not a floor whereon he may lay his head.' No doubt Mr. Schonfield is inclined to see in this last clause an authentic touch of the Master, and accordingly to derive support from it for his theory of a Hebrew (and not merely an Aramaic or Syriac) original.

Certainly the addition of the word 'floor' seems to lend a new pathos to the utterance. It is suggested that the reference is to a paved recess in the common khan or caravanserai of the village, raised a foot or two above the level of the courtyard where the cattle were tied; there the traveller would find for the merest trifle a place on which to lie and sleep. And yet Jesus could not afford that merest trifle!

But is it the point of the utterance that Jesus was stricken with poverty? As Montefiore remarks, He never seems to have been at a loss for friends or lodgings. Is it not rather that He warned the scribe who wanted to follow Him that He was living at the time a life of wanderings, having no fixed abode? If that is the meaning, then the reference in the Hebrew Matthew to the 'floor' of the inn is perhaps not altogether apposite. Could He not always find accommodation there, should the worst come to the worst?

The realistic note struck in this old Hebrew text lends support to Mr. Schonfield's contention that the du Tillet MS. is very early (of the second century A.D., he thinks); but it may be gathered from the foregoing that we should have difficulty in allowing that the reading in 8:20 supports the argument for a Hebrew original. Indeed, it looks as though the translator has taken liberties with his text.

We should not underestimate the importance of this discovery for Hugh which was really a big turning point in his life. Elsewhere he writes about this:

Looking back on the first decade of my quest I could say with confidence that I had had a rewarding glimpse of the man and the Jew that Jesus had been. This was encouraging. There could be no doubt in my mind that this individual had really existed, and was here for the finding. But how was he to be reached, almost in spite of the Gospels?

Initially, as I could see much later in my life, I had been too starry-eyed, too thrilled by the idealism of the messianic, to be sufficiently analytical and objective. In this respect the fortuitous acquisition of an old Hebrew text of Matthew had been salutary: it had compelled me to study the Gospels more coolly and intently. I was a long way yet from competence to investigate adequately; but I could detect that the image of Jesus they presented had largely been overpainted and adapted, so that Jesus, like the Patriarch Joseph in Egypt, had become 'a stranger to his brethren'. The non-Jewish student would not be so acutely conscious of this transformation, since he would think it proper and appropriate that Jesus should be alienated from the Jews and from Judaism—not so much a *gentle* as a *Gentile* Jesus.[16]

Communication in the world was making great strides as in 1927 the Bell Telephone Company made the first successful long distance television transmission and the first transatlantic telephone call was made. Charles Lindbergh made his historic first solo nonstop transatlantic flight. In that year the League of Nations made a treaty abolishing all types of slavery. This was in a world whose population had now reached 2 billion.

---

16 Schonfield, Hugh J. (2004) *Jesus Man-Mystic-Messiah*, London: Open Gate Press, p.32.

The influenza epidemic was still taking a large toll of lives with 1000 people a week dying in Britain alone.

At the age of 27, Hugh's career as a historian and scholar was now beginning to take shape and 1928 found him reading a paper at the IHCA (International Hebrew Christian Association) conference in Hamburg from 16th-21st July. This meeting must have had a very charismatic nature because it was reported that "the opening meeting was one which thrilled each delegate in his innermost soul, because he at once realised that this was a historic gathering, the like of which has never been equalled in the history of the Church since the first century". At this meeting Hugh "pointed out that the needs enumerated in the address given by Sir Leon Levison were both great and urgent, and appealed to the members and associate members of the IHCA to render help by trying to arrange meetings in various churches of their own denomination, or in giving drawing-room meetings in their houses, so that the needs could be made known. In this respect he felt that everybody could render some service to the IHCA".

Perhaps today it is difficult for us to imagine what revolutionary happenings were taking place and rights which we today take for granted were only then just coming into force. For example, it was in this year that the United Kingdom lowered the voting age for women from 30 down to 21 making it the same for both men and women. In the USA, Al Smith became the first catholic to be nominated for president. On the technological front, the first colour television transmission was demonstrated and machine sliced bread was introduced for the first time in the USA. In the world of politics hopes for peace were always present and the Kellogg–Briand Pact was signed, the first treaty where those states which signed agreed not to use war as a means of resolving conflicts. As history has demonstrated, this has unfortunately not led to the abolition of war. Herbert Hoover became president of the USA.

This does not mean that Hugh could find no time for meditation and his artistic talents. An example is the following piece of serendipity with the historian's touch:

THE LADY-BIRD

A Springtime Secret.

Lady-bird, Lady-bird, fly away home!
Your house is on fire, - your children at home!

Most of us, in our childhood days, have chanted this quaint couplet, as we spied the little red insect with the black spots, during a country ramble. But how many have given a thought as to its real meaning? Yet, like many a nursery rhyme, the germ of a great truth is hidden here.

Years ago, the Lady-bird used to be known as the Lady-cow, and in the south-western counties of England it still goes by the queer appellation of God Almighty's cow. Dictionaries tell us that Lady-bird is only a contraction for Our Lady's bug, for we are dealing with neither a bird nor a cow, but a beetle.

How came it then, we may ask, that a beetle should be dedicated to the Virgin Mary? The answer is, that time alone is responsible, for originally, the Lady-bird was dedicated to the most venerable of goddesses long before Christianity was heard of. Thousands of years ago, Mother Nature was worshipped as "Our Lady", and her shrines may still be seen in many lands. She had many other familiar names, Isis, Istar, Astarte, etc., all signifying the same idea, - the great feminine productive principle. Both the cow and the beetle from different reasons were sacred to

Christian times

the Virgin Mother of the Universe as symbolising Nature's nourishing and—the latter productive qualities

Picture 12: Abstract Drawing by Hugh J. Schonfield

There is an older version of our rhyme than the one with which we are so familiar. It runs:

Lady-cow, lady-cow, fly away home!
Thy house is on fire, thy children are flown.
All but a little one under a stone:
Fly thee home, Lady-cow, ere it be gone.

Nature's house is the solar year, the fiery pathway of the sun, represented by the months or signs of the Zodiac which were anciently ten in number.

The little one under the stone signifies Nature's infant off-spring; life renewed after the hard winter; the green shoots appearing above the stony soil. With this in mind we may re-read our couplet as it has been restored by Hargrave Jennings[17]:

Lady-bird, Lady-bird, (Mother Nature) fly away home!
*Your house is **OF** fire (the annual pathway of the sun)*
*Your children (the Zodiacal signs, or months) are **TEN***

The Ladybird thus reminds us, as it reminded our ancestors ages ago, of the ever-glorious return of Springtime.

1929 found the young couple living at 134a Sinclair Road in Kensington and also at

Picture 13: The 1928 IHCA Conference

191 Brondesbury Park in NW London. They equipped their home with furniture from Maple & Company Ltd. A home was now necessary as the first daughter Marion was on her way.

This year was the year of the Wall Street Crash which marked the beginning of the Great Depression. Riots broke out between Palestinians and Jews set off when British police took down a screen which Jews had put up in front of the Wailing Wall in Jerusalem.

---

17 Hargrave Jennings (1817-1890). He was a Rosicrucian and occultist. Reference to this is to be found in Jennings, Hargrave (1887) *The Rosicrucians: Their Rites and Mysteries.*

The foundation of a family does not seem to have hindered Hugh's energy for writing and research as his second book, *The Lost Book of the Nativity of John* was published by T & T Clark in that year. He also wrote an article in the December Expository Times under the rubric of *Should "Things Strangled" be omitted from Acts xv. 29?*. The article is quite Christian in its approach and employs the term 'Lord Jesus'. This article is reproduced below in its entirety:

> Article in *The Expository Times* December 1929
>
> Should "Things strangled" be omitted from Acts xv. 29?
>
> By Hugh J. Schonfield, London.
>
> In the course of some recent studies in the Sermon on the Mount I made a discovery, though perhaps this is rather too strong a term, which happens to throw light on the vexed question of the text of the Apostolic decree in Ac 15. The new evidence which I am able to bring forward seems to show that the Western Text is right in omitting "things strangled" from the number of prohibitions. The late Professor Peake discussed the problem in a recent article.[18]
>
> "The question as to the decree and the four prohibitions," he wrote, "is one of the most tangled problems in the history of the early Church. There is, in the first place, a serious variation of text. According to the generally accepted text we have apparently three food prohibitions combined with one ethical. But there are very early and important witnesses which omit the reference to "things strangled." If this text is correct, it is still possible to suppose that, apart from the ethical, we have two food prohibitions. But the removal of "things strangled" makes it possible to take all three as ethical, that is, as prohibitions of idolatry, murder, and impurity."[19]
>
> It is well known that the evidence of the earliest MSS is against the omission, while the external evidence is in favour. If "things strangled" is retained, it is very difficult to regard the decree as historical. As Canon Wilson says: "There is the incongruity, which must have struck every one, of coupling with these food-laws the prohibition of fornication, as if it were on a level with them. There is the unaccountable omission of all mention of circumcision, which from 15^5 we see was the thing chiefly insisted on. There is the inconsistency of saying in the decree that "they would not trouble them which from among the Gentiles turn to God," and then imposing on them food-laws which there is evidence to show were not generally observed among the Jews of the Dispersion, as seems also to have been admitted by St. Peter (15^{10}). There is the statement, in the Bezan text, of Ac 21^{25}, "we sent, giving judgment that they should observe nothing of that sort. "There is the strange statement (in 15^{31}) that, when the decree was reported at Antioch, "the multitude rejoiced for the consolation." There is the still more inexplicable fact that St. Paul, shortly afterwards, when the question about the eating of meat "sold in the shambles" (1 Co 10^{25}) which had been offered to idols, does not allude to this decree, while he absolutely forbids (1 Co $10^{20\text{-}21}$) sharing in idol feasts. And, finally, there is the fact that no Western Father, or apologist, or hostile critic, ever alludes to such a food-law as enjoined on Christians. If it ever existed it was ignored from the first."[20]

---

18 'Paul and the Jewish Christians,' *Bulletin of The John Rylands Library*, Jan. 1929, pp. 31-62.
19 P. 45.
20 The Acts of the Apostles, translated from the Codex Bezae, Introduction, pp. 16-17.

In his next paragraph the same writer concludes that "if the words "things strangled" were not in the decree, the natural interpretation of the decree would, beyond all question, have been that it forbade the three great sins of idolatry, murder, and fornication; and was, in fact, a purely moral law."[21]

Professor Peake found it "extraordinary that the Gentile disciples should be told that nothing more would be required from them than to abstain from idolatry, murder, and fornication. The reference to murder in particular," he felt, "is difficult to accept. It is hardly credible that it should be necessary to prohibit this in Christian Churches."[22] He therefore decided "that the text with four prohibitions is correct, three of these having definitely to do with forbidden forms of food."[23]

Will not the difficulty be overcome, if it can be proved that it was just these three ethical commandments that were regarded by the Pharisees and by the Lord Jesus Himself as fundamental for society? So we have it already in the Mishnah:

"Captivity enters the world on account of idol-worship, fornication, and bloodshed."[24]

Elsewhere, it is said, "Whoso slandereth his neighbour committeth sins as great as idolatry, fornication, and murder".[25] And, indeed, so fundamental were these three commandments regarded by the Rabbis in the stress of the times that they declare, "Any sin denounced by the Law may be committed by a man if his life is threatened, except the sins of idolatry, fornication, and murder".[26]

To the Jewish religious authorities, then, the commandments concerning idolatry, fornication, and murder were τούτων τῶν ἐπάγκες 'these compulsory things,' exactly what the Jewish Christian elders and apostles call them in the decree (15^{28}).

The Sermon on the Mount is evidence that this view was held by the Pharisees at an earlier date, for Jesus, in setting forth the righteousness of the Law which should exceed that of the Pharisees, comments first on these very same commandments; murder (Mt 5^{21}), fornication (Mt 5^{27}), and idolatry (Mt 5^{33}). It may be objected that the last deals not with idolatry but oaths. But this is answered by understanding that Jesus condemned swearing on the ground that it indirectly countenanced idolatry. The heathen might suppose, if Jews swore by any created thing, that they too were polytheists. And if Jews accustomed themselves to such oaths they might be led to use the oaths of the heathen as well, and so God's name would be profaned. Hence the Rabbis forbade partnership with a heathen, "lest at any time the heathen should impose an oath on the Jew, and he be obliged to swear by the heathen's idol; and the Law says (Ex 23^{13}), 'Make no mention of the name of other gods, neither let it be heard out of thy mouth'".[27]

We may infer, I think, that Jesus knew of the Pharisee teaching on the fundamental character of these commandments.

---

21 Ibid. Canon Wilson notes the association in Rev 22^{15}, "Without are the fornicators, and the murderers, and the idolaters."
22 P. 47.
23 P. 48.
24 Aboth, v. 9.
25 Ercch. fol. xv. B.
26 Sanhed. fol. lxxiv. A.
27 Sanhed. fol. lxiii. B.

Picture 14: Cigarettes

Professor Peake admitted that ethical prohibitions would harmonize better with all the circumstances than food-laws, but he was too honest a scholar to adopt this interpretation without a valid reason and merely to evade a difficulty. Perhaps the additional evidence which I have adduced may be found adequate to show that after all there is justification for omitting "things strangled," and that on this issue, at any rate, the Western text is to be preferred.

Around this time, an interesting new development come to pass which demonstrates Hugh's interest and capability in English literature. It was at this time that he made the acquaintances with Leonard and Virginia Woolf and published *Letters to Frederick Tennyson*. He had found this collection of unpublished letters written to Fred Tennyson the poet, eldest brother of the Poet Laureate, written during the period between 1831-1884[28].

In an article in *The Church Overseas* where Hugh commented on an article by Dr. Montefiore[29] in the *Hibbert Journal* of April 1929. Hugh expressed some understanding for Jewish conversion to Christianity and he seemed to support the idea of missions to the Jews. He concludes,

One last word. Unless the Jewish people ranges itself on the side of Christ, Christianity is a failure and the angelic song of "peace on earth" is a dream of idle shepherds. The hope of the world lies in a converted Israel, not assimilated but still distinct, fulfilling its mediatorial office among the nations. I can agree with Dr. Montefiore that a reconciliation between Christ and his people will not come from Jewish missions. It must come from within.

It was certainly a time of much literary activity and he wrote quite a number of articles about advertising standards and methods at this time, including a lengthy article in Punch, March 12th 1930, on the National Savings *Magic Stamp* poem used in its campaign:

Buy a magic Savings Stamp,
Stick it on your card -
SIX-PENCE WEEK-LY
It isn't very hard.
Ten years roll away -
How the money's grown!

28 Advertiser's Weekly, July 5. 1929.
29 Claude Joseph Goldsmid Montefiore (1858—1938)

FIF-TEEN POUND-NOTES
All your very own.

This was the year when the Moon moved closest to Earth (Perigee) whilst at the fullest phase of the Lunar Cycle. This is the closest moon distance at 356,397 km in memor-

Picture 15: Hadleigh Castle Essex – Water Painting by Hugh Schonfield

able history so I guess anything could happen although I doubt it was the motive for Hélène, who had some valuable jewellery, for them to decide to take out an insurance policy to cover them with the County Fire Office Ltd. to the sum of 120 pounds!

However, it was the year of Gandhi's famous Salt March and this would have been an event which certainly would have been of interest to our couple. It is amazing in any life story of a famous person that it is always a combination of the significant and the trivial. At the same time, the National Socialist Party gained 100 seats in the German Reichstag and with hindsight we know what forebodings this entailed.

In 1931, the cooperation with Leonard Woolf intensified and they jointly issued a magazine entitled *The Search, A Quarterly Review*. Only four issues of *The Search* were published between January and October 1931 (Volume 1, Numbers 1-4). The relationship between the editors and Leonard Woolf was not smooth and the Hogarth Press published only the first two issues. "*The Search* aims at presenting its readers, in form as readily assimilable as possible, with the researches and conclusions of modern scholarship in the domains of Religion, Philosophy, Science, Literature and Art." (From inside front cover). According to Harvey, Hugh was joint editor with E.J. Langford Garstin who was a member of "Alpha and Omega", a circle of occultists interested in hermetic magic and associated with Alastair Crowley. Whilst the magazine was described generally as "devoted to the discovery of Truth in Religion, Science, Philosophy, Literature and Art", it was particularly interested in esoteric religious knowledge."[30] This could be another reason why Hugh did not get on too well with his co-editor.

In this year, he and Hélène attended the 3rd Conference of the IHCA. Helen was given a book with an inscription by Leon Levison, *Songs in the Night* by M. E. Logie-Pirie.

Hugh had played an important role in the foundation of the IHCA and had also shaped many of its tenets although his suggestion was rejected by the Commission put in place to define the tenets of faith. Harvey states:

> His contribution also reflects an orthodox Christology, with Jesus as "God's son," the "one mediator between God and man" and the incarnation expressed by "God was manifest in the flesh and we beheld His glory – the glory as of the only begotten of the Father, full of grace and truth"[31]

His thinking on the role and person of Jesus was already taking shape and a book was published in 1932 by the Search Publishing Co. entitled *The Speech That Moved the World*. Because of its controversial nature he decided to author it under his pseudonym *Hegesippus*. The Catholic magazine *Tablet* was very upset by its content and published a critical review:

> Here is an interpretation of the Sermon on the Mount by an anonymous writer. The erroneous theory which colours his thesis is that "Christianity was never intended to be a religion, but was a governmental system based on the principle of Divine Sovereignty." It was "an integral part of the great Jewish patriotic and theocratic movement." Christ was just such a Messiah as the Jews of his day expected; one who should deliver his people from the Roman yoke and then establish the kingdom of God on earth. What is called the Sermon on the Mount is really a political speech!—or so "Hegesippus" affirms. "It should be possible, as Jesus intended, for all men of all creeds to be Christians—followers of the Messiah—without prejudice to the religion which they profess, whether they are Jews, Mahometans, Buddhists or Hindus." It is strange that a "Speech which moved the World" should have suffered worldwide misinterpretation until an anonymous writer took up his pen nearly two thousand years after the Sermon was preached. H.T.[32]

There was a generally reactionary spirit about at this time both in politics and religion. The Archbishop of Canterbury forbade Anglican Church remarriage of divorced persons, for example. There were other developments which would have a considerable bearing on world events and influence our subject person in the future such as the World Disarmament Conference in Geneva in response to the demand made by Germany for equality of status abolishing Part V of the Treaty of Versailles, which had disarmed Germany and the French demand for security, maintaining Part V. The Germans walked out of the conference on the grounds that their wish was not being

---

30 Harvey, Richard (2002) *Passing over the Plot? The Life and Work of Hugh Schonfield (1901-1988)* in Mishknan, Issue No. 37, 2002, p. 40.
31 Harvey, Richard (2002) *Passing over the Plot? The Life and Work of Hugh Schonfield (1901-1988)* in Mishknan, Issue No. 37, 2002, p. 43.
32 *The Tablet*, 3rd December 1932. http://archive.thetablet.co.uk/article/3rd-december-1932/30/so-now-we-know. Accessed 24th July 2014.

complied with but they were later offered a compromise.. By this time the foundations stones for Adolf Hitler's plans to grasp dictatorial powers had already been laid and the Weimar Republic had de facto ceased to be.

In 1932 Aldous Huxley published *Brave New World* and Hugh and Hélène's second daughter, Joyce was born whilst the young family were living at 75 Woodstock Avenue in Golders Green[33], London. Hugh also found time to write an article for the Exchange and Mart about his discovery of the an early work by Lewis Carroll:

Early Work of Lewis Carroll

How a Bazaar Reader Profited from a Find

by Hugh Schonfield

My discovery of a collection of five volumes of letters from the Tennyson family found in an old furniture shop was told to readers in *THE BAZAAR* last October. My good fortune, however, has not deserted me, for I have recently made another find which is of special interest this year, in view of the Lewis Carroll centenary celebrations.

Rummaging in the box outside a second-hand booksellers shop in the City, I picked up two volumes bound in one of *The Train*, a monthly magazine published as long ago as 1856-1857. The price asked was two shillings. Glancing through the pages I noticed several contributions by Lewis Carroll. Of course, I bought the book, and proceeded to investigate. I learned on reference to Carroll's *Life and Letters* that he had used the famous pseudonym for the first time in writing for *The Train* and, indeed the final choice had rested with its editor, Edmund Yates. Dodgson, to give him his real name, was then only 24 years of age.

Carroll's contributions consisted of five poems:- *Solitude* (March, 1856); *The Path of Roses* (May 1856); *The Three Voices* (November 1856; *The Sailor's Wife* (May 1857); *Hiawatha's Photo* (December, 1857); and a tale..... (October... *Novelty and Romance*..., 1856).

By a coincidence the centenary of Carroll's birthday fell due on January 27 of this year shortly after I had made my find, and I decided that it might be worthwhile to publish the poems and tale for the first time in one volume with the original illustrations of Charles Bennett and William Mc. Connell, increasing the usefulness of the book by appending from Carroll's life and passages from his works referring to trains or railway traveling – subjects in which he had been interested since, as a boy of 12, he built a toy station in the garden of his father's rectory at Croft.

He also published a book entitled *The New Hebrew Typography* in which he makes suggestions for a modern Hebrew typeface. This book is still cited today. A review stated:

"*The New Hebrew Typography* with an introduction by Stanley Morison and numerous Types designed by the author and drawn by Bertram F. Stevenson."[34] British biblical scholar Hugh Schonfield (1901-88) endeavoured to create a type for a nation without an independent home (at the time): the Hebrew nation. Playing off German modernists who called for a "New Typography", Schonfield promoted his *New Hebrew Typography*. For this campaign, he regularized and Romanized the forms of

---

33 The area is noted especially for its large Jewish population.
34 Excerpted from the Face the Nation exhibit at the University of St. Thomas, http://www.goodreads.com/book/show/18375083-the-new-hebrew-typography (11.11.2013).

the Hebrew letters. The contrast between horizontal thicks and vertical thins that characterized Hebrew writing for millennia, for example, was inverted into horizontal thins and vertical thicks, matching the typical treatment of the Latin letter in European types. Like the modernists, Schonfield advocated reform for the sake of rationalization and contemporaneity—but he also seemed to argue in his designs that revising Hebrew letters into the forms that gentiles can recognize as familiar and comfortable might ease the assimilation of a Jewish minority in Europe.

1933 was the year in which Adolf Hitler was appointed Chancellor of Germany, which was to change the fate of the world and especially the Jews in Europe. I cannot help wondering how Hugh would have felt about this event at the time or whether he could imagine the horrors which were about to befall the world and especially the Jews. After all, it was in this year that the building of Dachau concentration camp was completed and a one-day boycott of all Jewish-owned businesses in Germany was organised as well as the banning of the kosher ritual of shechita. Albert Einstein was certainly aware of what was happening and fled from Germany to the USA. Hugh seems to be living life as normal, diversifying once again and becoming a shareholder with 100 pounds in a venture called "Abraham's Vineyard Ltd". He published two further books, *The Book of British Industries* through Denis Archer (UK) and *Jesus Christ XIX Centuries After* through his Search Publishing Co. He wrote later[35] regarding the former, "in the post-war years I devised and published at my own cost *The Book of British Industries* to assist economic recovery".

Franklin Roosevelt became President of the USA in that year with the main concern being to fight the economic depression which still continued. Prohibition in the USA was lifted yet Cannabis became illegal. This law would be used later in an attempt to silence one of Hugh's famous followers, John Lennon.

By the time 1934 had come, Hitler had established himself as "Führer" whilst the Soviet Union had joined the League of Nations which Germany had previously left.

Hugh was managing director of the publishers Dennis Archer but this was sold to Hutchinsons in 1934 being reported in *The Bookseller*, Wednesday, September 19th 1934 thus:

> HUTCHINSON'S GAIN ANOTHER IMPRINT DENIS ARCHER LTD. TAKEN OVER
>
> *The Bookseller* understands that the firm of Denis Archer, Ltd., has been taken over by the Hutchinson group of publishers.
>
> Denis Archer is one of the younger publishing firms in London and, in the short life as an individual firm, published a number of books which met with success. Among these may be mentioned *The Junior Outline of History, The Child's Own Limerick Book, The Book of British Industries, Stable Money, Jacob Across Jabbok, The Evening Standard Books of Short Stories, The Oriental Caravan, Hosanna and Stir.*
>
> It published The World of To-morrow, memorable as an example of book-production of a revolutionary kind. With the Book of British Industries, the firm rendered a service in bringing together the greatest company of industrial experts in the country.

---

35 This was a note (date unknown) addressed to Ambrose (Appleby?) where he states that 'there are of course things about my history in a British national context, which mostly will not be known to you.

Towards the end of last year the house gave signs of being stabilized, after the normal vicissitudes of "growing pains".

Mr. Hugh Schonfield, its managing director, reporting progress last November in *The Bookseller*, wrote: "The past year, from the aspect of mind and body, is one which both the directors and the staff would fain forget. It has been a period of long, feverish activity, late hours in the office and little relaxation out of it. Printers and binders have viewed our haggard faces with grave concern and wondered at the full sixty seconds worth of work that we cram into every minute. Despite the depression and despite our handicap of youth, we are now forging ahead."

About the same time the firm announced its intention of specializing in good humorous fiction, and Miss Cicely Courtneidge, the world-famous comedienne, joined the Board of Directors in an editorial capacity. The firm was also associated with the institution of a publishing venture for the production of new novels at three-and-sixpence, to be sold to libraries.

Despite hard work on the part of the directors, increase of capital and an encouraging amount of success, large difficulties remained in the way, and a few months ago the firm of Denis Archer, Ltd., was forced to call a meeting of its creditors.

The Hutchinson group of publishing firms includes Messrs. Stanley Paul, Messrs. Selwyn & Blount, Messrs. John Long, Messrs. Rider, Messrs. Jarrolds, Messrs. Hurst & Blackett, etc.

Obviously, Hugh was interested in finding a new occupation and applied in November of that year to the Colonial Office with a report on the English book market in Palestine and suggesting they employ him in the Educational Department in Palestine for this purpose. It would seem that Hugh was intending to move to Palestine. There was no vacancy as it happens. However, he still planned to visit Palestine.

In 1935, Hugh received an invitation from the Northcliffian Old Boys' Association in Hampstead addressed to him at Halcyon Book Co. Ltd. Holborn. I was not able to trace this association nor any information of him having attended a school under this name. He is addressed as "Mighty Oak Schonfield" in the invitation which included an old school tie for him to wear and as the headmaster wrote that Hugh should come along as his "guest", it would seem that this was an honorary association.

The Halcyon Book Company declared itself insolvent in the December of 1935. It is also not clear what role Hugh may have played here. Probably he was working in the office as an editor and it may have been a temporary job after Denis Archer folded up. The company published such books as the *Regent Encyclopedia of Empire Postage Stamps* and *Milestones to the Silver Jubilee. A Diary of a Nation* by Dent H.C. (Ed.).. The themes do not seem to have been those which would have fitted particularly well to Hugh's profile.

The plans for travelling to Palestine started to materialise and he received a letter from the Office of the Commissioner of Jerusalem dated 15th January 1935 saying that the facilities for travel had been granted (Sir Leon Levison had telegraphed them on Hugh's behalf). He was offered a place with *The Palestine Post*[36]. Hugh wrote an extensive series of three articles on the subject of selling books in Palestine in the Publisher's Circular and the Publisher and Bookseller, June 1935, so he was obviously able to make use of the research work mentioned above.

---

36 Letter from G. Agronsky 10.2.1935.

Picture 16: Design for a Palestine Stamp by Hugh J. Schonfield

He was working on a translation of the Psalms and an Orient Version of the Old Testament. With respect to this project, he was in correspondence with Dr. J. Rendel Harris, the well-known bible scholar of the time. J. Rendel Harris, through contacts to the Monastery of Saint Catherine on Mount Sinai, had been instrumental in the discovery of the *Sinaitic Palimpsest*, the oldest Syriac New Testament in existence[37]. We have not been able to locate the manuscripts of the above translations by Hugh and as far as we are aware, they have never been published.

An interesting point which Rendel Harris makes in his letter to Hugh of the 2nd July 1935 is the mention of a discovery made by Hugh "on the other side of Jordan". Rendel felt that Hugh had found the survivors of the Desposuni and wished that he had been able to follow it up. He goes on to say, "Nazareth is a hard nut to crack. It would be very interesting if we could trace our Lord's origin in contact with the Greek civilisations of Decapolis. We should also have an explanation why the early Greeks fled into the regions of Pella". Obviously, by this time, Hugh had returned from Palestine after also having visited Jerusalem in the March of that year.

The connection with Rendel Harris and other scholars was an important factor in Hugh's thought development. He writes:

> Thus it was practicable for me to conduct the researches which were essential to comprehend the Mediterranean world at the beginning of the Christian Era, and to

---

37 cf. http://en.wikipedia.org/wiki/J._Rendel_Harris

become well-acquainted progressively with the land and conditions which Jesus had known. I was able to develop this equipment with the help of great masters like Sir Flinders Petrie, Rendel Harris and Crawford Burkitt, and by a number of visits to the Holy Land and neighbouring countries. I was fortunate, also, in that many important discoveries were being made in Bible lands.[38]

An article in the Sunday Dispatch of July 28th 1935 entitled *Christ's Childhood: A Discovery —Young Scholar Finds Evidence Of It In A Forgotten Town "Was Not Spent in Nazareth" - Bible Expert Supports New Theory* was certainly intended to cause a stir and showed at least that the press were also beginning to take notice of Hugh. As the title suggests, the article calls into question whether Jesus really spent his youth in Nazareth. Hugh is described as "a brilliant young Jewish scholar who is engaged on a new translation of the Bible". Furthermore he is described as a "smiling young man of 34, who looks even younger than his age, in his business office. During the day he is a business man. In the evenings and far into the night he works on his translation of the Bible". Hugh is quoted as saying, "I spent a considerable time in Palestine pursuing my studies. I happened to find this little town, El Husn and I believe the people there are descendants of the Nazarenes". Rendel Harris is cited as saying, "Mr. Schonfield has constantly been to me and written to me for advice. He is a fine Hebrew scholar and has translated into modern and intelligible English the whole of the Book of Psalms, which previously had been badly translated, much of it being still obscure". We can only hope that this manuscript comes to light one day.

Hugh's ability to understand and explain texts in oriental and other languages continued to develop. He himself wrote later:

> I discovered that I had the ability to paint much of what I saw in words, so that others could see with me; and from my youth I applied myself to those languages, Hebrew, Egyptian, Assyrian, Aramaic, Greek and Latin, that could unlock for me the portals of antiquity. Before completing my education at Glasgow University I had already discovered the importance of a neglected Hebrew manuscript of the Gospel of Matthew, and I was still only twenty-five when my translation of the text with a critical introductions was being published by T & T Clark of Edinburgh. This brought me into the valued friendship of men like Dr. H. Rendel Harris, Professor Burkitt of Cambridge, and Dr. W. Elmslie, and later of Dr. Travers Herford and Canon Lukyn Williams.

An article published in the Occult Review February 1931 vol. 53, which appears to be the only article written for this magazine, and which deals with a Jewish Rabbi named Elisha Ben Abuyah, includes an interesting statement:

> There is always something awe-inspiring in the picture of a man of seemingly settled convictions, acknowledged a doctor of divinity, suddenly conscious of the futility of the way he has for so long taught, abandoning his former religious associations, and going out less than the least of all his pupils to seek a more satisfying faith.

It could be conjectured that Hugh is identifying himself with this personality at this juncture of his life. At this point in time he was very much a Christian, albeit a Hebrew Christian. He had discovered Jesus as the Messiah, was embracing some of the Christian theology but at the same time, we can detect the thread of the messianic in his mode of understanding. This followed him all his life and as his studies progressed, he

---

38 Schonfield, Hugh J. (2004) *Jesus Man-Mystic-Messiah*, The Open Gate Press, London, p.4.

became intensively aware of the Jesus of history. For Hugh, Jesus was a real historical character who had a mission on behalf of his people – and the world.

It never continues to amaze me how Hugh found so much time for such a wide variety of endeavours. Of course, his helpmate Hélène was often very active in the background, giving him support as well as bringing up the children, but in 1935 their daughter Audrey was born so she would have been quite busy I am sure. So it transpired that we find them both present at the laying of the foundation stone of the New County Hospital at Banstead Wood (Princess Hospital for Children) on July 23rd 1936. This occasion gave them the opportunity to meet the Duchess of York.

This was the year when Edward VIII, son of the Duchess of York, came to the throne but also abdicated at the end of the year, choosing to marry the divorced American woman, Wallis Simpson rather than continuing as King because this would have conflicted with his role as head of the Church of England.

In this same year, the activities for the Hebrew Christian Association were also still taking much of the couple's time and attention. There was an intensive friendship with the Levisons.

Unfortunately, Sir Leon died on the 25th November of that year. Hugh wrote a poem in his honour which was published in *The Hebrew Christian*:

In Memoriam
Sir Leon Levison, Kt.
Lion, you were
And we, who mourn your passing,
Salute the courage in yourselves
Which withstood
Oppression and the slanderous word.

Statesman, you were
And we of lesser vision
Salute the builder in you
Who planned
Sanely and with practised hand.

Jew, you were
And we in race your brothers
Salute the mystic in you
Which, by grace
Saw Messiah with unveiled face.

Friend, you were
And we, whose hearts you captured,
Cherish the loving life of you,
Again made known,

Even by laying down your own.

Hugh J. Schonfield.

Hugh and Hélène also sent a letter of condolences to Leon's son Fred. In Fred's reply of the 7th December, he states,

> I'm awfully glad, Hugh, that you had that talk with Daddy when you were here. It will be a great encouragement to you to know that he sympathised with your dreams for the future of the Alliance's work in London; dreams that are partly to be realised in his own Memorial. Mother, too, rejoiced to read your words about giving yourself to the Alliance's work. That work is near to all our hearts, and it is such a work of God that we know He will bless it and enable us all to carry out whatever part of it He calls us to.

In this year he also worked on some translations of parts of the books of Isaiah and Ecclesiastes (the manuscripts of which seem to have gone astray). It would seem that Hugh was proposing a translation of the Bible including the Old Testament and was looking for a publisher to sponsor it. In this same year he also published the book *Richard Burton Explorer* with the publisher Herbert Joseph (UK) and *The History of Jewish Christianity* with Duckworth (UK).

In 1937, the foundation stone for the Temple of Peace in Cardiff was laid by Viscount Halifax. Opened in 1938, it was stated:

> The Temple will serve as the outward and visible sign of the allegiance and loyalty of the people of Wales to the principles and objectives of the League of Nations. It is not intended to be a dark mausoleum, and because dark clouds overshadow Europe, that is no reason why we should put up the shutters and draw down the blinds. On the contrary, this is the time for constancy and courage; this is the time when we, both as individuals and as a nation, should humbly re-dedicate ourselves to the service of the great tasks that lie before us. It is to be hoped that the Temple of Peace and Health will come to be regarded as the shrine of all that we hold most dear, and that it may prove to be of real service to the future welfare of humanity as the symbol of our determination to work for a better world.[39]

Whether Hugh was aware of this event or not, is not recorded but this building was to play an important role in Hugh's future and became the home of a historic event in his life.

1938 was also the year when Adolf Hitler took control of the German military and Austria was annexed by Germany. Hitler declared his intention to destroy Czechoslovakia. At the Evian Conference on Refugees convened in France, no country in Europe was prepared to accept Jews fleeing persecution and the United States was only willing to take 27,370. At the same time, Neville Chamberlain returned from negotiations with Hitler to declare "Peace in our Time". In Germany, Jews' passports were invalidated, and those who needed a passport for emigration purposes were given one marked with the letter J for "Jude" ("Jew"). 12,000 Polish Jews were expelled and it was the fateful year of the "Kristalnacht".

---

39 Leaflet: *A New Mecca—An Account Of The Opening Ceremony of the Welsh National Temple Of Peace And Health Cathays Park, Cardiff*

According to an article by Ben W. Fuson[40] written in 1963:

> Dr. Hugh Schonfield......1938 first conceived of the civilized world's need of an "independent and impartial Servant-Nation consisting exclusively of World Citizens. This nation would be without territory, because the world was its homeland; without armament, because its people could never make war on their fellows in any circumstances; without compulsive power, because its function was the antithesis of domination and oppression; without partisanship, because its mission was mediation and reconciliation."

An issue of the *World Citizen*[41] reported of Hugh that:

> In the autumn and winter of 1939 he developed his theme in a series of lectures given to a Discussion Group attached to a London branch of the Peace Pledge Union. The plan visualised the necessity for the creation, as a decisive intermediate step towards world unity, of a world functional body, organised on the lines of a nation, but representing an actual world citizenship, and embodying the principles of Service, Mediation, and Example. This Service-Nation would be recruited from men and women with a world outlook in all lands, released from State allegiance by naturalisation as Servants of Mankind.

In the White Paper of 1939, the British government restricted Jewish immigration to Mandatory Palestine. After the invasion of Poland, Britain, France, Australia and New Zealand declared war on Germany on the third of September.

Picture 17: A View of Goose Green Farm – Hugh J. Schonfield

---

40 Ben W. Fuson, Ph.D., born 1911 was Professor of English at Kansas Wesleyan Univ.,Salina, Kansas. Born in Canton, China and reared there; taught in China and India; Fulbright professor at Meshed University in Iran, Quaker. 1937 became president of the Fellowship of Reconciliation. Author of a number of books and became a prominent Mondcivitan.
41 The World Citizen, Special Merger Number. January, 1948.

The Servant-Nation Movement

So by now, the concept of a messianic Servant-Nation had taken on a concrete form in Hugh's mind. The Service-Nation Movement was a pre-cursor to the Mondcivitan Republic (Commonwealth of World Citizens) and came out of the Movement for a Holy Servant Nation founded by Schonfield which was active in the 1940s. His daughter Audrey reports from this time, "I remember him as a loving father and being involved in the "Feast of Frontiers" and the "Service Nation Movement". We would march, dressed up in international clothing. When we lived in Highgate we used to have a huge garden fete where all the people involved in the movement would be invited. Then there was a lot of interest in Esperanto and I remember my father being quite fascinated by the idea.". Hugh did find time for family despite the busy life he lead. Audrey reminisced that they would go on holidays together and remembers the large trunk they would pack with their belongings. She remembers going out in a rowing boat and describes him as a sort of "Victorian" father who was always writing. At the same time she remembers that he never brought religion and his thinking into family life. In fact she said that he did not encourage his daughters to follow in his footsteps - "we weren't boys!". This is partly what she means by "Victorian" - children should be seen but not heard. She also remembers him being rather untidy and that her mother preferred to have help in the home than buy another new dress (whilst down to one) – she was thus, as she says, a "pseudo son". Her sister Joyce did not go to university, which apparently she should of done, and Hélène did not finish university.

In some ways Hugh had an esoteric or spiritual leaning which included the vision he believed to have received of the servant nation. Once, whilst staying in a hotel, Audrey remembers that he had a dream of nuns walking through the rooms. The next day they discovered that the building used to be a nunnery. Such sentiments also included the belief in a benign influence that would provide as necessary.

However, as the reader will acknowledge, whilst the servant nation idea was nothing new in Hugh's head, it was now increasingly taking on a concrete form..

It was about this time that Hugh visited "Goose Green Farm" which was run by the pacifist Frank Newman Turner (1913 – 1964) who was one of the first British organic farmers and one of the first UK practitioners of acupuncture. His son Roger (who has also become a leading osteopath and naturopath) remembers meeting Hugh at this time as a small boy. Frank became vice president of the Movement for a Holy Servant-Nation whilst Hugh was president. Frank Newman Turner started to manage Goose Green Farm in 1940 (which also employed conscientious objectors during the Second World War) and later acquired it, where he was able to experiment successfully with organic farming and his concept of "health from the soil up". He started to publish a magazine entitled *The Farmer* in 1946 and so we see that in this circle of friends and acquaintances, the barebones for a new world concept were beginning to be developed.

Whilst on the farm, Hugh created one of his gentle water paintings:

Audrey remembers the Schonfield children being evacuated there for a few months in 1940. There was an Italian prison camp nearby and the prisoners helped on the farm. Apparently one of them actually fell for Marion and made a ring for her out of a piece of tin. He wrote to her after the war to invite her to Italy to meet his family. At the time she would have been about 13.

During 1940 he also edited the book *The Treaty of Versailles: The Essential Text and Amendments*. Published by the Peace Book Club. Also the book *Readings from the Apocryphal Gospels*, was published by Nelson (UK).

Growing food would also be an important issue as rationing was introduced in Britain in 1940. Winston Churchill became Prime Minister and Germany extended its invasion

Picture 19: Goose Green Farm by Hugh J. Schonfield

and occupation to include the Low Countries and France whilst the bombing of London and Coventry began. The Auschwitz concentration camp was opened in Poland in which over 1 million Jews were to die.

The Peace Book Club was founded by Hugh "as a means of studying the problems of War and Peace in view of the spirit of Aggression and Domination acutely represented by the Totalitarian Dictatorships and the Master-Race theory."[1]

His brother Geoffrey was an army captain and was obviously serving in Normandy. He wrote to Hugh and Hélène on the 7th June 1940, the letter passing through the censors. He was doing the job of assistant area Commandant.

The D Day landings on the Normandy beaches were a significant turning point in the war, starting the Battle of Normandy and finally resulting in the restoration of the French Republic.

In 1941 the book *Italy and Suez* was published by Hutchinson and Penguin wrote saying that they would not be able to reprint a Spanish edition of the Suez book due to paper shortages.

It is amazing that he managed to find so much time for his various pursuits but one underlying idea would not leave him and that was the idea that there had to be a servant-nation as part of what he believed to be God's plan for mankind and as the road to peace.

---

1 In the leaflet *New Hope for a World at War* published by the Commonwealth of World Citizens (date unknown).

The involvement with Frank Newman Turner and others led to the formation of the Society for the Constitution of a Holy Nation of which he was president and Frank (whom he addressed as Newman) vice president. It was run from his home in London.

The object of the society was declared on its headed letter paper as:

> To create, by the will of God, as an instrument for the promotion of world peace and justice, a free nation, pervasive and universal, dedicated to the service of humanity, to the function of international mediation, and to the demonstration of a pattern of nationhood.

The Quakers were very attracted to this idea and would host meetings about the subject. A press cutting from an (unknown) newspaper received kindly from Roger[2], the son of Frank Newman Turner, demonstrates how far this concept had evolved:

NEW NATION FOR NEW WORLD.

SOCIETY OF FRIENDS' MEETING AT BRIDGWATER.

The achievement and maintenance of peace through the medium of a Service Nation was the subject of a public meeting organised by the Society of Friends at Friends Meeting House Bridgwater, on Sunday evening.

The speaker was Mr. Hugh J. Schonfield, author and lecturer, with Mr. Newman Turner in the chair.

Opening the meeting, Mr. Newman Turner said that at a time when the world was consumed in war, it was the particular duty of Christians to think ahead to the peace and the manner of its achievement. Christianity was a world religion, and there was an obligation on Christians, as follower's of the Prince of Peace, to have a world outlook.

Mr. Hugh Schonfield devoted the first part of his address to a review at the political history leading to the present crisis. Whenever one nation or a group of nations had set out to dominate or control a part of the world another nation or group of nations had united to prevent it. This was the process known as balance of power, which had been the principle governing world affairs up to the time of the League of Nations.

The League of Nations had been a great step forward towards world peace, but it had failed because of the divided loyalties of the representatives to the League. It had been impossible for the officers of the League to act impartially, because as nationals of a particular country they could not avoid being influenced in their decisions by the interests of the country which they represented. The Permanent Court of International Justice had likewise proved only a partial success because of its difficulty in attaining a position of strict impartiality. The world was now rapidly approaching a stage where there would be no neutral country or organisation to which the warring nations could turn for an impartial settlement or mediation of their disputes. It seemed obvious then, that before a stable peace could be established, and certainly if it were to be maintained, there must come into being a body of people devoted impartially to the service of humanity, having no ties of nationality, but being true world citizens, who could act as spokesmen for and servants of mankind. The Service National Movement, of which the speaker is president, had been brought into being for the constitution of such a body of world citizens whose lives would be devoted to the service of humanity, the mediation of international

---

2 http://www.newmanturner.com/roger/proBio.html

disputes, and the living out of a pattern of nationhood. From the religious approach this would be recognised as the ancient Divine plan of world government so often referred to in both the Old and the New Testaments as the Holy Nation—a people drawn out of all the nations of the earth to be a Servant-Nation through which peace would be found.

By 1941[3] the Society had a mailing list of some 300 persons and organisations and they were getting a considerable response to the memorandum which they had sent out. The magazine *The World Citizen* was now being prepared and they were receiving membership contributions and subscriptions. A conference was scheduled for September and being hosted at the Friends House on 6th September[4] and is presumably the meeting reported above.

That summer Hugh and Hélène spent their summer holiday with the Newman Turners at Goose Green Farm. They found the holiday very refreshing and "each day was a holy day of rest, communion and love"[5].

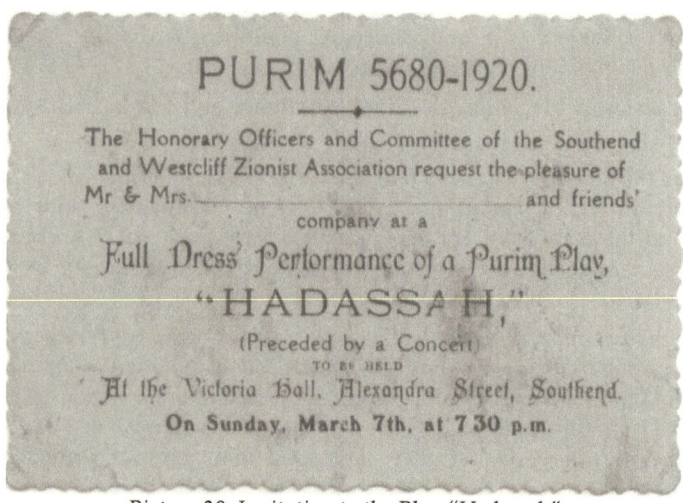

Picture 20: Invitation to the Play "Hadassah"

By October of that year they had received the offer of a house in Heston Middlesex from a Herbert Ede which they wanted to use as a service centre. The house was partly mortgaged and it was necessary for the trustees to cover the risk of the mortgage payments. However, the house was partly let and there was an income from rents to cover this expenditure[6]. The Society continued to grow and gained renowned persons to its membership such as Mr. Alderman[7] the technical engineer in charge of construction of the new Waterloo Bridge[8].

---

3   Letter from Hugh to Frank Newman Turner dated 12th April 1941.
4   Letter from Elfie (M.E. Price?) to Frank Newman Turner dated 21st June 1941.
5   Letter from Hugh to Frank Newman Turner dated 6th August 1941.
6   Letter from Hugh to Frank Newman Turner dated 3rd December 1941.
7   cf. Alderman, P.R. and Prior, F.E. (1947) *Temporary Works and Constructional Devices Used in Connexion with the Construction of the New Waterloo Bridge. Works construction division.* In ICE Engineering Division Papers, Volume 5, Issue 15, 01 January 1947, pages 3–40
8   Letter from Hugh to Frank Newman Turner dated 15th October 1941.

The Servant-Nation Movement

By the end of 1941 the Society was negotiating incorporating the Peace Army and its Chairman and other members were joining the society as a preliminary step. So-called "service sections" were springing up across England and a person named Walter was offering his home as a place for convalescence for members. Hugh was very happy to experience this spirit of love in the group[9] and I am sure he saw parallels with the early church experience.

Members were also encouraged to send food parcels to Germany and enclose a card specially prepared about the movement. The scheme had actually been imitated by the Peace Pledge Union and there seem to have been considerable connections between the two groups. The text was:

> The Service-Nation Movement exists to create a true world citizenship, by uniting individuals of all races who have a world outlook in a new nationhood for the service of mankind. The Service-Nation—a nation without territory or armed forces—is the first practical step towards world unity and the abolition of war. It will act as a mediating agency between the nation-states, and as the active promoter of the welfare of all sections of humanity. Membership of the Movement is open to all who wish to associate themselves with its objects. Naturalisation as world citizens will be available to those who desire it when the Service-Nation is constituted. SERVICE-NATION MOVEMENT 20, BUCKINGHAM STREET LONDON, W.C.2.

Hugh and Hélène also spent the Christmas that year with their children at Goose Green Farm. As an aside, it might be worth mentioning what Audrey relayed on to me that her mother Hélène was not a person to outwardly show affection yet would at times display a fiery temper whilst Hugh was a very emotional person who would cry easily. Joyce would often get at loggerheads with her mother whilst Marion would act as nursemaid for the other children.

This period is well summarized in this extract from an article which appeared in 1983 from the German group of the Mondcivitan Republic in 1983[10]:

> In the autumn and winter of 1940-41, while the bombs rained on London in the Battle of Britain, a handful of people periodically made their way to each others homes through the darkened streets, sheltering temporarily on occasion in porch and portico from falling shrapnel, with houses crumbling into ruins often only a few yards away. They met to promote the Society for the Constitution of a Holy Nation, formed on September 8, 1940. Audrey pointed out to me that they never sought refuge in an air raid shelter but would sit under a large oak dining table whilst their mother read *Peter Pan* to them.
>
> The tiny Society's first publication was another pamphlet by Hugh Schonfield, "The Holy Nation and its Mission". Here the Employment of the adjective "holy" was explained. "Holiness", said the author, "is the conscious direction of our powers and capacities to the performance of their pure and proper functions. The most exact machine cannot be holy, for it is not in conscious control of its purpose. This applies also to the lower organisms. But men and nations have the endowment to function consciously, though it is still only partially developed and they can accordingly achieve good or evil results in the utilization of their possessions and po-

---

9 Letter from Hugh to Frank Newman Turner dated 3rd December 1941.
10 http://www.schonfield.org/about/the-servant-nation/mondcivitan-republic/germany/newsletter-1983

tentialities. The holy nation, therefore, is one in which not only are the parts knit together through the cultivation of the group soul, but in which every activity of nationhood is consciously employed for its true end."

The writer went on to consider current ideas for the creation of an International Authority after the war.

In the efforts to define the International Authority there is evidently considerable confusion of thought, due to the attempt to make it both representative and independent.

If the authority had only to act in an advisory capacity no serious difficulty would arise, but then also its usefulness would be very slight. It is because it has to be invested with plenary powers that its nation and composition cause so much heart-searching. There is the instinctive dread of creating a monster, and the anxiety not to give full play to rivalry and jealousy through attempts on the parts of larger states to make the Council an instrument for self-aggrandizement.

It would appear that while it is easy to define the spheres in which an International Authority could successfully operate, and the purpose for which it is essential, there exists so much mistrust of any such body as it has been imagined as to negate the prospect of its practical organization. The mission of the Authority commending itself so much to reason and good sense, it can only be assumed that there is a serious fault in the conception of its nature. The Fault is twofold. It consists, firstly, in the supposition that an International Authority must be one in which the nations jointly participate, and, secondly, in the belief that it must have coercive powers to enforce decisions on recalcitrant states. Facing the facts of the situation it is obvious that the kind of authority most likely to succeed is one which requires the minimum of cooperation from the nations and interferes least with their affairs. Preferably it must be able to establish itself independently and without any preliminary of world conferences, covenants or pacts. If such a thing could be possible its members must be world representative and world-minded. Then, the authority must have so patent a moral and ethical basis as to earn the admiration of men everywhere, and be so beneficent in character, with a program solely of service, as to secure ever wider consent to its proposals and be voluntarily entrusted by the nations with mandates and Commissions. Finally it must have a constitution which makes it the peer and equal of the nation-states so that dealings with it can be conducted through the ordinary machinery of government and diplomatic exchanges. Needless to say, it must be unsupported by any physical force, its function being to win respect for international law.

The concept of the Holy Nation answers to these requirements in every particular as no other sort of international authority does or can. Once peace is established no objection to its institution would be raised in any quarter. There are thousands of able men and women with a world outlook in every profession and occupation, who for the good of humanity would be ready to apply for naturalization as soon as their citizenship could be accepted."

These words were written in 1941, looking forward beyond the strife of World War II, and illustrate how we were beginning to seek to define our position.

At this time through invitations to address meetings and the circulation of literature the Society acquired some new recruits not only in London but throughout Great Britain. The membership made up in enthusiasm what it lacked in numbers, and a year after its inauguration the Society was able to hold its first conference at the beginning of September 1941 at Friends House (the Quaker headquarters in London).

The movement had quite a number of prominent supporters including, as Audrey remembers, Sir Robert Mayer, who died at the age of 105 in 1985 and was famous for organising classical concerts for children and was patron of Britain's famous youth concerts[11].

In the August Hugh gave many addresses on the Holy Nation including one at the Cambridge Convention on Foundations of Peace organised by the Vedanta Movement, and at a meeting of the Christian Party at Oldbury (near Birmingham).

In a lengthy article in *The World Citizen* Vol. 1, No. 4 Hugh describes the vision of the Holy Servant-Nation which so shaped his thinking. The following extract sums up how his spiritual and political ideas had now taken shape:

> Gaze, then, into the future, and you will see our nation at work, labouring at world education, administering international law, protecting minorities, promoting the just distribution of goods and services, combating disease and all social evils, fostering the arts and sciences, drawing the ends of the earth into an ever closer union until the day can dawn for the world commonwealth, for that order which has been spoken of as the Kingdom of God and the Brotherhood of Man, and our arduous mission will be ended.
>
> At this blackest epoch of human catastrophe the light of a new faith, a new hope, has been kindled. It will grow steadily brighter until its rays light up the globe. It is the long awaited answer to aggression and domination, the answer of all-prevailing love.

---

11 http://www.nytimes.com/1985/01/20/world/sir-robert-mayer-is-dead-at-105-patron-of-british-youth-concerts.html accessed 12th July 2015.

The Work of the War Years Continues

Around this time Hugh had started working as a lecturer for the forces for whom he worked on and off during the war years. In 1942 he was receiving a salary of 650 pounds as a full time lecturer. Obviously Hugh did not see a conflict between this work and his work for the peace movement and the Servant-Nation. Everyone was expected to be involved in the war effort in some way and even Princess Elizabeth registered herself. He may also have felt a commitment to Jewry as the Holocaust was now in full swing with the open Nazi declaration of its intent to exterminate the race. It was now public knowledge with, for example, leading clergymen and political figures in the UK holding a public meeting to register outrage over the persecution of Jews.

By this time, the USA was getting deeply involved in the war and the first troops arrived in Britain. It is worth noting that the war also caused the creation of many worthy institutions such as the charity Oxfam which exists to this day.

The Service Nation Movement, as it was called at that time, remained active during the war years and Hugh was editor of the bi-monthly magazine *The World Citizen* and regular meetings would be held. In the magazine from July-August 1942 the plan for a "Mutual-Service Agency as the basis for a National Economy of World Citizens" was broached which would open membership to a wider group. This was to take the form of a trust manned by Service Nation Movement members. This could be seen as the first inception of what was later to become the World Service Trust. There was also an article in this edition of the magazine proposing involvement in organic farming, which undoubtedly was influenced by Frank Newman Turner mentioned above but also by Victor Leroux who was warning of the ultimate detrimental effect of chemical fertilisers used in farming. Hugh and his associates, particularly Newman Turner, were thus at the forefront of promoting organic farming which has continually developed to this day.

In the *World Citizen* of Jan-Feb 1943, Hugh seems to expect and hope that the war will come to an end that year. However, he sees – and prophecies – that this would only be a temporary peace because there is the need for a completely different solution. In an article in that magazine he also states:

> I make frequent train journeys, and often read a newspaper on these occasions. Studying the news I find myself automatically adopting a very insular attitude of pleasure or censure about current events; and I have consciously to pull myself up short, and say: "Now read that over again not as a British subject but as a world citizen, and see what your attitude is then." I find this a very salutary corrective.

In the issue of March-April 1943 we find the following:

"SERVICE ABOVE SELF"

Service binds, while force rends asunder

Service heals, while force wounds and destroys

Service knows no enemies, entertains no jealousies, accepts no distinctions

Service melts where force hardens

Service proves where force promises

Service convinces where force threatens

Service brings light into darkness, order into chaos, hope into despair

> Service is the only quality, which can make authority endurable and endure.

These lines by Hugh J. Schonfield from the *Memorandum on the Furtherance of Peace and Social Justice through a World Authority* (published by the Society for the Constitution of a Holy Nation) were chosen by Rotary International, Chicago, as the text of their Christmas Greeting to all Rotarians in that year.

In 1945 he received a letter from the "London Regional Committee for Education Among His Majesty's Forces" confirming termination of contract "for the time being". It included much praise for his work. It would seem that Hugh had decided on this course of action because he had so many engagements and that his health was suffering from the overload.

And Hugh could become quite indignant at the injustices and expressed his disappointment with the Archbishop of the Anglican Church in the May-June edition of that year of *The World Citizen* thus:

> Recently in the House of Lords proposals were made by the Archbishop of Canterbury and Lord Rochester for the rescue of Jews and other peoples from territory occupied by the Nazis. The speeches are now available in pamphlet form—*Nazi Massacres of the Jews and Others* (Victor Gollancz, 2d.).
>
> The archbishop makes out an eloquent and persuasive case against further delay and suggests that the scheme of visas for entry into this country should be revised and that we should admit "all those who are able to get here—they would not be very many—who have husbands, wives or sons already here, and especially those who have sons actually serving in our Forces."
>
> I confess to surprise that the Archbishop should so phrase his proposal as to limit the practical application of charity. If there be a Jewish woman, a Czech child, or a Polish peasant in danger of death or torture then we should offer them hospitality even though we run risks in so doing.

In the September of 1943 a conference was planned to be held in London for the members of the Service Nation Movement. This was the year that the Soviet Union announced that at Stalingrad, 175,000 had been killed and the German sixth army was defeated. But the protests against the Nazis and the calls for peace were increasing. In Sofia 36 people were executed and 200 arrested in anti-Nazi protests alone. On the other hand, war violence was becoming more intensive by 1944 with massive bombing of Berlin and the Normandy Coast by the British Royal Air Force and of course the famous "D-Day" landing.

On the 8th May 1945 the Germans finally surrendered. The war in Europe had cost between 50 and 85 million lives. This was a clear call that the world needed a different approach to war and peace but the conflicts have continued to this day.

The same year also witnessed the first atomic bombings of Hiroshima and Nagasaki in Japan by the USA, which caused the deaths of hundreds of thousands of civilians. The Japanese surrendered in the August of that year, officially ending the Second World War.

There was now increasing pressure to find a solution to the Jewish issue after all they had suffered in the Holocaust. Hugh wrote a suggestion (letter of 2nd October 1945) for immediately settling 75,000 Jews or more from Europe in Palestine, temporarily using a part of Transjordan. He posed the idea of a Federation of Palestine and Transjordan and the Jewish and Arab autonomous areas with Jerusalem as the extra-territorialised federal capital. Later the Jews should be allowed to return to Palestine, and their place would be taken by Palestinian Arabs, who would be settled permanently on the productive farms and orchards already created for them. He felt that the Jew would be willing to make this sacrifice for their distressed brethren in Europe. Unfortunately his suggestion was not taken up.

The same year also saw the publication of *By What Authority* through Herbert Joseph (UK).

The Service-Nation Movement was continuing to take shape and they were able to send a resolution on Poland to Sir Anthony Eden, then Secretary of State which was also acknowledged.

In 1946, the Servant-Nation movement sent a letter to Aneurin Bevan (a Labour Party member and Minister in Clement Attlee's government, who believed that the Second World War would give Britain the chance to create a new society) enclosing a memorandum on Palestine. By this time the Movement was publishing its own bi-monthly periodical entitled *The World Citizen* already in its third year. Tony Deeson was appointed Organising Secretary. The magazine included interesting and informative articles from a Service-Nation viewpoint on world affairs. A number of the articles were also produced in French.

The finalising of the war in Europe left a vacuum for new strife and it was in this year that Winston Churchill first coined the phrase "The Iron Curtain" perhaps heralding in the era of the "Cold War". At the same time there was a growing movement towards more international cooperation and the year marked the inaugural session of the International Court of Justice and the League of Nations was integrated into the United Nations.

Hugh's workload did not decrease and he was asked by Encyclopedia Britannica to write an article of 500 words for the series of four volumes *Ten Eventful Years 1937-1946* on the history of the Suez Canal. The letter was addressed to 5, The Riding, London NW11, where the family must have been living at the time.[1]

Louis Golding[2], a famous novelist of the time, wrote to Hugh about his review of The *Jew of Tarsus* which was published by Macdonald (UK) in 1947, and stated that he may be cited as saying, "A book uplifted in spirit and profound in scholarship". He was also to receive a letter from James Parkes[3] on the subject in November, which stated that he was not only in agreement with Hugh but also felt that the book should have paid more attention to Paul's theology on atonement. He found the section in the book which dealt with the mysticism of Paul and its Jewish background in Adam Kadmon to be most interesting. Parkes was very much against the missionising of Jews. I wonder if he had been aware of Hugh's work in this area during his early years.

1   The original letter is archived at the National Maritime Museum. Cf. http://collections.rmg.co.uk/archive/objects/467509.html
2   Louis Golding (November 19, 1895 – August 9, 1958) was a British writer, very famous in his time especially for his novels, though he is now largely neglected; he wrote also short stories, essays, fantasies, travel books and poetry. He was born in Manchester into a Ukrainian-Jewish family. (http://en.wikipedia.org/wiki/Louis_Golding, 14.11.13)
3   James Parkes (22 December 1896 – 10 August 1981) was a clergyman, historian, and social activist. With the publication of The Jew and His Neighbour in 1929, he created the foundations of a Christian re-evaluation of Judaism. (http://en.wikipedia.org/wiki/James_Parkes_(clergyman), 14.11.13)

Hugh's understanding of St. Paul is interesting with respect to his biography. Power cites a passage in his book:

> We have seen him as a rather lonely boy, brooding over his people's wrongs and the unique and difficult Jewish position in a hostile heathen world. He was fervently religious, eager to pursue the quest for God to the uttermost, not only of theological argument, but of strenuous and dangerous mystical exercises. His mind was excited with those questions affecting the function of Israel and the fate of mankind which figure so prominently in the apocalyptic writings and in the Jewish contributions to the Sibylline Oracles. He recognised that his position as a Pharisee adept, a citizen of Tarsus, and a Roman, gave him a special, and indeed a Providential status. Was it unnatural for this man to think that he might be the chosen instrument to inaugurate the fulfilment of Israel's mission, to declare God's name among the heathen, and bring in the era of peace on earth?[4]

Owen Power goes on to comment:

> This picture of Paul as a Jew and a Roman citizen with a messianic mission to bring Jews and Gentile together in a new era of world peace reverberates strongly with Schonfield's own sense of destiny—a Jew and a British citizen at the time of the Holocaust with a messianic mission to bring Jews and Gentiles together in the Servant-Nation.[5]

Having known Hugh personally, I have often asked myself how far Hugh actually identified himself with St. Paul. Hugh's stature and demeanour is perhaps what I would associate in my imagination with the character of Paul. Just as Paul was an outsider in his own religion, so was Hugh for the same reason that he saw Jesus as the Messiah. I am sure he admired the character of Paul even if he did not always agree with him:

> However, as far as Schonfield is concerned, Paul's Messianism ends in failure because Paul turns his back on Jesus to follow a faith of his own invention so Paul's universalism needs to be replaced by his own "message of Messianism for modern man".[6]

James Black (Moderator of the Church of Scotland), commented on the book that he found it interesting and most informative although he did not accept all of Hugh's views and ideas. He felt nevertheless that healthy difference was stimulating and the book would certainly lead many people to examine their own standpoint afresh.

Hugh decided to make an attempt to get into politics where he no doubt felt he could be of some influence. He was adopted as the prospective candidate for the Liberal Party for Enfield[7].

On 3rd January 1946, his father, William Schonfield died aged 76.

---

4   Schonfield (1997) *Proclaiming the Messiah: The Life and Letters of Paul of Tarsus Envoy to the Nations*, London: The Open Gate Press, p81 in Power, Owen M. (2011) *Hugh Schonfield: A Case Study of Complex Identities*. A thesis submitted to the University of Manchester for the degree of Master of Philosophy in the Faculty of Humanities, p. 45.

5   Power, Owen M. (2011) *Hugh Schonfield: A Case Study of Complex Identities*. A thesis submitted to the University of Manchester for the degree of Master of Philosophy in the Faculty of Humanities, p. 45.

6   Ibid.

7   Letter from Charles Frank Baron Byers, M.P. British Liberal Party politician, made a life peer in 1964.

The Work of the War Years Continues

The Jewish Ex-Serviceman's Legion had earlier written about Major Schonfield who had been vice-president of the league:

> Major Schonfield is believed to be the first Jew to join the London Scottish—in 1892—and became lance-corporal in his second year of service. He was gazetted to the old 17th North Middlesex as 2nd Lieut, in 1896; in his first year he passed the

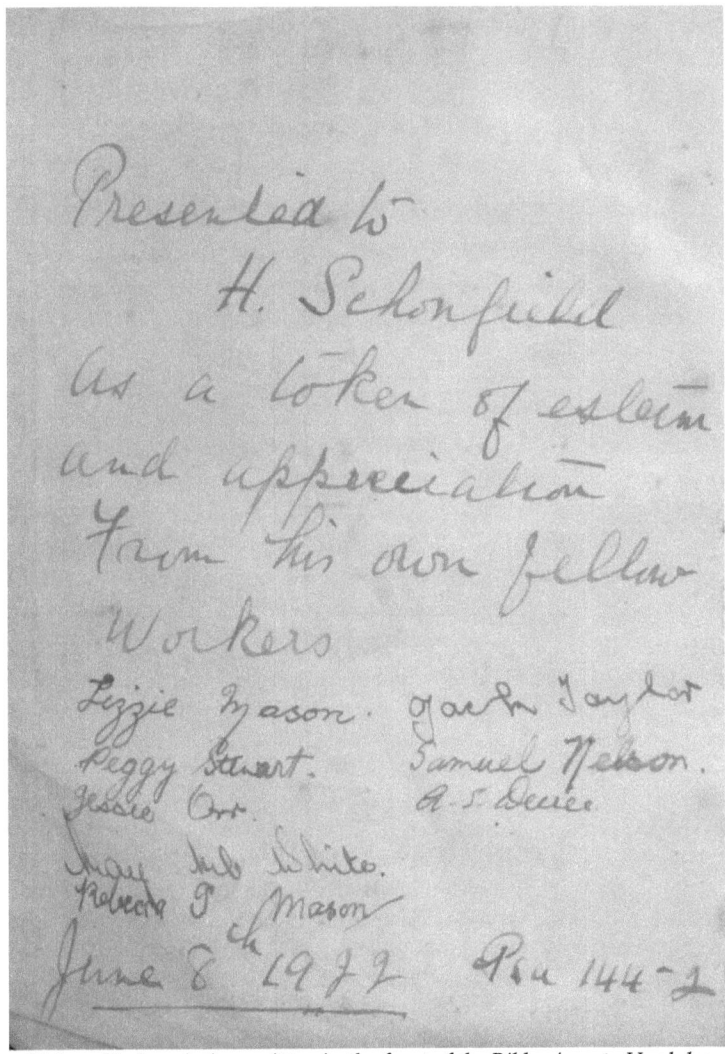

Picture 21: Inscription written in the front of the Bible given to Hugh by his colleagues

School of Instruction with a "special mention," and gained the Aldershot Certificate as Instructor of Signalling. In the following year he was appointed Brigade Signalling Officer with the honorary rank of Captain.

He transferred to the Territorial Force in 1908 and was promoted to Major in 1909, gaining high commendation from both Brigade and Divisional Commanders for his scheme for the training of specialists; he retired in 1911 and joined the T.F. Reserve.

On the outbreak of the Great War, Major Schonfield was appointed to command a Battalion Headquarters Depot. In 1915 he was appointed to raise and command a Third Battalion. Gen. Sir Francis Lloyd, commanding the London District, said that he raised more men in less time than any other battalion in London. Col. Patterson, in his book on the Jewish Regiment, says: "Major Schonfield...worked untiringly to promote the interest of the recruits (Jewish) and to imbue them with a good soldierly spirit while they were passing through his hands in Chenies Street." Owing to heavy strain of work he was compelled to relinquish the command.

Although he volunteered for active service, it was considered that his administrative and training abilities were more useful at home, and continued to hold similar positions throughout the War, gaining special commendation for organisation of the Signal Service in the Thames Section. He was demobilised in 1919 and awarded the Territorial Force Decoration.

Major Schonfield continues his deep interest in his old Regiment as the Chairman of the Past Officers Association. It is interesting to note that the annual chanukah military service was due to a letter sent and published in the "Jewish Chronicle," by Major Schonfield, under the nom-de-plume of "skean dhu"—the suggestion being taken up by the late rev. Francis L. Cohen.

Major Schonfield has recently returned from Palestine where he kindly extended to the Menorah (Jewish Ex-Servicemen's) Club greetings on behalf of the Legion. His visit to Palestine and position as Vice-President of the Jewish Ex-Servicemen's Legion proves a practical concern in Jewish affairs—he is always willing to give time and energy to our movement.

With this solid military career and strong connection to Judaism, he must have looked upon his son's exploits into Christianity and nonviolence with some considerable disdain.

1947 heralded the beginning of many changes in England. As a matter of fact, it was the worst snowfall in the 20th Century in the United Kingdom that winter and travel was considerably disrupted. This did not hinder plans for the nationalisation of coal mines but not only in England were changes afoot. Poland became a communist country and peace treaties were signed in Paris between WWII allies. The International Monetary Fund was created in that year also so there were a number of signs of a greater internationalism and some hopes of peace in the world, although we find the use of the term "Cold War" being applied to the increasing conflict between the USA and the Soviet Union. This was to last until 1991. What would have been very relevant to Hugh was that the Dead Sea Scrolls discovery became known. It would also have been of interest to Hugh that the ship "The Exodus" left France for Palestine with some 4,500 Holocaust survivors. The ship was captured by British troops and was refused entry to Haifa. The United Nations that year voted to partition Palestine between Arabs and Jews, leading to the creation of the State of Israel.

The year of 1948 found our subject still involved in the Bible translation and Professor Elmslie of Westminster College, Cambridge wrote to him[8] whilst he was living at 30,

---

8   Letter dated 14th April 1948. Professor W.A.L. Elmslie was professor at Westminster College, Cambridge, 1899-1949 who was highly regarded for his scholarly work in Old Testament studies. It is interesting to note that 'On 12 July 1924, Professor W. A. L. Elmslie of Westminster College, Cambridge, wrote to Herbert Loewe, then Reader in Rabbinic Studies in Oxford, explaining that there had been much heart-searching in the English Presbyterian

Wood Lane Highgate, encouraging him in the work and recommending the work be published because "Altogether, my belief is that the publishers could not find anyone better equipped to undertake the projected work".

A letter in similar vein was also received from Rev. G. Randall Jones on the same subject, encouraging him in the task. Talk is of a "Bible" translation in both letters but it seems to have emerged as a translation of the New Testament only.

Despite all these positive reflections and the vast amount of writing and research undertaken, Hugh had to work hard to make a living from his writing. It was not always easy to find a publisher and he had as yet to build a reputation in the USA for his books. Macmillan published *The Jew of Tarsus* in the USA in 1948 but attempts to find a publisher for *Jesus: A Biography* in the USA proved unsuccessful.

The process of change in Britain continued with the railways being nationalised and the National Health Act being passed. On the world scene, events such as Mahatma Gandhi beginning his fast unto death to stop partition violence and later being assassinated, would be encouraging Hugh and others to see what action they could be taking in this atmosphere of world upheaval. Soviet Communism was spreading into eastern Europe with countries like Hungary and Czechoslovakia joining the block. This was beginning to be aped in Europe with the signing of the Brussels Treaty which could be seen as a building block of the European Union. The World Health Organisation and the World Council of Churches were also established at this moment in time. The Universal Declaration of Human Rights was adopted by the UN. There was an increasing pressure for de-colonisation and we see the world moving very much into a new era.

Now the plans for creating a Commonwealth of World Citizens were taking shape and Hugh issued an open letter as "International Historian; Deputy-Chairman, World Citizenship Movement; Executive Member Crusade for World Government, etc.". which opened:

> Although this letter stands in my name, I am writing for others as well as for myself, some of whom have been distinguished for almost lifelong devotion to the cause of world unity. These have ranged themselves beside me as a result of the initiative I took recently in acquainting some who know me with my intention to work for the establishment of a Commonwealth of World Citizens.

It seems that he had taken on board a lot of people from the various World Citizenship movements which were springing up. It is rather difficult to have expected these people on the whole to be familiar with his messianic vision which was based on his understanding of the historical events of Israel. In the important essay *The Biblical Concept of a Servant-Nation*, he states, when relating the historical development of the Servant-Nation idea:

> But there is indicated also a new development of the nation. "The Lord God which gathereth the outcasts of Israel, saith, Yet I will gather others to him, beside those

---

Church regarding their 'relations towards Judaism'. A sub-committee had been appointed 'to think things over and to make any suggestions it may feel useful or possible'. 'In face of sheer unbelief, the materialism and moral evil in the world', Dr Elmslie deplored the mutual ignorance and misunderstanding in which Jews and Christians had been content to live, and pleaded for thought about these matters on both sides. He ended with an invitation to Mr Loewe to meet the members of this sub-committee.'"(http://www.jhse.org/book/export/article/19024)

that are gathered unto him."[9] Not only Israelites by race, but Israelites by faith, will form the holy nation and priestly kingdom. "I will send those that escape of them to the nations.. that have not heard My fame, neither have seen My glory; and they shall declare My glory among the nations... And I will also take of them for priests and for Levites, saith the Lord."[10]

Here in these post-exilic prophecies the Servant-Nation first begins to assume a new character. The composition of the nation is expanded to include an influx of Gentiles.

By 1950 the nuclear arms race started after the Soviet Union tested its first atomic bomb in 1949 and the US President Harry Truman ordered the development of the hydrogen bomb in 1950. Albert Einstein warned that nuclear war could destroy the planet. The Schumann Declaration proposal was made, the initiator of the European Union. We should not forget however that the WWII had only really come to an end in Europe and Japan and the Korean War continued with Chinese (now communist) involvement as well as the strife in Vietnam.

---

9   Isa. 66,19-20.
10 Rom. 2,26 on Isa. 59,20-21

The Commonwealth

By 1951, Hugh's dream of creating a politically evident Servant-Nation came to fruition and he was able to address the First Assembly of the Commonwealth of World Citizens in Paris on November 11th of that year[1]. We have to understand the importance of this happening amidst all that was happening in the world at that time and the considerable upheaval which had been brought about by the Second World War. The advent of the nuclear arms race would make the need for finding new ways to solve conflicts, as is still true today, imperative. Nuclear testing was becoming a regular occurrence. The fact that the United Nations had got involved in the Korean War was a clear example that it could not be that impartial spokesman for mankind. A different approach was called for and this inspired Hugh more and more of the necessity of building an impartial servant people.

In the following year he was nominated for the Nobel Peace Prize. Amongst all this, his heart was still close to his dear Hélène and he realised what an important role she had played in his life. In a letter to her, to be opened in the event of his death, he clearly stated his love for her and his children. His family needed him alive though as he was the main breadwinner of the family. Little did he know that he was to outlive her by quite a number of years. Hélène was also a source of inspiration as she herself had quite a literary flair it seems. The writer came across some short rhymes both she and Hugh made up (although I do not know exactly when they were written but with respect to the context, I imagine most were written as they was quite young). I have taken the liberty to reproduce some of these here as I feel that they give us an inkling of their serendipity, backgrounds and characters. I leave it to the reader to decide who wrote which as they are nearly all attributed to Hélène which does not always seem to tie up with the content:

THE PEDLAR

Hark! Somebody's ringing our bell.

Perhaps it's the pedlar with something to sell.

He's got laces and braces and dusters and pins,

And matches and latches and polish in tins,

But one day I hope if I ask him polite,

He'll bring me a dolly to cuddle at night.

THE WALLPAPER PATTERN

I'm counting up the roses in the pattern on the wall.

It's really very difficult because they are so small.

I've started at the corner and counted to the top,

Then down again and up again without a single stop.

But I can't get any further 'cos the washstand's in the way;

So I'd better leave off counting until another day.

---

1 This was also Armistice Day which marked the end of World War I on 11th November 1918.

Our Newspaper

We get a paper every day,
But Daddy loudly snorts-
"You can't believe a word they say,
They're always false reports".
So I've decided what to do
To please my Daddy most.
I'll print a paper that is true
And call it "Sonny's Post".

WE THREE

I want to go in the motor car
Mummy and Daddy and me.
Nanny can take some other boy
Out in the Park with my biggest toy.
Good-bye Nanny! See you at tea,
We're off for a drive now- just we three.

THE FROG IN MY BED

There's a frog at the bottom of my bed I knows
'Cos he's awfully cold
And nips my toes.
But when I jump in ever so quick
And push down my feet with a great big kick
Frog goes.

THE IDLE RICH

Joan Felicity Gertrude Trent
Lived in a flat with a largish rent;
Furnished throughout in the latest style
Out of what Papa called his "pile".
But Mama said "Oh George! How can
You talk like any working man!"

THE AEROPLANE

Airman flying ever so high,
Where are you going to across the sky?

Paris or Rome or Timbuctoo?
I wish 1 knew where you're flying to.
Cos' when I read my G'ography books
I'd turn the pages and have a look.

CAKE

One cake at home,
Two when I'm out,
Three at a party.
And Oh! what joy!
Four at a wedding,
When I'm page boy.

THE DIFFERENCE

Nanny says it's very rude
When I'm out to bolt my food.
But I think it's most polite
To show them that the food's alright.

Returning to 1951 and the need to provide income for the growing family, we find Hugh lecturing on a Greek cruise and giving talks to the passengers on the places the ship was visiting. He was not above taking on work to subsidise his other interests, many of which only cost him money rather than contributing to income. The year also saw the publishing of *The Suez Canal in World Affairs* by Valentine Mitchell (UK).

There were also continuing strong links with the Society of Friends and many Friends became citizens of the Commonwealth of World Citizens. One of these early Friends was the well known Quaker Corder Catchpool[2]. He died in a mountaineering accident in Switzerland in 1952 and an obituary appeared in the Winter 1952-53 Bulletin of the Commonwealth. Another Quaker who played a role in the Commonwealth and, if she had had her way, later in Hugh's life was Rose Chesney. She was temporary Recorder for the movement for a while but later emigrated to Australia.

Hugh also went on a short visit to Prague and East and West Berlin and was able to speak about the Commonwealth to representatives of industry, the universities and the church. It was reported that Hugh pointed out that the fears of the East about the aggressive intentions of the West were almost exactly the same as those of the West about the East, and that on both sides these fears were largely imaginary. The Commonwealth could perhaps do more than any other agency to bring East and West together and avert the horrors of a Third World War.

There were technological changes afoot which would improve travel and communications. In 1952 the first passenger jet service commenced between London and Johannesburg, transatlantic flights started and colour television sets went on sale in the USA the following year.. This is a fact that Hugh and Hélène were able to exploit in their many

---

[2] cf. http://www.quakersintheworld.org/quakers-in-action/234 accessed 9th July 2014

travels and in television broadcasts in the pursuing years. It is worth noting that the European Parliamentary Assembly opened that year also.

In the year of the death of Joseph Stalin, 1953, another Servant-Nation milestone was placed when the Second Assembly of the Commonwealth of World Citizens was held in London on November the 14-16th. Many of the admirers of his scholarly work would not have been aware of this priority agenda for Hugh which was the result of his dream.

At this time Hugh had some involvement with Caresse Crosby who was a rather controversial figure and best known as the first patent recipient for the modern bra. She was very much a world citizenship activist, founding "Women Against War" and decided to merge her organisation with the Commonwealth of World Citizens (which was later renamed the Mondcivitan Republic). In the *Bulletin No.5 Spring 1953* (of the Commonwealth of World Citizens) it was reported about some land that she had made available in Greece:

> The flag of the Commonwealth will be hoisted over our land at Delphi in Greece on May 24. This will be an historic occasion, and we understand that a film will be taken of the event. ....Caresse Crosby, who will be in Delphi about three weeks in advance, will do everything possible to arrange car service and reasonable accommodation. It is entirely due to her courageous initiative, vision and energy that we have been able to set a footprint in the soil of this ancient centre of civilization.

In the *News of the World* March 5th 1955 it was reported:

> American World Commonwealth Citizen—a beautiful edition of Eleanor Roosevelt —is 64-year-old Mrs. Caresse Crosby, of Washington, D.C., founder of Women Against War; friend of Somerset Maugham and various literary and artistic personalities on both sides of the Atlantic; author and publisher herself.
>
> She will be in London next month on her way to Greece where she has bought a piece of land for the Commonwealth at Delphi, adjoining a gift of land from the mayor of that ancient city. Some time in the future the two sites will be built on and will perhaps house the World Commonwealth University that Citizen Professor Rudolph Berthold of Graz University, Austria, is planning.

Caresse Crosby was elected as a Speaker to the Assembly at the Second General Assembly of the Commonwealth of World Citizens in 1953 but she was unable to do this due to health problems and Hugh stood in for her. There was a dispute with the Greek government about the transfer of the land ownership in Delphi to the Commonwealth[3] Her appeal was turned down. In fact at one point she was refused entry into Greece.

In an obituary we find:

> We deeply regret that we have to report that two more valued citizens have been taken from us. Caresse Crosby died in January in Rome at the age of 77. She will be remembered by many for her burning zeal in the cause of world peace and world citizenship, and as the Presiding Officer at
>
> our Constituent Assembly in 1956. She was a most remarkable woman not only distinguished in her many pioneer activities, including the arts, but for the fortitude with which for so many years she triumphed over great physical disabilities.[4]

---

3 *La Mondopolo*, February 1954.
4 *The World Citizen*, No. 1 1970.

On the personal side, it was this year when Hugh's mother died on 8th April at the age of 80. He also went on a trip with Hélène to Copenhagen on Servant-Nation business from where he wrote a postcard to his daughters Joyce and Audrey which carries the picture of Hans Andersen's mermaid and on which he wrote:

> Going to Tirole Gardens for a "One World" celebration.

From the 4th to the 10th September 1954 Hugh attended the fourth World Parliamentary Conference as Vice-President of the International Arbitration League. The League was later to become integrated into the Mondcivitan Republic which, as we shall see, was about to be constituted.

He was also a member of Civil World Aid (based in Johannesburg, South Africa) which was described as "an independent organisation working under the flag of the Commonwealth [of World Citizens] and carrying out Social and Relief Work for the whole of humanity". Among its members are Lord Boyd-Orr, Henry Usborne, M.P., Hugh Schonfield (United Kingdom), Baron Allard (Belgium), Prof. Gokhale (India), Prof. Eya Ita (Nigeria), Prof. Ismail Wieslaw (Poland). Some of the other countries represented are Sweden, South Africa, Denmark, Germany, Israel, Japan and the U.S.A."[5]

The advent of the Rock and Roll era was heralded in with Bill Haley and His Comets and their hit record "Rock Around the Clock". Developments from this music were to become a great influence in the future alternative movements and would be the basis of the music of the Beatles and of John Lennon, who we will meet later in this book.

Hugh's media engagements, particularly with the BBC were on the increase and would keep him very busy. On 1st February 1954 he gave a talk entitled *St. Matthew's Gospel in Hebrew:* "In the sixteenth century there was published in Paris a Hebrew version of the Gospel according to St. Matthew. Mr. Schonfield has examined the text and sees in it something other than a Hebrew translation of the Greek Matthew. In this talk he describes the style of the Hebrew document and the conclusions he draws from it"[6]. The programme was repeated on 6th May. On the 20th March he gave a talk on the Third Programme entitled "The Nazarene Gospel Restored" about the book by Robert Graves and Joshua Podro[7]. On 5th March he also took part in a programme with John Allegro on the Dead Sea Scrolls[8].

In January of 1955, Hugh travelled to Holland and Belgium in his capacity as Secretary of Planning for the budding Commonwealth of World Citizens. He was involved in setting up communities and exploring possibilities for a venue for the Constituent Assembly which was planned for 1956. A "Founding Fund" was set up to raise money for financing the Assembly and a reception was held in London.

The Authentic New Testament, the translation he had been working on, was finally published in 1955 by Dobson (UK) and the first copy was accepted by the Queen. He received a letter of congratulations from Louis Golding dated 4th April 1955:

> My dear Hugh,

5 *La Mondopolo*, November 1954 No. 8.
6 http://genome.ch.bbc.co.uk/57c131e9e007452a85c8ba4b2d5b1b6b. Accessed 24th November 2014.
7 http://genome.ch.bbc.co.uk/726126fa8de34e1d9a9715013bb87246. Accessed 24th November 2014.
8 http://genome.ch.bbc.co.uk/34e03b9d18f54647ad60464d1b788954. Accessed 24th November 2014.

I am delighted to learn that at last your great work is to see the light of day. I have known about it since the beginning—I don't mean since the beginning of The New Testament. I do congratulate you that at last it has reached fruition. You know how much luck I wish you—though this is the sort of work in which it is almost an impertinence to wish mere luck.

I haven't been terribly well for some time, but I am on the mend now.

You can rest assured that if I am well enough I shall be with you, please The Lord, on April 14th.

Greeting to you both,

Yours ever,

Louis

Recognition started to come from the most unexpected quarters and on the 5th December 1955 he was awarded "Doctor of Sacred Literature, Honoris Causa" by St. John's University, Ambur, India[9] in recognition of his translation of the New Testament – the first Jew to attempt this task.

Letters of congratulation and reviews from many bible translators and scholars such as William Barclay and J.B. Phillips came pouring in. J.B. Phillips later compared the translation to his own: *In a sense Dr. Schonfield's method is diametrically opposed to my own. I have done my best to "short-circuit" the centuries so that the message of the New Testament appears fresh and meaningful to the people of today. But Dr. Schonfield, while removing obscurities by the score and translating for the most part with great clarity, has been concerned to preserve the historical setting in which the New Testament documents were first written. I believe that both our intentions are good and valid ...... This type of translation into English preserves the true historical sense without making one feel that the language of 1611 is the only reverent vehicle for conveying the truth of nearly 2000 years ago.*

Plans for the Servant-Nation were moving ahead and Hugh was able to give the opening address at the Third General Assembly of the Commonwealth of World Citizens in September of 1955.

Recognition for his translation of the New Testament came in 1956 from the Archbishop of Canterbury (Geoffrey Cantaur) in a letter of 19th October 1956 thanking him for the copy of the Authentic New Testament and stating "It will stand as an eloquent testimony of that fellowship between Jews and Christians which both of us are so anxious to encourage.".

An article appeared in the Times of 14th July 1956, "Dr. Hugh Schonfield observed history was being perverted by film and novels on an increasing scale. People took this pseudo-history for the real thing, he said". Then there is mention in the East Anglican Times of August 1956, "Professor Hugh Schonfield the Hebrew Scholar tells me that his next book is on why the Dead Sea Scrolls were hidden in a deserted cave 2,000 years ago. The book will be published in the autumn. Professor Schonfield has spent several years studying infra-red photographs of the scroll fragments of some 300 books already discovered. "Most scholars assume that they were buried hurriedly to prevent their capture by an advancing enemy", he said. "But I think that hundreds of the books were

---

9   Power, Owen M. (2011) Hugh Schonfield: A Case Study of Complex Jewish Identities, p.10. (information furnished by Boston University archivist). I have been unable to actually trace this university. This may have been incorporated into another university such as the University of Madras or Delhi in the meantime but I have not been able to verify this.

written especially to instruct some future generation on how to meet the end of the world". With a wry smile he added: "Perhaps it is significant that our generation has found them".

The New Testament translation inspired the talk given on the 31st January 1956 on the BBC Third Programme entitled Jewish Benedictions and Doxologies: "Dr. Schonfield, who is a Jew, has recently undertaken a translation of the New Testament, which appeared as The Authentic New Testament. In making his translation he noticed the accuracy of the Gospels in quoting Jewish prayers current in the first century. In this talk

Picture 22: Hugh signs the constitution of the Republic

he discusses some of the forms of benediction and doxology employed in the synagogue and in daily life, and illustrates from the New Testament their use by Jesus and in the Epistles of Paul.[10]"

Furthermore, in an article in *Advertiser's Weekly*, October 26th, under the title "Bible Authority is Copywriter" we find the following: "Copywriters, as a class are more often skilful than scholarly. One who is both is Dr. Hugh J. Schofield (sic. Schonfield), author of two new books displaying much classical and Biblical learning—Dr. Schonfield started his professional life as a copywriter with the old Holford Bottomley advertising agency. Later he joined the promotion department of Northcliffe Newspapers under John

10 http://genome.ch.bbc.co.uk/cc6bfcc53fdf4267bae5463bed00f049Accessed 24th November 2014.

Coope, on whose behalf he wrote a whole series of advertisements to advertisers which appeared in *Advertiser's Weekly* in the early 30's. Since then he has been awarded an honorary degree of Doctor of Sacred Literature by St. John's University at Delhi, and has become an authority on the interpretation of Biblical and historical documents and literature".

There would often be occasion for Hugh to comment on other's contributions to scholarship or politics and he would write the odd letter to the editor of magazines or newspapers. One such example is a letter written to *The Listener* on 23rd August 1956:

"The Gospels and the Rabbis"

Sir,—I was very pleased with Professor Daube's able talk on "The Gospels and the Rabbis" (Third Programme, August 16), illustrating the need for a thorough study of Jewish sources in relation to the exposition of the New Testament for which I contended in my recent translation of the Christian Scriptures.

> From such studies, however, an important and neglected inference is to be drawn, namely, that the original structure and content of the Gospel owed much to intellectual Jewish members of the Church, the priests, scribes, and Pharisees who joined the Jerusalem Community. Only they could have been sufficiently well-versed in such matters as Professor Daube adduced.
>
> Yours, etc., London, N.6 Hugh J. Schonfield

However, apart from all these exciting developments, something much more important to Hugh was taking shape, namely the establishment of the Commonwealth of World Citizens. Now the Commonwealth was actually coming into being and Hugh addressed the Constituent Assembly on August 27th and made an address on the Constitution on the following day. The Principles of the Commonwealth were expressed thus:

NONE ARE ENEMIES

1. The Mondcivitan Republic[11] (Commonwealth of World Citizens) acknowledges none as enemies, no matter what they may do; for to admit the existence of an enemy is to create a barrier, darkening understanding, breeding hatred, and giving encouragement and licence to cruelty and inhumanity.

NONE ARE FOREIGN

2. The Mondcivitan Republic recognises none as foreigners, or of a lower dignity, since all belong to the same human race. There shall be identical treatment of those outside the Republic as of those within it, treatment that is founded on reverence for the human personality.

SERVICE TO ALL

3. The Mondcivitan Republic shall ever promote and actively assist measures for the welfare and equitable unification of mankind, and shall at all times respond to the extent of its ability to calls for aid in emergency or catastrophe.

COMPLETE IMPARTIALITY

4. Neither the Republic, nor any of its citizens, shall under any circumstances engage in war or in preparation for war, or in aggression, or wilful mis-representation. The Mondcivitan Republic shall ever hold itself free from all alliances, agreements

---

11 The Commonwealth gradually became renamed as 'The Mondcivitan Republic' from the Esperanto 'La Respubliko Mondcivitano'.

The Commonwealth

and contractual obligations, whether open or in secret, which can have the effect of favouring any group, party, section, or State, or any interests whatever, to the hurt or detriment of any others.

and WORK FOR PEACE

Picture 23: "Lyons" A Design Study by Hugh J. Schonfield

5. The Mondcivitan Republic shall study to be impartial and humane in all its relations, and shall labour in the cause of mediation and reconciliation.

TRUE DEMOCRACY

6. The character of the Republic is democratic and co-operative, based on mutual service and respect, holding all men in honour in public and private.

EQUITY AND JUSTICE

7. In its government and internal economy the Mondcivitan Republic shall continually seek to cultivate and display those standards of conduct which are equitable and just.

The establishment of this nation was the pinnacle of Hugh's achievements. It was to be the concrete realisation of the messianic hope and brought to fruition all the ideas and thinking which he had so painstakingly researched and experienced. The movement reached a level which it was unfortunately unable ever again to attain. In the introduction to the Commonwealth Constitution we read:

Why is this happening? And what does it mean? As founder of the Commonwealth of World Citizens, and to a large extent the architect of its Constitution, it devolves upon me to answer these questions as exactly as possible, and to explain the position of World Citizens in relation to the States of which at present most of them are nationals.

I wish to make it immediately clear that the Constitution is not a blue print for World Government. The structure it will create is that of an additional world institution in the sphere of government, but not one that requires the adhesion of sovereign States or seeks to impose any direct obligations upon them. Neither does it represent any attempt to change their political structure or intervene in their internal affairs. No higher authority is set up in the international sphere comparable to the United Nations, only an auxiliary authority at the service of every nation.

The idea of the Commonwealth of World Citizens has been no secret for a good many years, though comparatively few have known what was taking place. Everything connected with this enterprise on behalf of mankind has been stated openly from the beginning, and it has been a fundamental principle all along not only that nothing should be concealed, but that there should be nothing to conceal. That is why in 1944, when the project was taking shape under the auspices of the Service-Nation Movement and the Second World War was still in progress, all the Allied and Neutral Governments were informed of what was intended. And that is why in 1951, when work began in London to put the plan of the Commonwealth of World Citizens into operation, the British Prime Minister and Foreign Secretary were duly notified of what was being done. It would have been most improper to start to build a new people on British soil without reporting the fact to the Government. Both letters were acknowledged from Downing Street without comment, and the Commonwealth of World Citizens was thus free to go ahead.

I think that this may be regarded as some indication that the Commonwealth of World Citizens is an agency without any inimical or undisclosed designs. In time past it would not have been at all necessary to mention this; but in these days of acute suspicion, both in official and unofficial circles, people find it difficult to believe that a world organisation for humanitarian objects is simply what it purports to be, and has no hidden motives or secret partisan connections, and is not in any sense being used for some subversive activity. It is part of the curse of this generation that such an attitude should govern and continually poison human relations, and that groups should be working against one another to an extent which affords some justification for it. It is obvious that without a recovery of mutual faith and goodwill, inspired by a new spirit of friendly cooperation, the whole fabric of organised life on this planet is threatened. It is by no means least among the functions of the Commonwealth of World Citizens to promote the growth of this spirit not only by precept, but by a living example.

The publicity received about the constituted Republic was to attract many new citizens and create much activity. Local communities started to spring up as this one reported in the *Cornishman Penzance* dated 6th September 1956:

FELLOW SPIRIT GUEST HOUSE CENTRE

A move to Open One in West Cornwall

A move is contemplated to establish in West Cornwall as part of the new effort to found such communities throughout the world, a "fellow spirit guest house community centre" under the auspices of the Commonwealth of World Citizens, which, it will be remembered, held their Congress in Cardiff recently.

Mr. Jack Monro, of 12, Peverell Road, Penzance, who was elected an Executive Council member after the Congress, is going into the possibility of establishing the guest house in West Cornwall, which will be run as a business arrangement.

He told "The Cornishman" on Monday that the movement was founded by Hugh J. Schonfield, the professional historian, in 1940, and was known as the Holy People. The name was changed to World Service People, and then to its present name of Commonwealth of World Citizens. The founder is one of the experts working on the Dead Sea Scrolls.

The Executive Council met after the Congress, and one of the matters discussed was the starting of local communities in all countries and districts possible.

This was all happening and was very pertinent in a world still besieged by strife. The so-called Suez Crisis would have been of particular pertinence to Hugh. President Nasser of Egypt had declared that he would conquer Palestine. Nasser nationalised the Suez Canal which led to plans by the United Kingdom, France and Israel to invade Egypt. In fact Israel actually invaded the Sinai Peninsula, pushing Egyptian troops back to the Canal and Britain commenced the bombing of Egypt to force the reopening of the Canal. The UN called for the withdrawal of troops. Hugh must have felt that the time was more than ripe for a mediatory Servant-Nation to appear on the world scene. Proposals for a settlement of the Suez Canal dispute were formulated by Schonfield and published in *The Times*, 14 August 1956. According to the *Progress Report issued in May 1958*, this had been distributed officially as a proposal coming from the Commonwealth of World Citizens as had proposals for the Israel-Palestine and USA-Soviet Union issues. So Hugh was acting in his official capacity. He felt this was the sort of work that all citizens of the Commonwealth should be doing but did not realise that most did not either have the experience nor the connections to do.

That same year saw the Soviet Union suppress mass demonstrations in Georgia, labour riots in Poland and the Hungarian Revolution. There were also change scenarios happening back in Britain which may have done something toward the air of optimism. Britain's House of Commons abolished the death penalty only for it to be turned down by the House of Lords. I cannot help wondering what Hugh would have felt about the release of the epic film *The Ten Commandments*. Such technological developments as the first commercial nuclear power plant opening at Calder Hall in England were promising endless cheap power (which in the meantime has turned out to be a myth).

Parallel to his bigger dreams, Hugh had to continue the writing career which was the source of his livelihood and of course an area of major interest. As we are beginning to see, the two things were by no means disconnected. In 1956 the book *The Secrets of the Dead Sea Scrolls* was published by Vallentine Mitchell UK and by Yosselof (now Barnes) USA in 1957. The book *The Suez Canal in World Affairs* was also translated and published in India. Hugh was also asked to write a series of a further 12 articles for the Evening News for the series *The Bible was Right*.

He was continually lecturing on his scholarly specialities and, for example, he gave a lecture to the Women Citizens' Association on the Dead Sea Scrolls, as reported in the Barnet Press on 17th November.

In December he spoke about the Commonwealth at the Friends' Meeting House in Manchester.

Obviously Hugh did not have enough to do! He was also president of the International Arbitration League (which was founded in 1904 by Sir William Randal Cremer) and would have also have to attend meetings regularly. In 1957 discussions were taking place for a cooperation between the League and the Commonwealth and on the 27th September an extra-ordinary meeting was held to discuss this. By this time, the League was falling into decline so some new action was demanded.

The plans for building a Servant-Nation continued with the first parliament of the Commonwealth of World Citizens in Vienna in 1958. They received a letter of congratulations from the Westminster Bank in Highgate from manager Alan Leach.

Hugh got involved with Sir Victor Gollancz (an old Pauline) and the Jewish Society for Human Service (JSHS). Gollancz had founded this organisation in 1948 with Rabbi Leo Baeck and the organisation was based on the "universalist ethic of Judaism" to offer impartial aid to both Jews and Arabs in Israel. This was a continuing key concern of Hugh's and it is no wonder that he should want to be involved in this movement. He was concerned that the newly formed State of Israel should live up to its calling although he must have been pretty clear that the terms of a State's need to protect its territory would likely be in opposition to a "true" Israel which would, like his Commonwealth, have no need for territory or borders. But like Hugh, Gollancz had been involved with the founding of the Association for World Peace (AWP) and later the international charity "War on Want". In searching the Schonfield archives, the author came across a letter dated 21st December 1959 addressed to Mr. Gollancz seeking help for an Arab girl and which was passed on to Hugh asking for a contribution.

All of this led to much travel and we find a hastily written postcard from Munich around this time:

> Wednesday Evening
>
> Now at Munich staying with Heinz[12] who sends his heartiest regards. Arrived last night from Baden-Baden. Have people to see here.
>
> Then travel to Cologne Friday.
>
> Have to get up at 6 a.m. And travel all day. Stay in Cologne Saturday and take the night train. Should be home about 5:30 pm time for talk and television. My train due Victoria 3-5 but may be late. This is last line from your wandering kid. Got all your letters.

---

12 The name is rather illegible. I cannot imagine that this was the Heinz Müller we read about later.

Bundle love, Smike[13].

Then there is a postcard from Paris dated 30th March 1957 with:

a line from the top [Eiffel Tower] *as souvenir.*

From Amsterdam dated 24th August 1957:

Having a good crossing. Excellent lunch. Hope you had a good time with Sandbanks. Will write very soon. Love to Joyce and own Kin. Smike.

One has to remember the world scenario at that time. There was a paranoiac fear (probably somewhat justified) that the Third World War could break out at any time. This is best illustrated by the following article about *Operation Dropshot*[14]:

Operation Dropshot was the United States Department of Defence codename for a contingency plan for a possible nuclear and conventional war with the Soviet Union and its allies in order to counter the anticipated Soviet takeover of Western Europe, the Near East and parts of Eastern Asia expected to start around 1957. The plan was prepared in 1949 during the early stages of the Cold War and declassified in 1977. Although the scenario did make use of nuclear weapons, they were not expected to play a decisive role.

At the time the US nuclear arsenal was limited in size, based mostly in the United States, and depended on bombers for delivery. *Dropshot* included mission profiles that would have used 300 nuclear bombs and 29,000 high-explosive bombs on 200 targets in 100 cities and towns to wipe out 85% of the Soviet Union's industrial potential at a single stroke. Between 75 and 100 of the 300 nuclear weapons were targeted to destroy Soviet combat aircraft on the ground.

At this time there was some trouble with the International Arbitration League of which Hugh was president. An agreement to cooperate with the Commonwealth of World Citizens had been made but in the meantime, the League had been included in a bequest by a Mr. Fallows, a League member (which had been the subject of a complex legal battle). Now some of the League council members thought that the money could be used to revive the League whilst others thought cooperation with the Commonwealth should be pursued and the money transferred. Hugh was accused of bias so in a long letter of 15th November 1958, he tendered his resignation. Hugh felt that he had to point out that the Commonwealth had already been established in 1950, before he was elected president. He stressed that the proposal was not for a merger but only mutual advantage and that the League should retain its independence. A considerable amount of correspondence ensued but finally the League was incorporated into the Commonwealth and ceased to exist as a separate entity.

The importance of the International Arbitration League should not be underestimated and it had enjoyed a long history. In the Jubilee booklet from 1920 we read that the League had been founded by Sir William Randal Cremer on July 21st 1870 and was his life's work. He later received a knighthood and in 1903, the Nobel Peace Prize. In the booklet it states:

Before he came to the work of his life he had a useful preparation as a politician and social reformer. He acted as secretary of the Workmen's Committee on behalf of the Northern States in the American Civil War, became secretary of the historic body known as the International, helped to organise the reception to Garibaldi in

---

13 His cosy name between the couple
14 https://en.wikipedia.org/wiki/Operation_Dropshot

London, was a leading figure on the Executive of the Reform League, and unsuccessfully contested Warwick twice as a Parliamentary candidate.

The League produced a regular periodical called *The Arbitrator* from 1872 until its dissolution. It was the instigator of the idea of a League of Nations:

> Within eight months of the initial meeting the League had to its credit a modest but practical plan for the creation of an international authority, a not unworthy forerunner of the Covenant of the League of Nations, now, happily, an accomplished fact. There is a close resemblance in some of the operative clauses of this scheme and the institution brought into existence at Paris.

In 1958 the famous peace symbol was created being designed for the Campaign for Nuclear Disarmament (CND) and which gradually was adopted by other peace activists. We have to remember that nuclear testing was being carried out intensively at this time. The growing protests against, particularly amongst the youth, may have triggered the beginnings of the future protest movements. The protests may also have influenced the agreement by the USA, Soviet Union and Britain to cease testing for three years.

The Bible Was Right which had been published in 1956 by Frederick Müller USA, now appeared in 1959 as a paperback with Signet Books USA. It seems that slowly but surely, Hugh was gradually establishing himself as a writer of format on the US market.

Quite a milestone in international affairs was the establishment of the European Court of Human Rights in 1959. Such developments were a more positive contrast to the continuing threats of the Cold War, the continuing development of intercontinental rockets and the spread of nuclear weapons. The Dalai Lama was forced to flee from Tibet under the increasing domination of Tibet by China and the resulting uprising.

Hugh never ceased in his efforts to promote the Mondcivitan Republic. He often would travel with Hélène visiting communities and one of these trips was reported in the Republic's magazine:

> The summer of 1959 afforded my wife and myself an opportunity to visit two of our Communities in Italy, and on the way I was able to attend the Conference of the World Association of World Federalists at Oosterbeek near Arnhem in Holland. It was a pleasure to meet Prof. Knap at the Conference, Mr. Sam Hammond, Minister of Finance of Ghana. I also met again Mrs. Esther Peters, whom I saw last at the Peoples World Convention at Geneva in 1950. She gave me her application for Citizenship and is going to take up residence in Canada. I am glad to say that our outlook was much more in evidence at the Federalist Conference this year, so that its main emphasis was on how to promote a sense of World community and how to assist the underprivileged countries.
>
> At the end of the Conference, before joining my wife in Italy, I spent a pleasant weekend with Joachim Müller and his family at Cologne. Herr Müller, who has long worked in the cause of world government, has now become a citizen: his wife, some will remember, was able to attend our parliament at Vienna as an observer.
>
> My next rendezvous was with Hélène and our daughter Joyce at the station at Bologna, where we were warmly welcomed by Deputy Maria Sciabica. She and her husband Vicenzo, whom we met for the first time, are the life and soul of the Bologna community. Both were tortured in concentration camps during the war, and therefore know far more than most of us the evils and the horror of international conflict. We discovered that this magnificent couple have really given their all for

our Commonwealth, health, strength and means, assisting personally some of our people who are destitute or unemployed. They have inaugurated a fine social service system with another citizen Dr. Chiaburri giving his medical services free. We had two meetings with the Community at Dr. Chiaburri's house, and all the citizens insisted on escorting us back to our hotel on the final occasion.

In 1960 Hugh was appointed chairman of the newly established H. G. Wells Society of which he had been co-founder. The objects of the Society were "to promote and encourage an active interest in and appreciation of, the life, work and thought of Herbert George Wells". A periodical *The Wellsian* was launched as the organ of the Society."[15]

The writer had the good fortune to make contact with David Bailey who was able to re-

Picture 24: Prospect Cottage

call the contact he had with Hugh during the 1960's and he relates:

> I had the pleasure of knowing this gentleman for a few months during the early 1960's. I was an apprentice at the time in the chemical industry—just an ordinary young lad training for an ordinary job. My pal at the time worked in central London as an office boy at Reuters—he asked me if i would like to come along to a preliminary meeting of a group proposing to encourage working youngsters to pursue their hobbies by meeting professional people already established in that particular field. The point of contact and the person behind this wonderful idea, was a lady who ran a small publishing business whose name I sadly forget. As I recall, the premises were a small office somewhere near the British Museum. At this meeting, attended by myself, my friend and one or two other people (not a very good start really) this "lady" informed us that, by the nature of her business, she knew several professional people who would be very keen to "encourage" working class youngsters – they included a west-end producer, a reporter from a national newspaper, a world-class athlete and an "archaeologist". I was very keen, my hobby was ancient history, and I secretly wanted to be an archaeologist, but being a working lad from just beyond The East End, I knew this ambition was only ever going to be a dream and would always be limited to visiting The British Museum every Saturday subsidised by what was left over from my poor apprentice wages.

15 *La Mondcivitano*, 2nd Quarter 1961

A week later the first full meeting of the newly formed "Encouragement Hobby Club" was held attended by about ten or fifteen young teenagers and the professionals. The group who chose "ancient history"—about six of us, were introduced to Dr Hugh Schonfield. Personally I had no idea what a famous person he was, he mentioned he had written a book or two about archaeology of the holy lands. This branch of the club arranged to meet at his house the following week for the first "lecture". I walked into his house in London and was bowled over by the historical pictures and his classy furniture. It was outside my experience as you can imagine. Dr Schonfield spoke about his excursions into Egyptian tombs! He showed us a wooden carving which was found in a tomb and a secret compartment he had discovered within it about the dead sea scrolls and their significance in biblical history. I hung on every word. My jaw remained firmly open throughout! This man was my hero! When the meeting finished, Dr Schonfield gave me a shard of pottery that he had found in the holy lands. It had an imprint of the potters finger at its base and I still have it! Dr Schonfield suggested that at the next meeting (a surprise to me) I spoke about an area of ancient history that I had some knowledge of to the fellow members and he would, of course, come along too. He was sure he would really enjoy it!

I spent the next week in a cold sweat! I re-read the few books I had on the history of Roman Britain after work and spent several whole nights writing and re-writing my notes—how could I possibly follow the "lecture" given the week before? I had never been so nervous in my life! The big night came—I had at least twenty or thirty A4 sheets of notes and crossed-out paragraphs! Dr Schonfield smiled confidently throughout my over-long presentation. I shall never forget his kind words when it was all over—he thanked me in front of the small audience of youngsters remarking that he had "learnt a couple of things himself this evening" etc. and he "applauded the hard work I had put into preparing the talk". A few more evenings of various lectures from other historians, some attended by Dr Schonfield, followed.

The "club" for many reasons I forget now, evaporated but my memory of Dr Schonfield remains. That brief meeting with that great person inspired me for the rest of my life. I remain an amateur archaeologist and historian after a lifetime in the pharmaceutical industry. I sometimes give talks on local history and something of the "enthusiasm" that I heard from that first "lecture" I heard at Dr Schonfield's remains with me. I wished I could go back in time to thank him.

Fame Starts to Spread

It was in this year that he published the wonderful piece of literature, his translation, *The Song of Songs: The Immortal Marriage Song of Love* which was brought out by Elek Books in the UK and the New American Library (Signet Books) in the USA.

His fame started to grow in the UK with a BBC TV programme on the Dead Sea Scrolls in March of 1959. The film was produced "by Kenneth Brown followed by a studio discussion between Kenneth Harris of the Observer and R. D. Barnett, F. F. Bruce, John Allegro, Dr. Hugh Schonfield, and Rev. M. Black on some of the historical and theological issues which these discoveries have raised"[1].

Hugh and Hélène had purchased a small country house where they lived some of the time which was called "Prospect Cottage" in Tintern. Hugh needed a retreat where he could study and write in peace and also spend some quality time with his beloved Hélène. Nevertheless the house was to see many visitors and, for example, Donald Hanby, of the Commonwealth of World Citizens, would visit them there. It was marked on the postcard picture reproduced below:

Hugh and Hélène's daughter recollects:

> I was just remembering the two holiday homes my parents had. The first was in Tintern, Monmouthshire and was bought after we grew up. It was a semi-detached house next to a pub called "The Moon and Sixpence" and was quite near the Abbey and built into the hill. I remember there was an old lady who was too infirm to walk up and down anymore and so had not seen the village for several years. My mother used to do charity teas with the vicar's wife in the front garden. They loved spending time there, but of course my father didn't drive (he never possessed a car except for the one he had bought with his brother and drove down a hill and crashed) so it was quite a journey by train. All the family and friends were always welcome to stay and enjoy the countryside.

Hugh's involvement with the situation in Palestine and Israel caused him to visit Nablus in Jordan regarding an educational project. He was able to hold a meeting with the High Priest of the Samaritan Community Isaac Amram Cohen (from 1961-1980) and was fascinated by their history and traditions which seemed to have survived the centuries. The High Priesthood has remained in the same Pinhas family for 112 generations and the current High Priest is the 132nd since Aaron, brother of Moses, promised the priesthood to his grandson Pinhas (Num. 24:12).

The Middle East continued to be one of his major concerns and area of expertise and he was asked to hold a lecture in Sutton-in-Ashfield entitled *The Epic of the Suez Canal*. He received a fee of 22 guineas for his efforts but he was undoubtedly more interested in the opportunity to share his vast knowledge of this subject.

Yet Israel continued to call him and in 1962 he returned, this time to Jerusalem and once again to Nablus where he met Amram Isaac Cohen, president and High Priest of the Samaritan Community and author of the book *Mount Gerizim, The One True Sanctuary* (1910).

---

1   http://genome.ch.bbc.co.uk/34e03b9d18f54647ad60464d1b7889.54 Accessed 24th November 2014.

The books, *A History of Biblical Literature*, in the USA, and *A Popular Dictionary of Judaism*, *UK*, were both published at this time.

We find a note in his diary from 1962 that he was to hold a talk on Wells and World Citizenship at County Hall on the 9th January, had an appointment with lawyer and friend Ambrose Appelbe on the 15th January and held a talk *Why I translated the New Testament* at Hope House. He wrote on the back of the diary:

> Build a better world with the Mondcivitan Republic. The imperative world-wide nation that serves all mankind.

An ITN TV news clip dated 28th August states:

> Citizens Meet Wales
> Cardiff, Wales—World Citizens Meet Various Scenes; GV Ext. "Temple of Peace" MS Women enters, CU Flag "Mondcivitan Republic", MCU Constitution (on Cushion) Placed before President, LS Pres. Speaking, Four Shots MS Pres. Dr Schonfield Speaking, MCU trans-african delegate takes Oath (Mr. S.F. Odusiga) MCU Deleg. Two Shots, CU North American Delegate (Peter Gerard) takes Oath, Two Shots, CU Ben Willis Fuson, (American West) Takes Oath.[2]

So we can see what was always going on in the back of his mind whilst involved in all these other activities. There was always this permanent link between the learning which was coming out of his historical research and the future of the world through the Servant-Nation. World affairs such as the Cuban crisis at this time would also have impressed upon him the urgent need for the Servant-Nation.

Around this time the American involvement in the Vietnam War commenced. This was to become a major factor in the alternative peace movements and the subject of increasing protests. John Lennon became the ad hoc leader of the movement to get the USA out of this war and to put an end to it but at this time the Beatles were very much in their early days and just auditioning for Decca Records and producing their first records.

As an aside, it is worth noting that Ambrose Appelbe and Hugh were both involved in the project to establish an International People's College for which a trust had been founded with such notable trustees as Dame Sybill Thorndike and Rev. R.C. Sorensen M.P. In a brochure issued by the trust, Hugh is listed as being on the Foundation Committee.[3] The project had been initiated by a Mr. De Bevere and the trust was entitled "International People's College Trust" and in the brochure, Hugh is also listed as Vice-Chairman.

Another note in a diary reads:

> The Christians of Paul's time did not grasp what he was trying to convey, which was founded on Jewish mysteries. When the Church got round to Paul again after flirting with gnosticism it misunderstood his great passages in ignorance of their origins and used him to oppose their own theology.

> We [consider] Paul as an authority on what Jesus represented. We ought to take note from Paul's words that his conception of Christianity did not come from Jesus but came by a revelation. "Though we have known Christ after the flesh we know him so no more". So he did not concern himself with Jesus but with the Christ of

---

2 http://www.itnsource.com/en/shotlist/FoxMovietone/1963/08/28/158565/?s=hugh %20schonfield. Accessed 24th November 2014.
3 Part of a brochure included in the Epitaph to E.A. De Bevere.

Messiah idea. The only contact with Jesus was the primitive teaching of his death and resurrection and ascension.

Christianity is the message of Jesus which has become lop-sided, it is the messianic idea with a pagan slant or tilt.

The Passover Plot Era

Around this time, something dramatic started to take place – something which was to change not only Hugh and Hélène's lives and affluence but also to start one of the biggest New Testament controversies which exists to this day. It was something, often totally misunderstood, for many extremely enlightening. It was the book which was to change the life (and perhaps cause the death) of the most famous popular musician and composer in modern times – John Lennon.

For Hugh (and Hélène) it would mean countless speaking engagements, television and radio appearances, life threats, travelling and encounters. It even culminated in the production of a Hollywood epic film and documentary films.

Thus it was that in 1963 the excitement and potential in Hugh's writing was beginning to be understood. - even by the publishing world. The British publisher Hutchinsons decided to make an offer to Hugh with an advance of one thousand pounds and 12.5% royalty rising to 17.5% for over 30,000 copies sold to write the book which was to make him famous and controversial, *The Passover Plot*. Mark Paterson, his agent, said that "the advance would be one of the highest paid for an unwritten book". They were soon to discover that estimates of total sales which would amount to several million were very conservative, even if most of those sales were to take place in the USA where Hugh Schonfield's name as an author was about to break upon the American world of theology and literature.

As he stated later:

> Important discoveries were to flow from these researches affecting both Judaism and Christianity. Book followed book, notably Secrets of the Dead Sea Scrolls and The Pentecost Revolution. But the most popular was The Passover Plot, a book about Jesus which was to influence John Lennon of Beatle Fame and help to inspire Jesus Christ Superstar.

This was the year when US President John F. Kennedy was assassinated. This was seen as a blow to the civil rights movement.

By May 1964 the Nablus High Priest informed that the school project had been completed. This must have added to Hugh's feeling of achievement as it was something which was close to his heart. He also was becoming noticed by high society and Sir Kenneth Grubb hosted a reception in Hugh's honour. Apart from family members, a number of celebrities and old acquaintances were to attend, including Dennis Dobson, Lord and Lady Sorensen, Harold Rubenstein, Mark Paterson and his wife, Sir Guillum Scott, Lord Calecote, just to name a few. It is interesting to note that some of these attendees are to be found back in 1930 attending an annual general meeting of the Anglo-Jewish-Association, with Major Schonfield in attendance.

It is notable that Hugh was a smoker in those days but this was by no means unusual because it was not until 1964 that the US surgeon General Luther Terry reported that smoking could be a health hazard – something we take for granted today. Attitudes were changing and in 1965 cigarette advertising was banned on British television. Audrey remembers that the rooms always were filled with smoke.

The work in the Middle East had to continue and a trip was planned to Jordan for May 1965. *The Passover Plot* was now published in the UK and shortly afterwards in the USA.

The rapidly growing interest in the book led to its publishing in 1967 as a paperback by Corgi Books in the UK and Bantam Books in the USA.

In 1965 (International Cooperation Year) a garden party at 5, Lansdowne Road in Holland Park London was organised under the "Feast of Frontiers" in aid of the World Service Trust. Lord Sorensen opened the party and guests were expected to appear in national costume. There would be a number of events at this address including a Mondcivitan Christmas Bazaar on November 21st. These events were intended to raise funds for the World Service Trust. In the BBC Home Service radio programme *Home this Afternoon* on 15th December Hugh gave a talk about the Dead Sea Scrolls[1].

Not only Hugh but Hélène also got involved in the media work for the Commonwealth and was asked, as President, to take part in an interview in Woman's Hour on the BBC Light Programme as "Mrs World" on 15th December 1965[2].

On the international scene there was still a desperate need for a neutral people and whilst the Vietnam War continued, trouble broke out in Africa when martial law was announced in Rhodesia (now Zimbabwe) and the white minority government of Ian Smith declared independence unilaterally. The UN accepted Britain's intention to use force if necessary.

In 1966 Hugh was asked to appear in the BBC TV programme "Meeting Point" on 16th January in an interview about *The Passover Plot* - "A controversial best-seller (to the surprise of its author) attempts to re-interpret the life and work of Jesus in the light of historical studies of his time, including the Dead Sea Scrolls. Dr. Hugh J. Schonfield author of the book discusses his ideas with Professor Christopher Evans, Professor of New Testament Studies, University of London King's College Chairman, Derek Hart, Producer, Peter Ferres"[3]. On the other hand, from a letter from Hutchinsons, it would appear that our author was not totally satisfied with their performance in selling the book and had expressed concerns that there would not be enough copies available to meet demand after the TV transmission.

A Maurice Lewin sent him a postcard on the 4th July in which he wrote:

> I thought the discovery of the Arabic manuscript will provide a trickle on your mill, and I hope that if its publication will provide some valid factual information you may be induced to consider more favourably my recent suggestion.

It is not to clear what the suggestion was because that correspondence seems to have got lost.

However, there were storms on the horizon as the book became subjected to heavy criticism by fundamentalist Christian groups. A legal battle with "The Plain Truth" and its publisher Herbert Armstrong for publishing untrue statements about Hugh and the Passover Plot ensued which ended by the magazine (reluctantly) printing a retraction. Hugh had enlisted the support of his lawyer Harold Rubenstein in this issue. Herbert Armstrong who died in 1986 had been described as "God's Apostle on Earth" and issued a magazine in the style of magazines like *Newsweek* or *Time*. Armstrong used it as a platform for his fundamentalist and dispensationalist ideas. Obviously he would not be too

---

1 http://genome.ch.bbc.co.uk/59d808e2e298423aac84029932961e86. Accessed 24th November 2014.
2 http://genome.ch.bbc.co.uk/1740c15693924f82a50f4b3cc9f2e8d7. Accessed 24th November 2014.
3 http://genome.ch.bbc.co.uk/59d808e2e298423aac84029932961e86. Accessed 24th November 2014.

pleased with the content and subject of *The Passover Plot*. Hugh's main contention though, was that the content of Armstrong's article was personally slanderous and untrue. As it turns out, Armstrong had not actually read the book himself and was just going on hearsay, and he managed to turn his retraction into an opportunity for his own teaching.

By October 1966, the publisher Bernard Geis alone was selling about 5-6000 copies per week in the USA and by the end of the year the book was already in its fifth printing. They were already looking forward to the completion of *Those Incredible Christians*. Unfortunately, Hutchinsons were not able to share the success of the Americans in the UK and interest remained at a relatively low level. It would seem now that Hugh's fame as an author was going to be established in the USA and not in his home country. It would seem that the controversy fired by the Christian establishment actually fuelled the fire which made the book so popular and which remains a classic to this day.

All the work involved in promoting his books meant that the couple needed a break and they were able to enjoy a short holiday in Yucatan in 1967. Hélène wrote an extensive report on their holiday. She starts off by writing:

> Oct. 11. Arrived at Merida. We walked off the plane as if into Kew Gardens hothouse. The heavy scent was unbelievable.

It goes on in a captivating manner and shows that Helen was also endowed with some considerable literary skills and we can imagine her picking over Hugh's manuscripts and suggesting better turns of phrase.

The New American Library published *The Readers' A to Z Bible Companion* in 1967. He was also asked to write an article on the *Passover Plot* for the US magazine *The National Explorer* of New York.

By March 1967, *Passover Plot* had climbed to number three on the *New York Post's* best seller ratings and number 10 on *Chicago Tribune* and was runner up after the top ten on *Publishers' Weekly* Charts. Sales had reached 89,000 copies and by August it was number one paperback on the *New York Post* best seller chart.

1967 was the year of the "Six Day War" between Israel and Syria, Israel annexed East Jerusalem and thus the Middle East continued to be an area of conflict. Nuclear weapons were also spreading and China was to test its first bomb. Yet growing sections of the younger generation were tired of all these conflicts and hoped for a better world. It was very pertinent when John Lennon's song *All You Need is Love* was released.

Popular Culture

Publishers Bernard Geis were now ready to issue a contract for *Those Incredible Christians*. In a letter to Mark Paterson from the publishers, Letty Cottin writes on November 13th 1967 regarding an article in the New Yorker magazine:

> Since Richard Lester knows John Lennon and John Lennon is a Passover Plot fan, and a disciple of Hugh Schonfield's, and since the movie sounds closer to Hugh's book than to "Salt of the Earth", perhaps you can sell Lester in buying both books and doing a combined motion picture treatment.

Here we have some of the first evidence for John Lennon's involvement with Hugh. Hugh was to have an important influence on Lennon's thinking which is apparent in songs such as *Imagine* which continues to be a major source of inspiration to this day. This influence should not be underestimated. In a study by Matthew Schneider of Chapman University we read:

> The starting point for the Beatles' careers as both creators and objects of conspiracy theories was the "bigger than Jesus" controversy of the summer of 1966. This episode in pop culture history was more than just the flash point for long-smouldering anxieties about the relevance of religion to postwar Anglo-American society. The uproar that erupted over John Lennon's statement that the Beatles were "more popular than Jesus" demonstrated for this pop-star cum social commentator that outbursts of hysterical celebrity worship—like the Beatlemania that greeted the group around the world from 1964-66—originated in the same psychic and cultural forces that in the past had produced periods of mass religious fervour. Thus Lennon learned by comparing his first-hand experiences of Beatlemania with the picture of first-century Palestine he found in Hugh Schonfield's 1965 book The Passover Plot, which Lennon read shortly before uttering his infamous remarks. Schonfield also taught Lennon, however, to view history conspiratorially—that is, to look for the ways in which the powerful weave the chaotic profusion of events, conflicting interests, and contradictory testimonies into an apparently seamless eschatological narrative. To manifest and capitalize on their quasi-religious importance in the lives of their fans, Lennon realized, the Beatles needed merely to provide a plenitude of tantalizing, apparently disjointed details; their adherents, like the early church fathers, could be counted on eagerly to weave from those data a personally and culturally meaningful narrative.[1]

There is a sense in which one might see an unintentional responsibility of Hugh for the murder of John Lennon. Wikipedia states that Mark Chapman was convicted for Lennon's murder in 1980:

> Mark David Chapman (born May 10, 1955) is an American prison inmate who was convicted for murdering John Lennon on December 8, 1980. Chapman shot Lennon outside The Dakota apartment building in New York City. Chapman fired at Lennon five times, hitting him four times in his back.[2]

---

1 Schneider, M. (2003) "What matters is the system!" The Beatles, the "Passover Plot," and Conspiratorial Narrativity in *Anthropoetics* 8, no. 2 (Fall 2002 / Winter 2003). http://www.anthropoetics.ucla.edu/ap0802/beatles2.htm, accessed 22.4.2012.
2 http://en.wikipedia.org/wiki/Mark_David_Chapman

Chapman was a fanatical evangelical Christian and refused to plead insanity, saying that he was acting out the will of God in murdering Lennon. He had been a big fan of Lennon but turned against him when he became an evangelical Christian. The final straw was the "more popular than Jesus" statement.

Lennon's son saw the matter differently:

> [John Lennon] was a countercultural revolutionary, and the government takes that kind of shit really seriously historically. He was dangerous to the government. If he had said, "Bomb the White House tomorrow," there would have been ten thousand people who would have done it. These pacifist revolutionaries are historically killed by the government, and anybody who thinks that Mark Chapman was just some crazy guy who killed my dad for his personal interests is insane, I think, or very naïve, or hasn't thought about it clearly. It was in the best interests of the United States to have my dad killed, definitely. And, you know, that worked against them, to be honest, because once he died his powers grew. So, I mean, fuck them. They didn't get what they wanted. Sean Lennon, quoted in The New Yorker, April 20, 1998.[3]

Matthew Schneider sees this as the result of a conspiracy theory approach but when one analyses the lines of the song *Imagine* one realises how near this is to the idea and principles of the Servant-Nation idea being taught by Hugh. Lennon was certainly in telephone contact with Hugh as he related this to the author on occasions. If one were to follow a conspirational approach, one could imagine that the establishment of a world order based on such principles could be seen as a threat to the status quo even worse than Communism.

At this point, Bantam Books were keen to promote the book and they proposed a trip to the USA financed by themselves followed by a lecture tour. A dispute about royalties broke out between Bantam Books and Bernard Geis which meant that Hugh had difficulty receiving his funds. Marcus Jaffe of Bantam tried to help out by paying directly. It would seem that a solution was soon found.

Hugh agreed to appear on the ABC Television programme *Looking for an Answer* with Robert Kee and Dr. George Caird. The programme was recorded on the 28th November. Hugh also appeared on a programme with David Frost. In 1968 Nahum Levison died and Hugh received a letter from his wife Margaret. Hugh had visited their home in Edinburgh in those early days. Hugh is quoted as stating around this time: *I have lived by the axiom: Hats off to the past: coats off to the future.*

Finally, *Those Incredible Christians* went to press with Hutchinson (UK), Bernard Geis (USA), Bantam Books (USA) and Corgi (UK) publishing in 1986 and 1969.

In March of 1968 Hugh received an invitation from the Oxford University Newman Society to speak at their Triennial Dinner. Guests on the occasion were such as Archbishop Cardinale, Lord Longford, Douglas Goodruf and Douglas Brown.

In the Schonfeld archives there is an interesting interview on the role of women carried out by a Rosalie Shonfield which the author does not believe to have been published. It contains a lot of insights into our subject's thinking and so it is reproduced below:

---

3   Schneider, M. (2003) "What matters is the system!" The Beatles, the "Passover Plot", and Conspiratorial Narrativity in *Anthropoetics* 8, no. 2 (Fall 2002 / Winter 2003). http://www.anthropoetics.ucla.edu/ap0802/beatles2.htm, accessed 22.4.2012.

Picture 25: Hugh and Hélène

Women, as a result of centuries of repression, are more conservative than are men regarding profound changes in the church, according to Dr. Hugh J. Schonfield, outstanding Biblical scholar.

Dr. Schonfield, British author of the tremendously popular The Passover Plot, recently toured the United States on behalf of his latest book, Those Incredible Christians (Bernard Geis, $5. 95). The latter book traces the first 150 years of Christianity, demonstrating by historical documents how the church came to mythologize and distort the man Jesus Christ, (in his earlier work, Dr. Schonfield's controversial thesis is that Jesus plotted his own death to confirm the contemporary Jewish belief in the Messiah.)

He has found in his lectures, and in radio telephone interviews, that the questions he receives from women differ in that they are far more emotional.

"But don't forget," said Dr. Schonfield, "that even in the pagan religions, women were chosen as priestesses—to perpetuate rituals—precisely because they could be counted on to keep a conservative view."

Thus, Dr. Schonfield explains, it is only with much required effort that women today are able to overcome repression in all fields.

However, it is inevitable that, "in the future, step by step, organized religion will dissolve," said Dr. Schonfield. "But religion is a thing apart from spirituality, which is gaining. Although twanging a harp aloft is no longer the issue, "Love your God" and "Love your neighbour" definitely is"[4].

Dr. Schonfield attributes changes in attitude toward traditional religion to the mass media. Extensive reporting of scientific progress has led to the realization that "the universe demands a different kind of mental bearing. Once you are convinced that the universe doesn't have a top, you begin to question the afterlife and miracles."

Scholars and clergymen have been hesitant to discuss these questions before the public—scholars because of their habit of "talking to themselves," and clergymen

Picture 26: Willi Haller

because of their own conservative interests (what might facetiously be called their "vested interests" in the church).

---

4 This goes some way perhaps to explaining the line "..and no religion too" in Lennon's song Imagine.

All this—plus mass social awareness—is what Dr. Schonfield believes makes his books, written for the laymen, so timely. And because he makes these issues known to ordinary men, Dr. Schonfield is convinced that he is following the intentions of Jesus, who is reported to have said, "What you hear in secret shout from the house-tops." And it also is said that "the common people heard him gladly."

Acceptance of Dr. Schonfield's ideas came almost forty years after he began working them out. Born in London in 1901, he was educated at St. Paul's school in London and at the University of Glasgow where, as a boy, he wrote his first book on the subject.

He has approached his subject as an historian, relying on archaeological discoveries culminating in the finding of the Dead Sea Scrolls and the ancient site of Masada.

His method was so revolutionary, so unrecognised and so frequently attacked that he, his wife, Hélène, and their three daughters, often lived in relative poverty.

"The girls felt acutely that their father's work was not given the recognition it deserved," said Mrs. Schonfield. "But Hughie never tried to influence their reaction or their ideas—and now they and our friends are so happy for him."

None of the girls—all married and living in London, Cambridge and Paris—have avidly taken up their father's pursuit. "One's children have to rebel against their parents," said Mrs. Schonfield. But they wouldn't be surprised if one of their six grandchildren became involved in religious history. "The alternation of generations," said Dr. Schonfield, "is a cultural, as well as scientific phenomenon."

In his work, Dr. Schonfield projects himself back many generations, psychologically to the times he is writing about. He becomes, as he said, "alive with the historical period".

Although he would have liked to have known Jesus, "I think I would have found him rather frightening," he said. "He was so intense in his ideas, it was hard to be in his company for very long. He would lapse into long periods of silence".

This human rapport with historical figures is warmly and clearly presented in Dr. Schonfield's books. He is able to write concisely for the layman—often a difficult task for a scholar—because, "I had the good fortune to spend the first years of my adult life working in an advertising agency—writing about products varying from savings certificates to records. They called me the "copywriter-theologian," and I had the distinction of being the first to have an ad reviewed in Punch".

Dr. Schonfield has heard his books discussed by scholars, clergymen, laymen, professors, students, Jews and Christians. He gauges general reactions by saying, "If faith rests only on blind adherence, my books will destroy that faith. But if faith is based on progressive evolution of individuals, then my books will validate that faith. And the latter is the faith we know through historical fact to have been preached by Jesus."

A film of The Passover Plot, scheduled for production by Twentieth Century Fox, will bring the demythologized Jesus to a wider audience. Dr. Schonfield insists an unknown actor must play the lead and that historical accuracy in dress and sets must prevail.

Films, books, America—has success spoiled Hugh Schonfield? No.

This is what he has been waiting and working for, but he continues to work hard and is extremely demanding of himself when interpreting his books.

Mrs. Schonfield, who he has known most of his life, takes notes on all questions put to him, so that he can study and refine his own thesis.

Their home base soon will be Malta, when they will move from a London apartment. There the Schonfields will live in a comfortable old house furnished with "what in this country would be considered antiques," and artefacts which must definitely be considered, according to Dr. Schonfield, "antiquities". ("You don't call a 2,000-year-old pussycat an antique," he points out.)

But Dr. Schonfield also is very much a man of his own time. Does he identify with Jesus or any of the apostles? "I identify with Hugh Schonfield".

And he is a man of the future. Choosing from a myriad of entertainments on a recent evening in Chicago, he enthusiastically decided upon "2001: A Space Odyssey".

Paraphrasing the title of his new book, Dr. Schonfield aptly acknowledges that he is leading an "incredible existence".

It was on April 9th 1968 when Hugh was to meet the person who really started to move things in a new direction – Wilhelm (Willi) Haller, a Swabian (South German) entrepreneur and visionary. I can testify to the fact that if it had not been for this connection, this book would not be being written today. Willi was responsible for the translation into German of several of Hugh's books and also extending the work of the Servant-Nation dream to Germany. However, it was a relationship of ups and downs as we shall discover in due course. It was around this time when Hugh also met Heinz Müller for the first time in a Zürich hotel.

Increasing Affluence

As mentioned in the above interview, the Schonfields planned to move to Malta. In order to organise things, they rented a house initially for a few months. They planned to build their own house which was to be named Villa Salvatore. This project had now become affordable due to their improved financial situation after decades of struggling to make ends meet.

His daughter Audrey recollects:

> Just after the war my parents took the family to see a holiday cottage in Littlehampton, I remember there was still barbed wire along the beach which was a bit disappointing. Which may have been the reason why all three of us squabbled and behaved very badly. So my father said it wasn't worth buying it.
>
> Eventually my parents sold the house in Tintern. My mother was ill for quite a long time with Hodgkinson's Disease and had several minor operations which may have influenced their decision to buy a house/villa in Malta where the climate was better. They would spend several months there and my father would write there. They started with a flat in Taxbiex then bought the house in Valletta. My mother loved growing her own veg with help from a local gardner and they had a wonderful lemon tree. My mother cooked there with lots of rosemary and I always have a bush in my garden because I so loved her cooking in Malta. She was very happy there and made friends with all the ex pats and especially De Valera's wife who was English and missed home. The labour Prime minister was prevailed upon to prioritise their application for a telephone. Quite a feat. Many years later when I was visiting Malta on business with my late husband Charlie, we met the very same engineer at a meeting who remembered being told to put the telephone in. He was now in Malta's broadcasting business. The Villa was now an office.

After an initial interest, Bernard Geis Associates decided not to publish the Authentic New Testament. Hugh felt terribly let down by Berney as he had promised Hugh that he would publish the book. On the more positive side, the news came that by January 1968 *The Passover Plot* had been on Bantam's best seller list for 21 weeks. But by March, the news from Hutchinsons was not so good, the sales of *Those Incredible Christians* were disappointing and they blamed this to the fact that *The Passover Plot* had a strong narrative in the first part relating to Jesus whereas this book was about an institution with less immediate appeal. The problem was not just in the UK. A letter from Letty Cottin Pogrebin of Bernard Geis Associates on July 29th 1968 warned that sales of *Those Incredible Christians* was not going well in the USA with only 350 books a week. Expectations were high after the success of *The Passover Plot*. In a letter dated March 11th 1968 they had already cancelled the publicity tour in the USA for *Those Incredible Christians*. In a PS (handwritten) the author of the letter wrote: "The American Booksellers Association feels that you're too controversial to serve as a convention speaker – and no amount of arguing could persuade them otherwise". It would appear that things were made difficult for Hugh's appearances on TV as, "several of the most important interview shows have been cancelled from television channels in a great rash of 'image adjusting'".

In the UK however, he was kept busy with, amongst other things, an appearance on the BBC programme "Subject for Sunday" on 21st April 1968 discussing *Those Incredible Christians* with Rev. Michael Green[1].

All the turbulence in his life as a writer could not deter him from continuing his altruistic work and he was no doubt heartened when he received a letter from the High Priest Amram Isaac Cohen about the still functioning school in Nablus and stating that the school celebrated Hugh's birthday each year.

The book *The Suez Canal in World Affairs* which had been published by Vallentine Mitchell (UK) in 1952 was expanded and republished as *The Suez Canal in Peace and War* by Valentine and also by the Miami Press in the USA in 1969. A review appeared in the Sunday Statesman on December 21st of that year. They reported the book as concluding that there really was not much real use for the Suez Canal despite all the tribulations. They described the book as "coldly accurate".

Inspired with the vision of a Servant-Nation, Hugh wrote a short book entitled *The Man for Mankind* which presented a fictitious presentation of the passion story. The author here feels that the section on Paul is particularly interesting, although it is never clear whether Hugh admired Paul or not (the author thinks that Hugh had some admiration for Paul also and felt that Christianity had misrepresented his ideas. Audrey confirmed this and that he felt himself to be in like manner, a Jewish follower of Jesus):

Picture 27: A Design by Hugh J. Schonfield

---

1 Edward Michael Bankes Green (born 1930) is a British theologian, Anglican priest, Christian apologist and author of more than 50 books (Wikipedia).

We had a Jew of the Roman world whose name was Paul. His visions revealed to him much of the truth. He understood that the people of God had to be re-constituted, if it was to perform its function. It would consist no longer only of those who were Israelites by descent. It would include many of all races who would become Israelites though allegiance to the Messiah of Israel, He carried that message from land to land, establishing small communities in the many cities he visited.

It was part of Paul's teaching that each of us needed to be reborn in the likeness of the Messiah. Or to put it another way the Messiah had to be born and grow in us,

Picture 28: House Salvatore in Malta

so that gradually we conformed to his image. The resurrection of Jesus would be the transformation that we would undergo in being converted to his character and quality.

Thus all the People of God will reflect the messianic identity. One man will have become one nation, and in the light of that nation all the nations will be illuminated and united in one world, whose capital is the New Jerusalem—the City of God.

This is what I pray for, my friend, the revelation of the Nation-Messiah, the Children of God. But that vision is for an appointed time the duration of which I cannot foresee.

Through the relationship with Willi Haller, Hugh made the acquaintance of Heinz Müller who was the owner of a large company and a neighbour of Willi's. Heinz was interested in Hugh's books because he had established a publishing house and had an interest in theological themes. Heinz obtained the copyright for *The Passover Plot* in German after a mainline publisher could not be found for Willi's translation which was being prepared. Heinz writes that it was "for the ones it was too controversial and for the others it was too much involved with theology and religion". He hoped to have the book printed and available for the annual protestant rally yet he expected much opposition. By the 30th May, Willi had completed the translation. As Willi was a marketing expert, he had prepared leaflets and people to distribute them as well as posters to display at the protestant rally. Not only that, he organised aerial advertising. The book was to be called *Planziel Golgotha*. Unfortunately, this turned out to be disappointing so Heinz then tried to launch at the Frankfurt Book Fair.

In the midst of this, Willi was busy setting up a new company to produce time recording equipment. This company eventually was to become market leader in its domain. Hugh was writing *The Politics of God* at this time, which was undoubtedly for him his most important book. Willi was eagerly awaiting it to start translation.

The previous setbacks did not deter Hugh giving Heinz the rights to publish the German translation of *The Politics of God* which Willi also was to translate. The book was eventually dedicated to Willi's newborn son, named after Hugh as Hansjakob Hugh Haller.

At the same time the German translation of *Those Incredible Christians* was published.

Hugh was playing with the idea of setting up a company in Switzerland, presumably for tax reasons and had asked Willi's advice.

Back in London, Hugh's expertise on and position as former historian of the Suez Canal was still being cited as the Canal was enjoying its 100th centenary. Again, Hugh expressed his belief that the Canal had seen its greatest days in an article in *The Times Diary*. Marc Jaffe of Bantam was also reporting that *Those Incredible Christians* was not selling too well. It was never ever possible to replicate the unique success of *The Passover Plot*.

Hutchinson's also had concerns about *The Politics of God* which had now been made available to them in draft. They passed on some rather fundamental criticisms of the book. Again, a letter of 15th December 1969 from Hutchinson's was sent where comments on the content of *The Politics of God* were made prior to publication. They did not really like the material about his personal experiences nor the idea of an appeal at the end of the book. Chapter 2 was much criticised and a rework suggested.

This element of the book certainly reflects Hugh's "missionary" zeal for a Servant-Nation and the messianic age but it also reminds us that this is what he actually was about. Power, who we have elsewhere cited has an even stronger opinion on this matter and writes:

> It would seem that all Schonfield's work was motivated by his self belief that he was the Messiah. Schonfield does not appear to have made any public pronouncement that he was the Messiah, then apparently, neither did Rabbi Menachem Schneerson (1902-1994), the Rebbe of the New York based Lubavitch movement make a public declaration that he believed that he was the Messiah either. Schonfield claims that his mission is "neither cultic nor egotistic", and it appears that he was content in the knowledge that he would not see the fulfilment of the Servant-Nation in his lifetime as he believed there is no short-cut to his goal which he describes as evolution and not revolution.[2]

Here I have to heartily disagree with Power. In no way did Hugh consider him to be the Messiah and we had a number of personal conversations about such issues. He never had any aspirations to be a guru or leader of a sect, he just had an absolute conviction about the need in the world for a Servant-Nation—he was purely a person called to make it apparent in his age. That of course could be a definition of *Messiah* but in which case there have been many. As stated elsewhere and cited earlier, he just saw him-

---

2 Power, Owen M. (2011) *Hugh Schonfield: A Case Study of Complex Identities.* A thesis submitted to the University of Manchester for the degree of Master of Philosophy in the Faculty of Humanities, p. 68.

self as Hugh Schonfield but we should not forget the "Joseph" in his name which he had always felt designatory.

And whilst reminding ourselves of this, the Joseph family on Hélène's side was also an ongoing interest requiring attention and one of the projects was the restoration of the Plymouth Hebrew Congregation Old Cemetery, a burial place of her forefathers and of historical importance for British Jewry. It was necessary for funds to be raised for this project and the Schonfields were expected to share in this.

The work in Germany was always a recurring theme and Willi Haller wrote to Hugh on the 7th March 1970 talking of his battle with Heinz Müller due to Heinz's insistence of taking a threatening tone with potential reviewers. The row between the two of them had gone so far that Heinz threatened Willi with dismissal from his job in the firm of Hengstler where Heinz was 25% shareholder. In this letter he is asking Hugh for advice in how to deal with the conflict. Two days later, Heinz also wrote to Hugh where he also speaks of a heavy quarrel with Willi. Fortunately the battle cooled down somewhat and by the end of May it would seem that things had normalized. It is not clear whether Hugh played a pacifying role in this or how he responded to Willi's appeal for advice.

Nevertheless, this did not change the fact that Schonfield's publishing agents were not satisfied with the sales of books in Germany despite the publishing of *Unerhöht diese Christen, Geburt und Verwandlung der Urkirche (Those Incredible Christians)* published in Germany by the Molden-Verlag.

Hugh and Hélène's interest were also focused elsewhere as they were busy with the construction of their new house "Villa Salvatore" in Malta.

The Politics of God

Hugh was always full of new ideas and he proposed to the publishers Hutchinsons that there should be a staged event with the Shaftesbury Theatre with the cast of Hair on July 25th although the author could find no trace of this having materialised.

It seems that some misunderstandings with the publishers Bernard Geis Associates in New York arose over the rights on the production of the film of the *Passover Plot* and the publishers were keen to make it clear that they had no objections to the project.

For Hugh, 1971 was a momentous year because it saw the publishing of *The Politics of God* by Hutchinson in the UK. *The Politics of God* was a different kind of book for Hugh and had a different aim from most of his other books. In his own words in an article written for *The Mondcivitan* in 1971, he explains this:

> I set to work on writing *The Politics of God*, a book which would bring the Mondcivitan Republic to the notice of the readership I had been able to interest as an author. The volume was published in Great Britain in July 1970 and in the United States in April 1971, and has been bringing us not a few enquiries and additional citizens. The effects will be multiplied when the book appears in paperback in May 1972.

He was increasingly in demand as a speaker and held a lecture at Eton College in March 1971 entitled, *Fraud and Forgery in Early Christianity*. Meanwhile, back in Germany, Willi Haller had commenced work on the translation of *The Politics of God* into German and had also composed a long letter to the wife of the German President, Mrs Heinemann, in which he discusses German-Jewish relations and *Planziel Golgotha (The Passover Plot)*. It would seem that this did not meet with a friendly response. In a later letter, Heinz describes his opinion that Hugh is the "Joseph" mentioned in a vision of the American Psychist Jeane Dixon (1904-1997). We can detect a certain "Hugh worship" on the part of Heinz in this letter where he states:

> May you remember that we discussed on our first meeting at Zürich the book about Jeane Dixon and her vision of February 1962. Her friend, Ruth Montgomery, writes there on page 170: "Jeane saw Joseph guiding the tableau like a puppeteer pulling strings". And she asked on page 172: "Why was Joseph in the vision?".
>
> I think, between you and us existed full agreement that no other man than you are this Joseph in the vision of Jeane Dixon? Why will you hesitate longer more to "pull the strings"? I myself am ready to enter the spiritual fight within Germany!
>
> But, it shall be only your own decision to give the signal or not. Somewhere in your Passover Plot, you quoted the German chancellor Bismarck about Disraeli: "The old Jew, that was a man!" Now, it seems to me that it is time to show the world that you are this man.

All this seems rather fanatical and I can find no evidence that Hugh actually replied to it nor what he may have thought of Jeane Dixon[1]. Nor am I sure what Heinz expected from him with "pulling the strings". It would seem that Heinz Müller had some end-

---

[1] According to Wikipedia, Jeane L. Dixon (January 5, 1904 – January 25, 1997) was one of the best-known American astrologers and psychics of the 20th century, due to her syndicated newspaper astrology column, some well-publicized predictions, and a best-selling biography.

time notions which, according to Willi Haller, meant that he had built an anti-fallout shelter in his house.

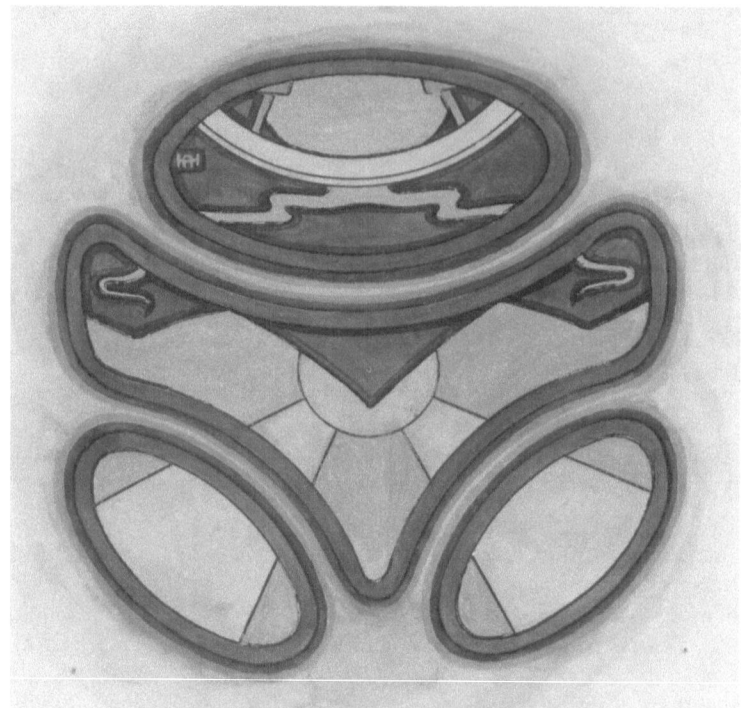

Picture 29: Abstract Design by Hugh J. Schonfield

As pointed out above, Willi had written to the wife of Gustav Heinemann, the German Federal President, who was a theologian. Apparently he considered her reply to be ignorant.

The year was also a milestone like so many we have in life. It was the year of his 70th birthday and Joseph Singer (his son-in-law and husband of his daughter Marion who was a photographer at 30 George Street, Hanover Square, W.1) proposed a toast at his birthday celebration:

> *When Hugh was a lad, he served a term*
> *as an office boy with a publishing firm,*
> *he cleaned up the galleys and manuscripts*
> *and scribbled all over the naughty bits.*
> *He scribbled away so industriously*
> *that he became a member of the literary.*
>
> *In writing books, he made such a name*
> *that a scholarly scribe he soon became,*
> *he went on to make a Hugh and cry*
> *by answering The Question Why.*

*He answered so convincingly
that now he is an authority.*

*Now, would be authors, whoever you be
if you want to rise to the top of the tree,
if your soul isn't fettered to an office stool
be careful to be guided by this golden rule;
Stick to what you know to be -
a matter of controversy!*

Picture 30: Mondcivitan Community School

1972 found Hugh planning a trip to Jerusalem in November whilst he was living at Hyde Park Square. He was in touch with Yigael Yadin[2] of the Institute of Archaeology who was conducting excavations in Jerusalem and was willing to show these to Hugh. It would seem that Hugh had also asked if the Institute could organize lectures but Yigael suggested Hugh contact Professor Werblovsky. A trip to Masada was also planned.

It is worth noting in this context that Yigael Yadin had prevented the controversial scholar Donovan Joyce from visiting the archaeological excavations of Masada in 1964. Joyce had also come up with the supposition that Jesus survived the crucifixion and actually died in Masada as the last of the rightful kings of Israel[3]. It became the essence of a best-seller *The Jesus Scroll*.

Interest in the Middle East conflict was increasing and Hugh was involved with proposals for Middle-East Confederation and the formation of a society at the beginning of

2 Yigael Yadin (1917 – 1984) was an Israeli archeologist, politician, and the second Chief of Staff of the Israel Defence Forces.
3 Cf. http://en.wikipedia.org/wiki/The_Jesus_Scroll

1972. It was through this work that he got to know his long time associate Joseph Abileah[4], a violinist of some note and founder of the Haifa Symphony Orchestra, who spent most of his life working for peace in the Middle East. Joseph was the first conscientious objector in Israel in 1948.

The correspondence with Heinz Müller did not abate and again Heinz wrote in July, encouraging Hugh to "pull his strings":

> Let me come now to the end of this letter. During my holidays of Corsica I had a lot of time to contemplate all these important considerations. Therefore, don't forget to pull your strings in the right time. Finally, don't forget Hans Naber[5], alias Kurt Berna (President of the Foundation of the Holy Shroud) and his message of Jesus in 1947. As I told you, this was the message of reconciliation to Judas (which may explain as well that Naber sometimes may be a difficult man to discuss and deal with as I experienced meanwhile myself). Don't make any mistake (also in undervaluing the importance of such people like Hans Naber and Rev. Wurmbrand[6])! For the real reconstruction of the drama of Golgotha we need all of these different peoples, Judas and John the Baptist as well.

Again, we have no evidence that Hugh took Heinz' advice on these things but Heinz certainly saw esoteric roles for himself, Hugh and Willi. Yet in the self same letter he mentions the disagreements he had with Willi. That is not surprising because Willi was a very down-to-earth person who approached things much more pragmatically.

Having now moved base to Malta, Hugh of course was bound to get involved in the project for the restoration of a Jewish cemetery in Kalkara by the Jewish Community of which Stanley Davis OBE was the hon. Secretary[7].

On the 21st May of that year Hugh appeared on BBC 1 in a programme entitled *The Origins of Christianity* where he debated with Albert Friedlander, Robert Murray and William Nell. The programme was repeated on the following day and as "The Search for Jesus of Nazareth" on 30th May on Radio 4.[8]

There was an esoteric side to Hugh's thinking as we have mentioned before and on to which Heinz Müller had probably latched. It was thus that in 1973 we find him getting

---

4   cf. Bing, Anthony B. (1990) *Israeli Pacifist: The Life of Joseph Ab*ileah, Diane Pub Co.
5   Hans Kurt Naber believed that Jesus revealed himself to him in 1947, telling him that he had survived the Crucifixion. Naber and Berna were apparently one and the same journalist (https://de.wikipedia.org/wiki/Holger_Kersten)
6   Rev. Richard Wurmbrand was an evangelical Christian with Jewish origins who suffered at the hands of the Communist Party in Rumania and was famous for his distribution of bibles.
7   http://www.aboutmalta.com/grazio/jewish.html
8   http://genome.ch.bbc.co.uk/906bff4015bc456497da542ba8715a87. Accessed 24th November 2014.

The Politics of God

involved with the Religious Experience Research Unit in Oxford[9][10]. Hugh was sharing some of his spiritual experiences as they were collecting data on this.

He and Hélène attended the 14th Triennial Conference in Sheffield of War Resisters International on behalf of the Mondcivitan Republic. He writes:

Picture 31: Group Picture

We were glad to meet some other Mondcivitans there, Satish Kumar from India, Donald Groom from Australia, and Bill Sutherland from Tanzania. Locally we were delighted to see Mr. and Mrs. Maurice Cole, who came round to greet us and attended an evening session.

The conference had attracted many young people who wanted a world free from war, and indeed free from most of the characteristics of organised society. They were largely in quest of a new Garden of Eden, a nature reserve from which all the competitive pressures of civilisation were excluded. They were all for a new society which they believed only revolution could secure; but they had given very little serious thought to how the world situation might be transformed.[11]

It was not always easy trying to steer this Republic and, as in any electorally based nation, it suffered from the inherent weakness that people would not only elect delegates but also expect the delegates to do all the work. It would be forgotten that people were not paid for their office and would have to do the work besides earning a living. Often a letter would come into the office from a citizen with ideas of what the head office should be doing. On one occasion, a letter came which started of with a list of what "headquarters" should be doing. Hugh commented, with one of his infectious grins, "never mind about what headquarters is doing – what about the hindquarters". Again, aided by his usual amusement at his own joke, we all burst out laughing.

---

9   Correspondence with Alister Hardy dated 24.8.1973.
10 The Religious Experience Research Centre was founded by the distinguished marine biologist Professor Alister Hardy FRS in 1969 as The Religious Experience Research Unit. He and his co-researchers began to gather a unique archive of accounts of religious experience and to publish research into the area. The maintenance of both the archives and the research and publications have continued. The Centre organises conferences and produces both books and a series of Occasional Papers on religious experience and spirituality.
    (http://en.wikipedia.org/wiki/Religious_Experience_Research_Centre – accessed 6th May 2014)
11 *The Mondcivitan, Autumn 1972.*

At the end of 1973, Willi Haller had left Hengstler to start his own company. This would estrange him from Heinz Müller and affect the future of their relationship. This new venture, Interflex, was to be a model enterprise based on Mondcivitan lines and which no doubt Hugh saw as the beginning of a Servant-Nation economy.

All the efforts of Hugh and others as well as the appearance of *The Politics of God* started to bring fresh blood into the Republic which was so close to his heart and the result of his life's work. In 1973 the Mondcivitan Community School was established in London based on modern pedagogic principles and the principles of the Republic. Ron Webb was responsible for this and was assisted by Charles Pooley. In describing its aims at the beginning of its second term, Ron Webb wrote:

> We hoped that if our methods were successful, the children attending the school would not fit neatly into the present framework of society but, having a broader educated experience, learning together in a truly democratic way, they would find themselves automatically working towards a new society based on mutual love and co-operation.
>
> It is intended that, although starting in a small way, the school should be a prototype for future independent schools seen as a part of the building of a Servant-Nation for the benefit of all mankind.[12]

It is notable that whilst an organisation which called itself "London Free School" (and had no connection to the Mondcivitan School) was founded in 1966 it did not actually establish a school as such[13]. The Mondcivitan Community School seems to have been one of the first of its kind—at least in London—because not only was it organised on democratic lines, it also had the aim to encourage an attitude of World Citizenship. Around the same time, In 1972, the White Lion Street Free School was started on not dissimilar lines[14] and there was a general interest in alternative education systems at the time.

The school was largely funded by Willi Haller personally and one can imagine Hugh's joy as he started to see the Republic taking shape. There were many other projects in this period including a charity shop, support of a children's project in Kenya and regular appearances of *The Mondcivitan*.

During these times Hugh and Hélène would often come to meetings which were held in Delancey Street. These were always occasions for serious business but it was never without a joke on the part of Hugh or some giggling on the part of Hélène.

Barry reminisced about his grandmother:

> Hélène too was one to break out in fits of giggles—to the extent that tears would roll down her cheeks as she laughed (a trait my mother and sisters have inherited). Many a time it was at her own expense—often getting a word wrong. My strongest memory was when I stayed with them and we were laying the table together for lunch. She was setting out glasses for water and set 4 down on the table for the diners. Suddenly she realised there was only the 3 of us and cried out, "oh dear—I've put out an extra loaf!" As soon as we realised she'd said "loaf" instead of "glass", she and I burst out laughing and it seemed to last for ages, extended further

---

12 *The Mondcivitan Bridge* 1973 Issue 1.
13 http://en.wikipedia.org/wiki/London_Free_School. Accessed 24th November 2014.
14 http://www.libed.org.uk/index.php/articles/337-white-lion-street-free-school. Accessed 24th November 2014.

as we explained the mistake to Hugh. She had no explanation as to why she has selected a word quite so far from her intention—perhaps she was thinking forward to needing to bring out some bread for us.

The Mondcivitan Republic held a meeting in England where there were delegates from around the world including Linda Chene from the USA, Herbert Moser from Germany. Toma Sik from Israel as well as Willi Haller and a number of younger people interested in the reactivation of the Republic. The group picture below shows Peter Deed on the exteme left and next to him Herbert Moser and Pedro Segura. Willi Haller is to be seen with his children in the foreground. Next to Willi we can see Phyllis Corke and Charles Pooley. Behind Phyllis is Sandy Engelking looking sideways and next to her Margareth Haller. Both Hugh and Helen attended this and played an active role.

Of course, despite the fact that the Schonfields were now basically residing in Malta, it did not stop Hugh from being active to promote the Republic. On the 14th November their friends Anne and Chris Langland arranged a meeting in their home where Hugh spoke about the Mondcivitan Republic.

Travels

He was continually travelling at this time and Malta was not the most central place to be doing this from. The author discovered a bill from Thomas Cook referring to planning an air flight from Malta to Zürich and then rail from Strasbourg to Paris and then Paris to London. As Willi Haller lived fairly near both to Strasbourg and Zürich, he visited Willi Haller and Heinz Müller on that trip.

At this time a novel appeared by Frank Yerby entitled *Judas, My Brother*[1]. Hugh felt that Yerby had stolen ideas from the Passover Plot and instructed his lawyer to take action. The lawyer wrote a mild letter to Mr. Yerby who refuted the accusation. As the lawyer felt that there was little chance of success to justify litigation, the matter was apparently dropped. Hugh wrote extensive reports on the book showing where phrases appeared to have been copied and obviously he was highly annoyed.

In 1974 *The Pentecost Revolution* was published by MacDonald (UK) and Macmillan (USA). Macmillan had suggested that the title of the new book be *Drunk with New Wine* but it was finally settled to call it *The Pentecost Revolution*. Bernard Hassan of Macmillan commented in a letter of 18th March on the fact that Hugh had felt hurt by Billy Graham's attack on him stating:

> As to Billy Graham, you may know that we recognize a certain cachet in this country to enemy lists. One of my DC friends was quite honoured to find himself on Mr Nixon's list, and several others were deeply hurt at being omitted. Since the reverend doctor is as close to a theological Nixon as this country will ever get (let us hope that a merciful God would not inflict worse...) you should feel profoundly honoured by Graham's diatribe.

In a short essay entitled *My Answer to Billy Graham*, Hugh wrote:

> Mr. Billy Graham the Evangelist has been pleased to attack me in a syndicated newspaper feature of his entitled *My Answer*. Someone who had read my book The Passover Plot apparently thought that my arguments against the resurrection of Jesus were quite convincing and put a question to Mr. Graham.
>
> If Mr. Graham had answered that my reasoning from the evidence left him cold I should not have objected in the least. He is perfectly entitled to his opinion. Instead he proclaimed that "the author of The Passover Plot is a skeptic who refused to accept the proof of honest research... and the existence of the facts makes no difference with a person whose mind has already been made up". Mr. Graham has never met me, and what he says is totally untrue. I never have been a skeptic, and my researches into the life of Jesus had been conducted over forty years with a completely open mind. In Mr. Graham's position he should not fear false witness against his neighbour, and that he has been ready to do so only shows him up as a man without scruples where his religion is concerned. Before he attacked me he should have been at pains to get at the facts.
>
> I have no need to speak on my own behalf. Here is what a former Professor of the Bible and Methodist Pastor has written about me, "In my opinion Dr. Schonfield is unique. He is the only Biblical scholar I know who is, at the same time, both a Jew by birth and heritage and a devoted follower of Jesus, by personal experience and commitment. So far as I know he is better qualified, both as a man and as a scholar,

---

1 Yerby, F. (1968) *Judas My Brother*, Doubleday.

to research the real Jesus than any other scholar in the field past or present. He has at his command more source material for such a study, better acquaintance with it, more ability to use it in an unbiased scientific manner".

The Passover Plot continues to be in enormous demand, and narrow-minded bigotry is powerless to stop it. Billy Graham's conscience should now be troubling him quite a lot.

An interview on the new book took place on Radio Four on the 2nd June and a USA tour for Macmillan from September 28th to October 21st.

Some of the activities on this hectic tour shed light on how strenuous this must have been for a man who by now was no youngster and did in fact result in a heart attack after which he had a bypass operation in the USA. His sister Marion flew out to be with her mother and it was at this point that he quit smoking:

New York:

Interview: National Catholic News Service

Interview: Warren Day, Ecumedia News Service.

WMCA Radio, Leon Lewis Show

Interview: Mt. Vernon Argus, Mrs. Helen Steiner

Boston:

Boston University Dinner-Top of the Charles The George Sherman Union

"Good Morning" WCVB-TV

Chicago:

"Some of My Best Friends" - TV interview NEC Studios

Chicago Tribune interview

American Jewish Committee Luncheon

Christian Bookseller Interview

"Extension 720," - Radio Show WGN Radio

Detroit:

Interview: The Jewish News

"Focus" WJR Radio with J.P McCarthy

Interview: Detroit Free Press, Eileen Foley

Interview: Detroit News, Nancy Manser, Church Editor

Los Angeles:

(Extra schedule)

Mineapolis:

"News and Views" KMSP-TV

WCCO-TV

"The Take-5 Show" Jane Johnston KFTP-TV

Mr. Carl Carlsen, St. Paul Dispatch

Minneapolis Star

Bob Allard Show KUXL Radio

Speech: Maimonides Institute of Jewish Learning

Close-Up Show, Jerry Jergensen WAYL

What's New Show, WTCN- Multimedia

Pittsburgh:

"AM Pittsburgh"

Interview: Pittsburgh Press, Mike Anderson, Religion Editor

Speak at Y-IKC

Return to New York:

"The First Estate" WNBC-TV

Speak at Metropolitan Synagogue with Rabbi Judah Kahn

Speak at Mid Island YMH, Wantagh

Breakfast Talk, East Midwood Jewish Center

Speak at Mt. Vernon YMHA

It was at this time that Heinz Müller decided to give up his publishing business due to the losses incurred with the Passover Plot (Planziel Golgotha). He was willing to pass over the rights to Verlag Gustav Lübbe – which actually happened.

Hugh in a letter of 3rd September 1974 felt that the book *The Sign* by Robin Maugham[2] used ideas from the Passover Plot for his book without any acknowledgement and was also worried about the idea that a film would be made of it, which he felt infringed his rights.

---

2 Maugham, Robin (1975) *The Sign Star.* W H Allen, London, UK.

The Delights of Hollywood

In September 1975 a contract was signed with Atlas Films in California to make a film of the Passover Plot. However, shortly afterwards, Hugh was taken into hospital. All the strain of travelling and holding interviews and talks had taken its toll on his health. He was also constantly worried that the film would be "done right". Fortunately, he was out of hospital by the 25th October when Mark Paterson cabled Coinduit in Beverly Hills that he would be flying out on the 29th. The meeting was about the filming of the Passover Plot and about the shooting which was to now take place in Israel rather than Egypt which had originally been considered.

Health was becoming an increasingly important issue and he suffered from a virus infection (letter 17th March 1976 from Malta). In a newspaper cutting from the *Observer Magazine* from 1976 (exact date not known), he was asked "Do you believe in an afterlife?" to which he replied, "I think it's a bit egoistical to assume that since we exist, we must matter eternally. I'd rather feel that we are immortal in the sense that each of us in our generation is contributing to the future." It would seem he was already thinking about these issues and had come to terms with them, which not everyone manages. Certainly he could chart his own contribution both to knowledge and he hoped, through the redefinition of the concept of a Servant-Nation, to a better world.

He could not relax about the film production and was really upset about the way the Passover Plot film was taking shape:

> Much of the film had been produced by that time and we saw a few sequences on screen, the Baptist episode and entry into Jerusalem. They had cast John the Baptist as the Tempter of Jesus in the wilderness. You can imagine how horrified I was when I could read the script in detail. It was the most ignorant and profound rubbish, not only false in almost every particular but written in quite deliberate contradiction of The Passover Plot. Jesus (called Yeshua) was being run around by the Zealots and in despair throws in his lot with them in a bid to stage a revolt, capture Jerusalem and turn out the Romans. Jesus thus becomes a militant freedom fighter which was the evident object of the script writer (a left wing pamphleteer as I learned). Michael Campus, an obstinate and wilful person, was determined to shoot the film without any apprehension that it was ludicrous and a travesty which would be laughed to death by the critics.

An article published in the Hebrew newspapers *Maariv* on the 19th January is not likely to have pleased Hugh at all as it contained all the usual editorial misunderstandings common with such reporting, including the fact that Hugh was now a "Jewish-American Professor called 'Jo Schoenfeld":

> A reconstructed Temple costing one million I£ [Israeli Pounds] is being built in the Exhibition Gardens in Tel-Aviv for the Jewish version on Jesus, which has already angered the Pope—The Passover Plot... The shooting started two weeks ago. A film which will probably rouse the ire of the Vatican but also the curiosity of a million Spectators.
>
> One hundred characters are taking part in the shooting and tens of bearded "hippies" assembled from the neighbourhood of Eilat, clad in sackcloth, and whose outlook fits the period of Jesus...

The Director of The Passover Plot Michael Campus is satisfied with their work, and they will be taken tomorrow to Jerusalem in two buses, and accommodated in a guest-house, which will be used in the shootings...

On Friday there were more shootings of The Passover Plot at Nuelba. In one day's photographing, which cost 1,000 I£ - 90 seconds have been added to the film....

The "dangerous" part will be played by a black Hebrew from Dimona, 196cm in height, known by the name of Avihail Ben Israel. A "tough guy" specialist in kiaff knife-fighting, Roberto Messina came from Italy to brief the actors... In The Passover Plot he kidnaps a boy while riding....

The Passover Plot is based on the bestseller by the Jewish-American Professor Jo Schoenfeld (sic). The Pope banned the book, but it seems that this has not affected its translation into 12 languages, and the selling of six million copies.

Menahem Golan told us about the film, which shooting during seven weeks will cost 2 million dollars. Four films have already been produced on Jesus, but this is the first time that a Jewish version will be shown on the screen... Most of the people involved in the preparation of the film are Jews...

The Last Supper is the ceremony of the Passover Eve. Jesus goes on pilgrimage to Jerusalem to incite the people of Israel to rebel against the Roman authorities. He rides a white donkey, as was done by the "messiahs" who were under the influence of the inspiration of the prophets... He doesn't die on the cross. His disciples take him down from the cross wounded, and hide him in a place where he dies of blood poisoning...

The Passover Plot was to be shot in Egypt... Menahem Golan who is well introduced in Hollywood succeeded in convincing investors that conditions are better in Israel, and that the production will be cheaper. In small Israel the actors are able to live at the Hilton 20 minutes drive to an archaeological site, a town, mountains and caves, or to the desert... says Golan.

Hugh's feelings seem to have been echoed in the report by Noreen Spall (Letter to Hugh dated 5th February) on seeing some scenes from the film, and this does not seem to have particularly increased Hugh's fondness for the film. She stated:

Although the scenery was impressive (and some of the camera work) the over-all impression to me was of a rather pedestrian production, at times naive and pretentious, with very corny dialogue (American slang). While I haven't seen the Lampell script I fear that what I saw closely resembled your description of it.

She was also critical of the producer saying:

I have changed my opinion of Wolf who this time seemed evasive and difficult (also to Milton and Israel). He was not in the least apologetic about his lack of communication and denied having received our letters and cables. I cannot accept this since we sent copies to Israel (the country) and California. He did admit to having received your first letter (enclosing the first part of your outline film treatment) and indicated (indirectly) that his and Mike Campus's conception of the film diverged so greatly from yours that he was uncertain as to how and when to use you as consultant. He did not say that in as many words but that was my impression.

I insisted that you must go to Israel just the same, pointing out the enormous benefit of your consultancy. He complained of the difficulty of arranging for your visit from Malta so I said you would arrange your own travel on the understanding that you would be refunded in Israel and compensated with your agreed fees to defray your expenses. He agreed to do this in front of Israel Katz.

I am sure your visit will be most fruitful and enjoyable even if you cannot get the right film made. They cannot fail to be impressed by what you have to offer, especially if you use your charm and persuasiveness rather than an aggressive or pained approach. I suggest that you insist on seeing the scenes we saw in London and more if they are ready.

It would seem that it was no longer to be a film based on the book but just a film carrying the same title. Nevertheless, Hugh and Hélène spent some time in Israel during the shooting trying to get the film changed and they traveled there on the 7th February. It was a continual cause of pain in the future that he would always be judged and criticised for this film which so misrepresented his ideas.

And things were not to get better. An article in the *Jerusalem Post* of the 14th May 1976 reported that the association of Churches in Nazareth were threatening to close churches and suspend services unless the Government bans filming of the unorthodox Jesus film *The Passover Plot*. Apparently the Ministry of Religious Affairs in Israel had received many protests, including ones from the Apostolic Delegate and a cardinal from the Vatican.

An article in the *Sunday Times* of the same date reported that Christian Clergymen in Jerusalem had asked the Israeli Government to stop the production of the Passover Plot which "depicts Jesus as an urban guerilla".

Hugh and Mark had not been shown the script before it was filmed so were not able to correct any of the errors. The *Jerusalem Post* published an article which included the statement that the film was based on the book – which Hugh denied. The film makers felt they were being dealt with unjustly and a row flared up.

But to be fair, it seems that Hugh may not have been the easiest person to deal with and the producers wrote to Mark Paterson on May 13th stating:

> Mark, as you can see from my letter to Dr. Schonfield, I certainly want to be polite and respectful to him in every way I can. However, statements from you like "the film shot bears no relation to the book" and a cable threatening "injunction proceedings" could make it difficult in the future to keep this posture!! We have complied with everything Dr. Schonfield wanted; we have saved all of his handwritten notes, scenes and pages; and when the final film is available, we will be easily in the position to compare his notes to what is on the screen.

As if these worries were not enough, Hugh had received a letter from Heinz Müller dated 31st March where he complained about his dispute with Willi Haller who had by now started his own company and his own publishing house (Mondcivitaner Verlag). He goes on to say:

> As before our houses stand only 80 metres apart as the crow flies. Yet between us a 100 metre deep chasm has opened up – largely invisible to the outside – and as far as I can see there are no signs that this chasm has become even one centimetre smaller during the last few months.
>
> It certainly is not my intention in this letter to quarrel with my fate that Willi has stood higher in your favour than I since our first meeting. It is equally true that it was through me that you and Willi met after I had initiated with very little delay, at

the beginning of 1969, publication of a German edition of your book Passover Plot on the occasion of the Stuttgart Evangelical Church Day.

Obviously Heinz was very bitter about things and probably Hugh's lack of acknowledgement of his prophetic interpretations of scripture which never failed to appear in his letters. Mark Paterson put it a different way, commenting in a letter to Hugh of the same date:

> I am enclosing a very strange letter from Heinz Muller together with a translation. He is obviously a dedicated man but shows signs of imbalance. I had no idea that he and Haller had separated.

Old skills and knowledge were always in demand and he was asked to give a lecture on the Suez Canal at the National Maritime Museum in London on the 28th September. The Schonfield archives relating to the research on the Suez Canal are housed in the museum today and are described as including the following items which are a witness to the work invested in that project:

> Photographs, postcards, illustrations and newspaper cuttings relating to the Suez Canal. Workman's token to the value of 1 franc issued during construction of the Suez Canal, 1865. Bearer bonds of the Interoceanic Canal Company of Panama, 1886. Card index describing items in the Schonfield Collection. Letter requesting the writing of an article on the Suez Canal for Encyclopedia Britannica, 1950. Typescript proposals for a settlement of the Suez Canal dispute formulated by Schonfield and published in *The Times*, 14 August 1956. Signed copy of Schonfield's book *The Suez Canal in Peace and War 1869-1969*. Typescript captions for lantern slides used in a lecture entitled *The Suez Story*, given at the NMM on 28 September, 1976. A sample of crystal from the dry bed of what was once the Canal of the Pharaohs. Black/white lantern slides: Wooden box containing 59 slides, as used in the above mentioned lecture at the NMM. Three small card boxes containing 13 slides (negative images) showing the Suez Canal and 16 slides covering the War in the Western Desert, 1941-42.[1]

According to a letter to Mark Paterson of July 3rd, he also had plans for a book with the title *War with the Beast*. The idea had been spawned by the church historian Stewart Perowne (17 June 1901 – 10 May 1989)[2] who apparently was "begging him for it: it was his idea". No book seems to have been written under this title however.

In this same letter he mentions that he had received a phone call from Ontario Television Authority to work on a six part TV programme on the life of Christ.

Of course even negative publicity can be effective publicity and all the controversy only led to even more copies of the books being sold and promoting Hugh's rise to fame.

In July Hugh received an invitation to view the first cut of the *Passover Plot* film in California. The premier was scheduled for 28th October.

The opposition from main stream Christianity on the film The Passover Plot did not abate. One of the strong voices was Dr. McBirnie of the (short-lived) Interfaith Committee Against Blasphemy who even published a leaflet on the subject. (There was a scandal about Mc Birnie who had been lent money between 1972 and 1980 to finance construction projects for his church. More than two dozen filed suit in 1984 to recoup

---

1   http://collections.rmg.co.uk/archive/objects/467509.html accessed 30th July 2014.
2   cf. https://en.wikipedia.org/wiki/Stewart_Perowne

their losses from McBirnie, who claimed he was bankrupt and had no assets. The courts found against McBirnie, saying that some funds were left in his various organizations[3]).

Also the Christian Apologetics Research and Information Service issued a leaflet *The Passover Plot: Resurrection or Recuperation?*. Hugh felt his ideas were misrepresented in the film and that people did not really understand the point he was making. On the other hand, a Mr. James H. Gill organised a counter movement "Americans for Fairness to Hugh Schonfield". Hugh sanctioned this and gave them express permission. Mr. Hill actually pulled back as he said he could not get a copy of the film *Sacrilegious Movies* from the broadcasting company. Hugh offered NBC an interview in London. Ben Fuson of Kentucky was very supportive of Hugh and wrote a number of letters to those he felt were making unjustified and uninformed comments.

Hugh wrote to Mark on November 25th because of a letter from the producer of the *Trial of Jesus* (Tadeusz Jaworski[4]) suggesting the idea of making a TV documentary on the Passover Plot with Hugh as narrator. In a further letter dated 25th December, he states that they want to do two specials, one on the Passover Plot and the other on The Pentecost Revolution. The film was finally produced as *The Jesus Trial (1980)* in a series of six episodes with the Ontario Educational Communications Authority[5].

Back home Hugh wrote to Mark on 6th November 1976. He and Hélène were just back from Los Angeles and going to Malta on the Wednesday. He stated that publicity was assisted by the cinema (at the premier) being picketed by young fundamentalists chanting and carrying Gospel banners.

Wolf Schmidt of Atlas Films finally found it necessary to make a written statement "To all Christian leaders and people of all faiths". He stated that their picture of Yeshua was of a charismatic, nonviolent and purposeful and loving man, and was anything other than "blasphemous". They further wrote:

> Yes, our film is controversial — especially in its essential message that risks must be taken in the name of freedom. And yes, The Passover Plot is revolutionary — embracing as it does Dr. Schonfield's description of the impact of Jesus of Nazareth:
>
>> *Wherever mankind strives to bring in the rule of justice, righteousness and peace, there the deathless presence of Jesus the Messiah is with them.*
>>
>> *Whenever a people of God is found labouring in the cause of human brotherhood, love and compassion, there the King of the Jews is enthroned.*
>
> There are those who still seem to want to block the free traffic of ideas and interpretations of Jesus. They even want to stop individuals from seeing films like The Passover Plot which might offer a view of Jesus different from their own. I hope your understanding of the Christian faith is a freeing one — one that enables you to reject such an approach and opens your mind to examine yet another view of that extraordinary person, Jesus of Nazareth.

---

3 Cited from http://articles.latimes.com/1995-07-08/local/me-21652_1_church-members accessed 7th May 2014.

4 Tadeusz Jaworski is an actor and producer, known for Vabank (1981) and Selling Out(1972) – http://www.imdb.comwww.imdb.com/name/nm0419552/bio?ref_=nm_ov_bio_sm, accessed 7th May 2014. The film was produced as *The Jesus Trial (1980)* in a series of six episodes with the Ontario Educational Communications Authority— http://www.worldcat.org/title/jesus-trial/oclc/7695188 accessed 7th May 2014.

5 http://www.worldcat.org/title/jesus-trial/oclc/7695188 accessed 7th May 2014.

In 1977 Hugh received Royal congratulations on attaining his Golden Jubilee as an author.

Villa Salvatore was at the point of nearly being sold. The sale may have been largely due to Hélène's health. It was thus necessary to make an inventory of its contents and to describe the layout which appeared as follows:

Ground Floor:

Small back bedroom

Corridor

Double bedroom

Drawing room

Dining room

Cloak room

Kitchen

Maid's room by kitchen

First Floor:

Single bedroom

Bathroom (en suite)

Corridor

Library

Library (External Terrace)

Kitchenette

Cupboard room next to kitchenette

Principle Bedroom

Bathroom (en suite)

Bedroom on half landing of small staircase

The house was nearly sold in 1977 but the prospective buyer, who was a tenant, discovered that a new public road was scheduled to be built right through the outer and back gardens and withdrew from the sale.

At the end of the year Hugh travelled to Australia, whilst the Passover Plot film was not doing well because it was largely banned including in Israel where an unnamed professor of Semitic Studies expressed the opinion that it bore no relation to the character of the book, considering it just to be cheap entertainment. Hopes were now set in the documentary film being made by the Ontario Educational Communications Authority.

In his diary from 1977 we find notes of trips to the hospital and doctor, of Malta 9th May and of leaving for Sydney on 19th November arriving 23rd November via Singapore.

Come 1978 and Hélène's health was worsening and it was decided to visit the Harry Edwards[6] Spiritual Healing Sanctuary in Guildford, Surrey. In a letter to Hélène dated 5th June about healing, mention is made of concentrating on her rib bones and that Hugh was having trouble with dizziness and faintness and was hoping for a cure.

6   Harry Edwards who was a spiritualist healer, died in December 1976 aged 83.

A letter came from the Texas State Library asking for rights to produce a tape version of The Passover Plot but no evidence is available that this was actually carried out.

There was trouble brewing though and Hugh was this time getting upset with BBC Television. In a strongly worded letter dated 5th February 1978 to Peter Armstrong Producer of religious programs at BBC Television, Hugh complained about the misuse and misrepresentation of all his work in a television program *Who Was Jesus?*. This was followed by another letter on 23rd March where he was disappointed that Armstrong had not retracted. There was much letter writing from the BBC but they were not willing to make a retraction.

Hugh was giving lectures in November in Geneva. Hugh met up with Dr. S. J. Samartha[7], director of the World Council of Churches who later wrote to him:

> I was glad I had the privilege of meeting you here at the Ecumenical Center even though it was for a very short time. I wish we had more time to discuss substantial issues concerning the meaning and responsibility of world citizens at the present time. I have gone through the pamphlets you left with me, particularly your address "What our time requires". It is obvious that unless people move beyond their particularities to the larger relationships within the world community, conflicts and tensions will increase. Therefore, the efforts you are making to bring together people within different nations to cooperate for common purposes for the benefit of humanity are very timely.

Villa Salvatore was sold to a Mr. Garzia and a permit of sale was received from the authorities. That was one thing less to worry about but I can imagine that it was quite sad for the couple to have to part with the property.

By now the Ontario Educational Communications Authority had finished the production of *The Jesus Trial* (based on The Man for Mankind) in three programmes: John the Baptist, John the Priest, Jacob or James brother of Jesus. It was first shown in Ontario on their educational network and had a tremendous response. Six video cassettes are listed at worldcat.org[8].

In a letter from Hugh about this, dated December 28th he jovially writes that "apparently I made a hit as a star performer". The film was aired in Toronto and sales negotiations with the USA were under way. *Man for Mankind* was in the development stages. In the same letter, Hugh blames the publishers for not doing enough for the marketing of his books – after the Passover Plot success expecting them to sell themselves. He goes on to say, "One day perhaps we may get someone who is excited about the importance of my unique approach and knows how to put it over in the right quarters and in the right way". In a handwritten note on this letter he writes, "Just heard. Hélène has to go into hospital – St. Mary's Paddington this afternoon and will be there until they can find out what can be done for her as a patient – possibly some days – or weeks".

In a circular letter dated December 1978, Tad Jaworski from The Ontario Educational Communications Authority, writes regarding the Jesus Trial:

---

7 Stanley Jedidiah Samartha (1920–2001) was an Indian theologian and a participant in interreligious dialogue. Samartha's major contribution was through the World Council of Churches sub-unit "Dialogue with People of Living Faiths and Ideologies" of which he was the first Director. (https://en.wikipedia.org/wiki/Stanley_Jedidiah_Samartha accessed 13.5.2014)

8 http://www.worldcat.org/title/jesus-trial/oclc/7695188

It has just been aired for the first time on our own Educational Television network within Ontario. We have had enormous response and more unsought publicity than one could ever have imagined. The reactions have ranged from demands to ban it on Television as being too controversial, to phrases such as "...a masterpiece". The reactions have really been quite bizarre. Considering this is a series about intolerance it has itself provoked far more intolerance than one could ever have anticipated. Letters, comments and articles continue to appear in the press almost daily on the subject of the series, and several weeks have now gone by since it was on the air, To sum up though I would say that the general viewing public have been most supportive and the series has been very well received.

We also discover that despite the fact that Tad plays it down in his letter that there was a lot of controversy about the series. In fact about the backer, Thomas Ide we read:

"Ide faced controversy in 1978 when he backed the production of The Jesus Trial, a series in which historical scholars staged a mock trial of Jews for the murder of Christ. The series was acclaimed by theologians and academics but was criticized by the Roman Catholic archdiocese in Toronto which pressured the provincial government to cancel the series. It aired but, the next year, the government of Bill Davis cut TVO's budget for the first time."[9]

Yet in another area, the expressionist painter Felix Topolski[10], who also painted a portrait of H.G. Wells, wanted to make paintings for Hugh's translation of the *Song of Songs*. However, he does not seem to have actually carried this out.

9   https://en.wikipedia.org/wiki/Thomas_Ide, accessed 14th May 2014.
10 Feliks Topolski 14 August 1907 – 24 August 1989

Tragedy Strikes

Then tragedy struck. Hugh's beloved wife and life companion, after a number of years suffering from Hodgkin's Disease, died on the 12th March 1979 aged 75. One cannot imagine what a devastating blow this must have been to Hugh as Hélène was always there in the background supporting him in all his endeavours and often accompanying him on his travels. He had known her most of his life and it was more than a marriage relationship – they were also mates in a common cause. She had stuck with him through thick and thin. They had shared hardship and prosperity together. As Audrey remarked about their relationship, "they adored each other". But now she was suddenly gone out of his life. Even though he had been expecting this for some time, it was now reality. He had previously written to Peter Deed (Secretary of the Mondcivitan Republic):

> Dear Peter
>
> We hope all has gone well with your visit to Geneva and with Willi.
>
> I am enclosing Hélène's report on our own visit for the magazine. We have been told that she cannot recover and is slowly and peacefully taking her leave. She has no pain; but courageously lent herself to the testing (successfully) of a new antibiotic never used at St. Mary's hospital before. It is her blood condition which has passed the point of giving her survival strength. I am with her every day. When she goes she would like the flag of the Republic to cover the coffin at the Crematorium during the service. You may imagine the horrible emptiness I feel. My darling can still see and converse with visitors briefly, but gets very tired quickly and I just sit with her a large part of each day.
>
> God Bless
>
> Hugh

Yet true to his principles, he asked that no flowers be sent but that instead a memorial fund be created in her name. The Mondcivitan charity, The World Service Trust, thus was renamed "The Hugh and Hélène Schonfield World Service Trust".

Daughter Audrey reminisced to the author what an important factor Hélène was in her father's life and offered a glimpse of her character:

> I can only say that Hélène devoted herself to my father, she loved him very much and supported him in all his work and I think he discussed everything with her. She fell in love with him as a child and there was no-one else in her life but him. They were pretty well inseparable. He always came first in her life even before her children sometimes. She was involved in the world women's movement at his instigation. She was quite shy and modest except that she loved clothes and we [daughters] have inherited that. She was a very English lady with her paper doilies and Lapsouchong tea, china cups and silver teapot and her trips "up West" with her sister and mother. We came too sometimes and had tea at the Lyons Corner House.

The ex-Prime Minister of the Mondcivitan Republic, Donald Hanby wrote an obituary on Hélène:

> **Reflections in Memory of a Dear Friend**
>
> Hélène Schonfield, who died in 12th March, 1979 aged 75, will be lovingly remembered by all who knew her.

My first introduction to Hélène was 21 years ago, at Rydal, the Sheffield home of Maurice and Doris Cole. Our hosts and their friends had provided accommodation and Quaker hospitality for a weekend gathering of Mondcivitans from Northern England. For many of us this was our first meeting with Hugh and Hélène. These were the exciting days following the Constituent Assembly at Cardiff's Temple of Peace and Health in August 1956 in the period leading up to the election of the first Mondcivitan Parliament which assembled at Vienna in May 1959. My first impression of Hélène was of a lady of intelligence and charm, with a very sincere interest in people she met, with a warm-hearted and friendly nature which immediately made everyone feel at ease. She was utterly devoted to Hugh and to his vision of a Servant-People.

Only Hugh himself could tell us just how much Hélène gave up to put Mondcivitan interests before all others. She performed many tasks, and frequently acted as an unpaid secretary. Indeed, I am sure she never received any reward for all her many services other than the satisfaction of knowing that she did her best in every respect. Whenever opinions might tend to diverge, Hélène so often enabled us to see one another's views the better and more charitably by a few timely words. In this sense she was an able and impartial mediator. But she would not hesitate to come to the defence of anyone whom she felt was in danger of being misrepresented or treated unfairly. She was a champion of the right of everyone to have their say, no matter who they might be. When meetings were over, Hélène would be amongst the last to leave, after joining in any tidying up or washing up that had to be done.

She was not without one interest which Hugh did not appear to share, and this was a love of Music. I recall happy occasions when I booked tickets for Hélène and other friends to visit the Royal Festival Hall, particularly for concerts of Mahler's works. How we chattered, in competition with passing trains, as we braved the crossing of the Thames by footbridge adjoining Charing Cross Railway Bridge at the end of the concert.

I had moved to London in 1960, where Hugh and Hélène became for me virtually another pair of caring parents, especially after the death of my mother. They were not alone in this respect, for I was even more indebted to our dear friend Frieda Bacon.

Visitors were always warmly welcomed, and I recall many happy gatherings, both large and small, first at Hugh and Hélène's lovely Queen Anne house in Highgate with the large garden and huge mulberry tree, and later at their flat in Hyde Park Square. On a deeply personal note, I especially recall how I met briefly my future wife when staying at Hugh and Helen's cottage at Tintern in 1964. When I later confided to Hélène that I had fallen in love she helped love along by inviting me and my young lady to be their guests for an autumn "blackberry" weekend at Tintern. My dear wife and I treasure our memories of a visit which brought us closer together, and we were delighted to have Hugh and Hélène at our wedding when we were married by Lord Soper in December 1965.

It was while Hugh and Hélène had the appropriately named Prospect Cottage, overlooking the River Wye at Tintern that Hélène had the idea of serving traditional home-made afternoon teas in the garden. I am sure many visitors to Tintern would remember the charming lady who served their tea and gave them a sincere country welcome.

It is now almost 11 years since I left London to settle in Worcestershire, and in recent years my meetings with Hugh and Hélène have become less frequent. In these later years, when Hélène already knew that she had a serious illness, she showed

Picture 32: Hélène in a serious moment

great fortitude. Certainly, I never heard a single word of complaint, and despite the advancing years one always felt that Hélène retained an air of youthfulness. She remained full of grace, and all of us who loved her will cherish her memory. My very deepest sympathy goes to Hugh and his family in their sad loss.

Rabi John Rayner made the following address at her funeral at the Golders Green Crematorium Funeral Service on 15th March, 1979:

Farewell to Hélène Murial Schonfield née Cohn

The sadness of this moment requires no emphasis. We all feel it poignantly – even those of us who knew Hélène Schonfield only slightly or saw her only occasionally. All the deeper is our sympathy for those who were near and dear to her: her daughters, her grandchildren, her sister and, above all, her husband. I say above all not only because he was her constant companion for 52 years, and not only because they had known and loved each other so much longer even than that, ever since a certain picnic in Richmond Park when they were young children, but because of the special quality of their relationship, which was a rare and beautiful combination of mutual affection, tenderness understanding, trust and devotion, and of shared interests, shared ideals, shared joys and shared enthusiasms. Among other things they worked together for such excellent causes as the World Service Trust, of which she became a Founding Trustee in 1956, and World Citizenship, and she always read the manuscripts of his books and made many valuable critical comments on them. After so long and close a partnership, the cessation of it must be for him a wrench of almost unimaginable severity. We know that in order to surmount it and to live on as she would wish, and as I am sure he will, serenely and creatively, he will need to call on all his great reserves of faith and strength. I believe, too, that he will be helped by the support of his family and friends and I hope that the knowledge that his sorrow is shared so sincerely by so many will also help to sustain him during the bleak and lonely periods which lie ahead for him.

But if those who were close to her are the most grievously bereaved because they have lost her, they are also the most privileged among us because they have shared so much of her life.. And therefore they have especially abundant cause for gratitude. Grief and gratitude are correlatives. It is the same human sensitivity which makes us susceptible to both and if we are honest with ourselves we must admit that we would not wish it to be otherwise.

Therefore let our service here today be not only an expression of sorrow but an act of thanksgiving. We are thankful that she lived as long as she did, for though she seemed so much younger, she was in fact nearly 75 and that her illness, which she bore so bravely for so many years, did not immobilise her until quite recently and that she died quite suddenly and peacefully in her own home. We are thankful for her qualities of mind and heart, for she was highly intelligent. She took a keen interest in almost everything. She loved art and music, she enjoyed travelling and meeting people, she was a person of great vitality and indomitable spirit, she was well read and well informed, and, never became old fashioned in her understanding and judgment. She lived fully and happily. Above all, she lived well, for she hardly ever thought of herself but demoted herself to the services of others, both individuals and humanity as a whole, from her own family and friends and a Ghanaean goddaughter to international organisations.

Of course these are only a few generalisations and I must leave it to those present to recall in their own minds, from their private memories of her, some of the innumerable details which make them valid. But they are, I think, sufficient to remind us all that, in her unassuming self-effacing way, she set an example that is worthy of emulation. When C. Day Lewis[1] gave his inaugural lecture as Professor of Poetry at Oxford he said he wished that writers would pay more attention to "what is lovable and admirable in humankind". I think we would all agree that she personified these qualities to a high degree.

Let us then resolve to remember her not necessarily every minute of every day but frequently, with continued appreciation and abiding affection, and with the resolve that her example and influence shall remain with us a permanent source of guidance, enhancement and blessing. And let us pray too, that in the world beyond time and space, the indestructible innermost essence of her being may endure for ever in

---

[1] Cecil Day Lewis – British poet.

Tragedy Strikes

perfect peace "tachat kanfey ha-sh' chinah", under the wings of God's eternal presence.

> The Service-Nation Movement exists to create a true world citizenship, by uniting individuals of all races who have a world outlook in a new nationhood for the service of mankind.
>
> The Service-Nation—a nation without territory or armed forces—is the first practical step towards world unity and the abolition of war. It will act as a mediating agency between the nation-states, and as the active promoter of the welfare of all sections of humanity.
>
> Membership of the Movement is open to all who wish to associate themselves with its objects. Naturalisation as world citizens will be available to those who desire it when the Service-Nation is constituted.
>
> **SERVICE-NATION MOVEMENT**
> 20, BUCKINGHAM STREET
> LONDON, W.C.2.

Picture 33: Card for Parcels to Germany

Amen.

Hugh desperately needed to get away from things and went to Malta for four weeks in April, staying with Robert Borwick's family. Writing to his daughter Marion on the 12th April he shared the thought:

> ...we had the fancy that when I was away without Mummy I carried her like a little kitten tucked in my inside coat pocket. I cherish that fancy now, and thus keep Mummy snug – or as we used to say Shnud^2 – and continually present. It helps.

There was a meeting of Hugh's Mondcivitan remnant in Aldingen at the Haller's house and Hugh was unable to attend. A postcard was sent to him on the 9th September signed by Willi and Margareth Haller, Hansjakob Hugh Haller, Steve and Sandy Engelking, Charles Pooley, Peter Deed, Kathrin Haller, Charlyne Valensin, Elias Engelking, Bastel Haller saying:

> We're having a good reunion here in Germany but feel sorry that you could not be with us. We all send you our warmest regards and our love.

---

2   Audrey pointed out that the word "Schnud" was an invention of her mother.

Life Must Go On

Hugh was forced to start a new life as a single at the age of 78 and moved to a flat at 1033A Finchley Road in London on 21st September of that year. It is not as if he did not have admirers who would have been willing to fill the gap left by Hélène. A letter of the 4th December 1979 from Rose Chesney stated her willingness to marry and be "a companion in old age". There was the hint that Hugh would rather accept male companionship than be alone and for a time the young man Didier moved into Finchley Road.

Marion's mother-in law A. Singer, who lived in Israel, pointed out that Hugh relied on Hélène a lot for her loving care. She thought that travel would help him a lot yet he was used to having Hélène on his side. So this is what transpired and he deepened himself in work and travel.

On the 22nd August 1979 he gave a talk in Geneva organised by Charlyne Valensin who was a great admirer and heartily supported his aim of building a Servant-Nation. The address was entitled *Holocaust and Us* and was attended by the Mondcivitan Secretary Peter Deed, my wife and myself, and the Haller family.

Charlyne carried out an interview with Hugh where he discussed his political and religious views.

1980 found our subject once again in Geneva giving a lecture entitled *Pentecost and the Essenes* at the Residence Universitaire in Geneva on June the 17th.

However, all the strain and deep sense of loss played havoc with his health and he was taken ill in Geneva, having to cancel a trip to Japan where he had planned to talk before the World Citizen's Assembly. He was attended to by Dr. Adrien Zaky on June 17th. Rose had arranged to meet him in Japan so this meeting did not transpire. She reiterated her willingness to look after him and was sad that he had not reciprocated. She pointed out in a letter of July 18th that she had only become physically attracted to him at the beginning of the year. In July (19th) he wrote to Marion (who he nicknamed "Weazel") and her husband Joe thanking them for looking after him and helping his recovery. He mentions having pain which was however subsiding.

But pain came from another quarter as Willi Haller wrote to him on the 14th July expressing the break with the Mondcivitan Republic and that he saw it as redundant in its previous form. He wrote a long letter where he carefully pointed out his stance:

> This is a very sad moment of my life and this possibly turns out to be a most disappointing letter for you. For years now I have more or less avoided the issues hoping that someone else would turn up and follow your footsteps but after your letter it is clear that you still put hopes on me and I accept that it might very well be "my destiny" to accept responsibility for our cause. I had hoped that I would not have to put my thoughts in writing but wait until you can come over to see us but now after I received the invitation from Peter [Deed] which is obviously from your hand I have reached a crossroad and have to make a stand as Luther did in front of the Reichstag in Worms where he said: "Hier stehe ich, ich kann nicht anders"[1].

He goes on to say:

---

1 Engl.: Here I stand, I can do no other.

I am still deeply convinced and this conviction grows as times goes by that your vision of a Servant-Nation joining together to save the nations forming a brotherhood of man in miniature and serving mankind is as valid as it ever was. Furthermore I am convinced that the Commonwealth of World Citizens and as it was later named the Mondcivitan Republic was a courageous and admirable effort to give this Servant-Nation a structural basis to grow and develop but I am afraid that this effort has contributed a great deal to our learning process and contributed a lot to its cause in its time but that this time has more or less come to an end and that new forms must emerge if our cause is to be advanced as it is required. ……

….The concept of the people of God, the community of the children of God, the Servant-Nation is something which goes beyond our capacity of perception. It defies clear structural definition. Who can claim to know or to be able to say who belongs to it and who does not. Obviously the dividing line cannot be drawn vertically separating those inside from those outside.

It has to be drawn horizontally right through everybody's heart making everybody potentially belonging to it and in reality sometimes yes sometimes no or partially yes and partially no. It is mysterious and it really is Utopia. We can be on the road to Utopia but we shall probably never be there. Any effort to give such a concept the name of an institution and the structure of an institution is like trying to put the ocean into a bottle.

It establishes something into a structure which at a given moment of history may be existing and right but which later on will no longer be adequate for a situation which may have drastically changed.

This must have been a devastating blow for Hugh because he really was convinced that Willi would take over the work from him. Unfortunately, like most great men, he was not able to part from the purity of his concept and allow for new perspectives as time changed. Willi mentions in his very detailed analysis that once the concept of World Citizenship was fashionable but in the age of cyberspace people generally saw themselves as part of the world and it was not necessary to express this idea in such a way today.

The book *The Riddle of the Empty Tomb* which was later re-titled as *After the Cross* was not selling well and the publishers A.S. Barnes closed down before 1982.

In a letter to Marsh of November 6th he mentions that he is still having after effects from his operation the previous summer. He had a French student staying with him for a month and hopes to have a Swiss student who will stay longer.

There was an enquiry from Ammirati and Puris Inc. for the film rights on the Passover Plot but the days of Hugh's best-sellers were drawing to an end it seems.

The last straw of the year was the death of John Lennon on 8th December 1980. As previously mentioned, John had been a follower of Hugh and had stated that his thinking was based on what he had learnt from his books. John had phoned with Hugh on occasions in the past.

To Hugh it must now have seemed that all had deserted him.

A real break and a holiday was now overdue and he embarked on a safari tour to Kenya in March 1981. He says that he went swimming every day and stayed at the Shelly Beach Hotel Mombassa.

Hugh planned to visit Willi in September and Willi offered to pay for his flight.

The Travels Continue

The next year brought more travels and he was in Cyprus in the January of 1982 with Dr. Lilian Starr.

On June 19th he held the annual Claude Goldsmith Montefiore Lecture after being invited by Rabbi Rayner of the Liberal Jewish Synagogue in St. John's Wood. In his profile for this lecture it mentions:

> Dr. Schonfield's concerns were not only with the past. In the post war years he launched an enterprise for world citizenship and international arbitration, and assisted personally in various crises, notably the Cuban Crisis, and in bringing about the Provisional Test Ban Treaty in regard to Nuclear weapons. He was nominated for the Nobel Peace Prize. His Jewish approach to World Peace was signalised by his book *The Politics of God*, and he was invited to preside over the centenary celebrations of one of his childhood heroes H.G. Wells.

H.G. Wells was certainly a recurring personality in Hugh's thinking and in this short piece he links Wells to the ideas of St. Paul:

> It is difficult not to be despondent about the state of human affairs. This is not because the problems requiring solution are so many and so complex, but because of the prevailing sickness of the human mind which will not permit them to be approached with wisdom and goodwill.
>
> One can understand now why H.G. Wells, that man of prophetic insight, should have written before be died nearly twenty years ago that brave and honest book *Mind at the End of Its Tether*. One can understand also that ancient vision of the Last Times expressed by St. Paul when he wrote to the Thessalonians of the Antichrist, "whose coming is after the working of Satan with all power and signs and lying wonders, and with all deceivableness of unrighteousness in them that perish because they received not the love of the truth, that they might be saved." The nations would be infected with "strong delusion, that they should believe a lie."
>
> What is so terrible about this present day and age is the widespread spirit of perversity which does not wish to hear or heed sound judgement, which mocks at what is honourable, wilfully propagates lies and half-truths, and seems incapable of seeing clearly and acting sanely. It is as if intelligence had become diseased, so that while it could function with startling acuteness scientifically and technologically, It was warped and corrupted in its consideration of the relationships of mankind. The political brain is aberrational, contorted with cunning. Interpreting data wrongly and reaching false conclusions, harbouring delusions that evil means are serving beneficial ends.
>
> "Evil, be thou my good," cries Lucifer in Paradise Lost. But political man is more bedevilled than Satan, since he has convinced himself that evil things really are good, and wrong things are right. He is zealous for what he genuinely believes to be good, and does not apprehend that there is bad in what he has espoused as worthy and just. What makes matters worse is that the power to distinguish between good and evil: is not blurred in respect of policies to which any section is opposed. It is blind only to the fallacies in its own position.

Almost immediately afterwards he went to Paris to hold lectures at the Université Holistique from 25th to 26th. Then from 9th to 12th July in the community founded by Marcel

Légaut in Mirmande in France. Talks were: "The messianic Plan. Palestine in the time of Jesus, and The new development of the plan". This was seen to be appropriate by Charlyne Valensin who had arranged for Hugh to give the talks because Légaut[1], whilst a devout Catholic, emphasised the humanity of Jesus, whom he saw more as a catalyst than as God incarnate. Charlyne wrote a short report after the event comparing the role of Hugh Schonfield with Marcel Légaut:

> From July 9 to 12, Hugh J. Schonfield had been invited to stay with the community founded around the French Catholic author Marcel Légaut, at Mirmande, an old typical French village in the Southern part of the country. Hugh Schonfield gave three main talks there on: The messianic Plan, Palestine in the time of Jesus, and The new development of the Plan.
>
> We shall briefly recall, for those who would not know, who Marcel Légaut is. This 82 years old man was a university professor of Mathematics who gave up his chair to become a shepherd. This sounds very romantic, but Légaut who is first and foremost a spiritual man had made the decision to respond to a personal call. He wrote many books, among them: *L'homme à la recherche de son humanité, Reflexion sur l'intelligence du passe et de l'avenir du Christianisme, Devenir soi ou rechercher le sens de sa propre vie.*
>
> Légaut, who remained a Roman Catholic, lays nevertheless the stress on the humanity of Jesus, whom he sees more as a catalyst than as God incarnate. Around him some lifelong friends cluster during the summer, together with many young people who are anxious to see a future for Christianity, mostly intellectuals, but also people from all walks of life.
>
> Now, what is the significance of this encounter from a Mondcivitan point of view?
>
> To me the Mirmande meeting seemed an important step towards establishing publicly our identity.
>
> We are frequently told: "You are not a religion, like Judaism or Christianity, you are not a State like the Vatican or the State of Israel, you are not an organisation like the UN which stands for the whole of mankind—who are you? On what authority do you speak for mankind?". The response Hugh Schonfield met at Mirmande was in itself the answer.
>
> It is always embarrassing for us when people say: "It is all very well to assert you are a universal people. But so say the UN officials, so say the Jews, so says the Church, so says Islam, so says Communism". And yet it should not be difficult for us to find the right answer, since Hugh Schonfield made it clear through his books that the Mondcivitan Republic came into being according to a messianic Plan. Therefore, our "universality" should recapture the essence of the Plan. And this was stressed at Mirmande.
>
> We cannot take action in the world to-day unless we know exactly who we are. And unless we translate our faith into deeds there would be no justification for our existence at all. And our identity springs out of the uniqueness of Hugh Schonfield's message, which is primarily concerned with reuniting the People of God, as a first and important step. Our identity must start with the bringing together of Jews and Christians, because Judeo-Christianity gave rise to our Western civilization out of which the so-called "international organizations" which are supposed to lead man-

---

[1] Marcel Légaut (1900–1990) French Christian philosopher and mathematician

kind came into being, as well as the people of other faiths and ideologies who relate genuinely to the Plan.

Now, could the Vatican, could the World Council of Churches or the Orthodox Patriarchate be a proper counterpart for Schonfield? None of them is primarily concerned in seeing mankind as a whole. But Légaut could be his Christian counterpart because he stakes his faith on his inner conviction, irrespective of institutions, of the universality of Jesus of Nazareth as the Messiah.

There is no getting away with it. Our identity, our taking action in the present world situation should be based on the knowledge of Judaism and Christianity we have got through Schonfield.

Now, Légaut comes in because of the amazing complementariness of the two men. Schonfield provides the frame, Légaut gives the flesh. In the same way as we can say that the People of Israel provides the structure of a nation, whereas the Christianity provides its inner contents.

Without Schonfield and his prospects for mankind, Légaut would seem rather pessimistic, laying the stress on individual fulfilment and ignoring the present political and other issues. Without Légaut—and the possibility of having a Christian counterpart equally concerned about the truth concerning Jesus—Schonfield would have less credibility among the Christians, and the Jews.

After the very moving talk of Hugh Schonfield on Palestine in the time of Jesus, the two men, emotionally shaken, embraced each other for a photograph. It turned out that the photo itself was very symbolic in its components. Two men—aged 81 and 82—embracing each other almost at the top of an uphill road. As if they had gone a long way before being enabled to meet—a way we shall all of us have to go through... a way which is the only outlet for mankind...

Charlyne Valensin.

In fact Charlyne was working very hard with increasing commitment and perhaps tried to bridge the gap between the two great men and wrote to Willi on the 3rd of July, after the Paris meeting enthusing with conviction that things were on the right path. She did not directly comment on the dispute and may not have been aware of it at the time as Hugh had a knack of keeping unpleasant things to himself, so as not to demotivate others.

According to a letter of the 20th September from Michael Baigent (who did not attend), Hugh took part in a debate at the Edinburgh Book Festival on 27th August 1982 on The Holy Blood and the Holy Grail with Richard Leigh and Henry Lincoln. This was chaired by Neville Barker-Cryer. Director of the Bible Society. Taking part in the debate were Hugh, Jonathan Sumption and Professor W.H.C. Friend. The announcement stated:

IMPORTANT ANNOUNCEMENT FOR ALL JOURNALISTS ATTENDING THE EDINBURGH BOOK FESTIVAL

THE EDINBURGH BOOK FESTIVAL—THE HOLY BLOOD AND THE HOLY GRAIL DEBATE

At 3.00 p.m. on Saturday 27th August, Richard Leigh and Henry Lincoln will be facing a formidable line-up of experts seeking to debunk the theories behind their hugely successful bestseller—THE HOLY BLOOD AND THE HOLY GRAIL

After topping the bestsellers lists on both sides of the Atlantic, and currently at No. 1 on the Canadian hardback bestsellers lists, the most controversial book to be published for many years now looks well on its way to the top of the U.K. paperback bestsellers after its publication on August 12th. by Corgi paperbacks.

Of Jews and Christians

In 1983 Hugh felt constrained to write a response to an article written by Cardinal Etchegaray[1] on the relationship between Jews and Christians. In this response he wrote:

> The Cardinal has not made the position sufficiently clear by wrongly equating Christians with Gentiles. He should have referred to them as ex-Gentiles. And he fails to point out that in the Apostolic Age, in the first century of the Christian Era, the great majority of the followers of Jesus were Jews whose religion continued to be Judaism. Christianity represented a position within Judaism, and had not yet become a religion in its own right, a new independent Faith. The argument of the first century was not about the relationship between two religions which had much in common. It was about whether Gentiles who had become Christians could be acknowledged as Israelites.

And continues:

> Something of tremendous consequence would have happened if the Christians could say to the Jews, "You are our brothers. We share the same ancestry and the same earthly destiny. Collectively we are the People of God". If this situation arose concretely and on a world scale it could not be ignored by the Jewish Community. There would be created a new fluidity with potentially radical adjustments of concepts and interpretations on both sides. The end in view would be the Kingdom of God on Earth, a world of peace and justice such as the prophets of old proclaimed —truly a messianic Age.

This underlines how Hugh was focused on the issue of the messianic people which can be traced as a thread throughout his works.

It was from March 24th to 29th 1984, after having a visionary dream, that he went to a Mondcivitan meeting in Cluny organised by Charlyne Valensin and attended by Willi Haller that he composed the following declaration:

> In this ancient and spiritual city of Cluny, in the year 1984 of the Christian Era, there is proclaimed again the messianic message of the deliverance of mankind from international strife through the ministry of a Servant-Nation.

On May 26th there was an interview with Hugh relating to Jews and Christians and the messianic idea which I have reproduced here because I think it might clarify the idea of a Servant-Nation which is what Hugh felt he was called to proclaim.

> **Question:** *Is it true that [in a messianic perspective] you are not considering the Moslems on the same level as the Jews and the Christians?*
>
> **Answer:** I am not considering the Moslems at all.
>
> **Question:** *But when you speak of the Jews and the Christians, you speak of religious things..*
>
> **Answer:** No, I am referring to the messianic idea. But it has been particularly developed through Judaism and Christianity.
>
> **Question:** *And not through the Moslems?*
>
> **Answer:** No. It has not been developed in any other religion.

---

1 https://en.wikipedia.org/wiki/Roger_Etchegaray

Question: *Wow! How would you explain that?*

Answer: But I must be clear. You see, at the present time, religions have been acting like sovereign States, in conflict with one another, and holding their own particular positions: "This is the truth, and what you have is not the truth!" And they are fighting one another. If we were treating the future on the lines of religions, we would be treating them on the same lines as in the UN [...] But, you see, in the uniting of the world, in the messianic teaching of the People of God, a nation is not something involving a contradiction of religions inside it. We are not fighting for one's superiority of something or another. Every individual inside a nation has freedom of conscience. They can worship in their own way in so far as they understand that the messianic is a divine political position. That is why I have called it "The Politics of God".

Question: *Is it why you often counterpose the two words "Romanism" and "Messianism"?*

Answer: Yes. Romanism, as represented by the imperial idea of the Roman Empire, is to have unity by superior authority that forces people together. We still have this idea of imperialism in human affairs. That is the very opposite [of Messianism], it is to control, to dominate; and, unfortunately, people are so attracted by this sort of thing that they try to put it even into space: you have the star wars, and these films which are made about fighting between the planets. Unfortunately, this is what is given our children to watch. It is not easy to eliminate, this idea of domination, and more especially in an age where the means of power are greater than in any other time [...] The conditions in the world as we find them are the cause why the message of the Servant-Nation has to come out again. It is the only possibility of changing the world structure. Without that, we would be lost, we would not know what to do, where to go. And this is so sad for young people who are growing up. They are saying: "What is going to happen to us? Shall we have life? Will it be taken from us? Shall we have work? What are we to do? Are we going to be destroyed in a bang?"

You are able to tell them: "No". But, of course, it is only faith, recognition of God that would enable you to appreciate this Plan. This Plan will triumph, because God cannot be defeated. This purpose will endure and fulfil itself. However, man at different times rebels.

Question: *But the idea of power control is just part of the whole human being. It is inside us. It is the battle inside the family between child and parents...*

Answer: This is what has to change, but it takes a long time. But we also recognize parental responsibility [...] Consequently, domination is a wrong use of parenthood. That is why families break up in that way...

Question: *I mean that it will be an internal battle, an eternal battle...*

Answer: I don't know about "eternal" because I don't know how long this planet is going to last. But I think it will certainly take a long time. It has already taken a long time. But you see what we read in the Bible that we have to assimilate: that a day is with the Lord as a thousand years. We have to have a different time sense.

Question: *Would you assume that the Planet would be destroyed one day?*

Answer: I am sure it will end when it has served its purpose. After all, it is a mortal thing. All mortal things must end. But what will be after that, I cannot tell you. What is the purpose, I cannot tell you at all. Why, out of all space, was this Planet chosen for this experiment which we are part of...

Question: *You said at the beginning that God indicated to men the purpose for which they had been created...*

Answer: As far as this Planet is concerned.

Question: *This Plan has been taught and spread around the Mediterranean at first. Now, has God given other indications to other nations outside the Mediterranean? I am referring to Buddhism and others...*

Answer: No. The answer is No. It has had to develop progressively from a central point outwards. I mean, when, after Jesus, the apostles went out to all over the world, carrying the message, they did not keep it in one country, and we know that the message was taken to India and to other lands. But the progress is that once the message has gone out to all the lands, then it has so to speak [?] communities throughout the world, which are representing the same thing. But [...] there is no force in this, we are not compelling. This is a mistake that the Christian Church has made when they sent missionaries. They tried to convert people to a religion they had never studied and never understood.[...] This is why today it is very difficult. It is not an easy thing for us to become a Servant-Nation, to give ourselves to the part of service, instead of control.

Question: *Suppose I am a Chinese or Japanese listening to you now. Would it not be necessary to give up cultural forms of the message, to have this Plan and this message acknowledged by the Chinese?*

Answer: We have not chosen any cultural form. We have citizens in all the different parts of the world. Because the Servant-Nation is something which transcends all the differences and resolves them in its own structure. You see, you are united first of all by a common ideal and a common function. To do that, you have to look at all the world with new eyes. You have to make yourself at home with all men, everywhere[...]

Question: *When you say "Israel will be a temple", do you think that the Third Temple will be constructed, or are you talking about a Temple which can be in the heart?*

Answer: I am talking about the Temple not made with hands. It is the atmosphere that we enter, and we recognize that this is a holy place.

Question: *Do you think that something is now already going this way?*

Answer: It is beginning to happen. It has to go through stages. Of course, I mean, when you think in terms of the Plan of God, you acquire in yourself a new timelessness. You are not thinking in terms of this year, or next year, or the year after. Things are working out sometimes quickly, sometimes over many ages.

Question: *It seems to me a real problem, the necessity of a land as a territory, which means a State, a political State, well the Sacred Land...*

Answer: You see, we think of a territory as of a Temple, and not of a land which is in contradiction with other lands. That is why I was speaking yesterday of the

Plan as it was in vision when the Children of Israel were taken from Egypt on the way to the land. And they had the Tabernacle in the desert. The tent is not a permanent structure. It was taken down and put up again at different stages. But the point was that people recognized: "This is not a territory" and they called it a "place of meeting". This is why the land is spoken of as a Temple, and Israel as a place of mission, that is where the teaching comes from the prophets, that the word of God will go out from Zion. And people would come from all the world to learn there, to meet one another. In the very last book of the Bible, the Apocalypse, in the vision of the new Jerusalem, it says that all the nations were saved.[...] And consequently, the world will become the Kingdom of God.

Question: *But this Holy Land has to be like the present State of Israel?*

Answer: Not necessarily.

Question: *May be not so large?*

Answer: It would always be a small place, which is not intended to exercise any power. It *must* be a small place.

Question: *In saying that, considering the disputes that are carried on about all this land at the moment and for decades, a transformation has to take place. But we have to be the means of that transformation...*

Answer: One of the things that the Servant-Nation has been doing through its representative there has been to create a new relationship between Arabs and Israelis. And we have Israeli and Arab citizens in our people. And one of our proposals has been that the country as a whole becomes, as we call it now, a Confederation.

Question: *I hope your proposals will succeed.*

Answer: As a Servant-Nation, we can do things like this, which other people can't. We have been doing many things which have been taking place in connection with the UN. Nobody else has been able to make these proposals and nobody else has been able to make the response as we have.

Question: *Would you tell us what you have done about Cuba?*

[...]

Question: *I would like to know the relationship between the idea of messianism and the first Assembly of Jesus in Jerusalem [...]*

Answer: The question was: "Was it necessary that people who were not Jews accepted Jesus as their Messiah, who was the King of Israel?" In order for him to be their King, anyone who joined had to become an Israelite. I think we have to understand this. This was not a new religion they were creating at all. They were dealing with the People of God. How could people who were not Jews become part of the People of God? By acknowledging the King of Israel as their King. Such was the conflict, because the people of Jerusalem said: "If you are going to become part of the People of God, you must be part of the Jewish people. You must accept the laws of the Jewish people as applying to you. In other words, you must become a member of the Jewish people by giving up being a Gentile." So, Paul said: "With so many people coming in, this is too difficult to insist upon." And so he said that he devised a method. He said: "Because Jesus, as the Messiah, had kept the whole law, everyone who comes into Christ is covered by his having kept the whole law."

It is worth noting in this context the remarks Hugh made about Moslem religion. Whilst it is generally accepted that Islam is not a messianic religion, it should be noted that Shi'a Islam exceptionally does have a messianic concept. This has been well discussed by Riffat Hassan. Hugh probably did not have an intimate knowledge of Islam but of course he was correct in terms of the teaching of the Koran[2]. Hassan concludes:

> I hope this article will stimulate at least a few openminded Muslims to reflect critically on the issues it raises, particularly on how they apprehend and relate to God and to reality, individually and collectively. Such reflection leads to greater self-understanding, which, in turn, brings about the self-security required for dialogue with other Muslims as well as with Jews and Christians. I also hope that at least a few equally openminded Jews and Christians will reflect critically on their own messianic ideas and beliefs to see if they can find significant parallels to messianism in Islam within their own religious traditions and experiences, which may help to deepen the sensitivity and empathy with which they look at and communicate with Muslims. Such reflection can lead to the opening of new avenues of understanding among the three religious communities —Jews, Christians, and Muslims—which, despite all their difference, share the same loving, merciful, dialogue-oriented God.

Often Hugh would jot down the odd idea that had popped into his head and the author found such a note on Christianity:

> What is Christianity? I have devoted more than sixty years to seeking the correct answer to that question. The truth has become increasingly clearer. Christianity is the pagan religious expression of messianic Judaism. This is both its strength and its weakness. Its strength in holding before mankind the promise of an ideal of peace and justice when all nations will acknowledge the One God: its weakness in seeing the Messiah as a human incarnation of God celebrated in a particular religious context.
>
> Jesus did not intend to make a new religion. Christianity is necessarily antisemitic because of its paganism, and claim to replace Judaism.

And again in another note we find:

> But then these believers, for the most part, are concerned to safeguard what they claim to be the fundamental doctrines of Christianity received by revelation. A good many Christian scholars do recognise that Christianity evolved by adaptation and accretion, and have been willing to say so openly, but frequently this admission is qualified by claiming that this was due to guidance by the Holy Spirit.
>
> Thus Christianity could go and had to go much further than the position occupied by Jesus himself. Very few have discerned that what Christianity insists on down to the present day owes a great deal to a Gentile attitude of mind which makes certain demands which have to be theologically satisfied.

In a letter to Charlyne dated April 12th 1984, Hugh mentions a Canadian Jewish friend who was later sponsoring the republishing of some of his books in the USA – a man by the name of Joseph Margulies and who was attending the talks in Geneva. He makes an interesting statement in this letter: "... there is a wish to put Religion and Politics in sep-

---

2   Hassan, Riffat (1985) *Messianism and Islam*, Journal of Ecumenical Studies, Vol.22 No. 2, Spring 1985, pp 261-291.

arate compartments. But of course we do not use Politics in the sense of Party Politics, nor Religion in the sense of conflicting Creeds". Joseph later considered the occasion to be a full success. Hugh also wanted to re-organise the speaking arrangements and tried to allay Charlyne's fears that the meeting would not be successful. He says:

.... It should not trouble you if only 10 are present.

But on a basis of faith, on which confidence should rest, you should not fear what I may say. If you do, it would be better to drop the project completely, for I may not be directed as to what I should speak about and in what manner I should express myself. Do you think I have no feeling for my audience? Would God have called me, would I be a Mondcivitan, if I had no care for my fellows? Take heart, and take courage!

We see once again the thing which was really moving Hugh. All his scientific and research work had culminated in this discovery and he felt he was called to proclaim it.

In this letter he also mentions that a Mrs. Arsac invited him to a short holiday before returning to London after the meeting. Willi was to talk at the end of the meeting on the theme "The People of God and the Nazis".

Willi had written to Hugh on the 31st January discussing their differences regarding the Mondcivitan Republic. It seems that Hugh could not abandon the idea of the Mondcivitan Republic as it had been conceived, even though it had failed in that form. Willi wanted to convince Hugh to look for a new interpretation. Yet we still find them both appearing together at this meeting. Apparently they had agreed to differ for the moment.

Jesus: The Evidence

In that year Bantam Books had written to Hugh about a suggestion of his to produce a book entitled *Sky Man* refusing to publish it but Channel 4, London Weekend Television, broadcast a series of programmes called *Jesus: The Evidence* of which Hugh was very critical and wrote to the broadcasters. He had worked on the series in the early stages back in 1982 and his books had been referred to but he had been "dropped" off the team – perhaps he was too critical of their approach as he was a stickler for precise historical representation. In fact, the magazine *Private Eye* reported on this referring to him as an "eccentric Jewish novelist" to which he took considerable exception. There was considerable communication on the subject. And he wrote to the producer on the 7th April:

> I am sorry to be troubling you when you must be extremely involved with the reactions to *Jesus: The Evidence* but I am sure you will have seen the reference to myself in *Private Eye*, where it is stated that I was "dropped" from the series. I enclose a copy of the letter I have sent to the Editor.
>
> It would appear that a great many things were going on relating to the series, of which I was not made aware, though I had devoted so much time and work to the series in its initial stages. But it is very detrimental to me as a scholar and historian to have it put about that I was "dropped", and I felt that it was rather "shabby" that I was not invited to the preview.
>
> I have devoted a lifetime—nearly sixty years in fact—to researching the subject, and no-one living is in a more competent position to speak to it authoritatively. In the circumstances I feel that the least the LWT can do is to invite me to be one of the participants in the discussion, which I understand is to take place at the end of the showing of the three programmes. Of course I shall be viewing the series with keen interest and attention....

In a "Right to Reply" on the same day, Hugh wrote:

> Dear Sirs,
>
> Hardly any of the theories put forward in this series will stand up to examination; but I will concern myself with the misleading nonsense presented in the Second Episode. It was as if Church and Synagogue had combined to assert that Jesus was something else than Messiah.
>
> I challenge Dr. Vermes to produce any document up to the time of Jesus in which the Messiah is presented as a warrior. To the contrary I can present Jewish sources which declare that he would be exactly the opposite, the Prince of Peace.
>
> When Jesus rode into Jerusalem on Palm Sunday this was in deliberate fulfilment of the prophecy that he would enter his capital on a donkey He did so to the plaudits of his followers and the people acclaiming him as Messiah. "If they are silent," he said, "the very stones will cry out." Jesus knew perfectly well the claim to be king in a Roman province was an act of high treason under Roman law for which the punishment was crucifixion. He was executed, not for being a magician or a prophet but as King of the Jews.
>
> Jesus did not allow himself to be addressed as Messiah earlier in his activities, because had he done so those activities would have been cut short by his arrest. But he did employ the harmless sounding synonym Son of Man, which would not give him

away to the masses or to the Romans. Similarly, he spoke of the Kingdom of God in parables.

Only at the end, when he was determined to suffer, did he accept to be acknowledged as Messiah.

As for Dr. Morton Smith, why was it not said that Clement of Alexandria, who referred to the secret text of Mark, was an eccentric Egyptian prelate and occultist. There was no mystery at all about the Kingdom of God, except when and how it would come about. It is clear from both Jewish and Christian sources that it represented the peaceful and just world order foreshadowed by the ancient prophets of Israel which would be inaugurated by the Messiah. It is a daily part of Jewish prayer (the Kaddish) and of Christian prayer (the Paternoster).

If what we are being treated to is "Evidence" then God help us. Most of the real evidence has unfortunately been ignored, and a great opportunity has been sacrificed. The writer may claim to know what he is talking about, having researched the subject for more than half a century.

Yours sincerely,

Dr. Hugh J. Schonfield

And to the magazine *Private Eye* he wrote the next day:

Dear Sirs,

In connection with the preparation of this TV Series for LWT you have referred to me (Apr.6) as an "eccentric Jewish novelist". Novelist I am not, having in a lifetime of authorship never yet attempted a work of fiction; but eccentric, yes certainly, since I could not achieve objectivity at the orthodox "centre" in my historical researches into Christian Origins.

Among my scholarly achievements has been the translation of the whole New Testament from Greek into English (*The Authentic New Testament*), and I have done much work on the Hebrew texts of the Dead Sea Scrolls.

It was because of my special knowledge and equipment that I was called in at the inception of the *Jesus: The Evidence* plan. I think I was rightly dropped from direct participation when the series, as I gather, was directed towards more speculative and fanciful ideas and theories. One must count among these the propositions of Orthodox Christianity.

I should say that I did not see in advance, and have not known anything positively, about the final contents of the programmes, but it is something of an achievement to have the theme of the real Jesus ventilated so widely and publicly. It may do something quite dangerous: it may make people think, often though—as yet—they are not put on the right track.

Yours faithfully,

Dr. Hugh J. Schonfield

So we can see that Hugh was quite willing to defend himself when necessary. He was actually quite a humble man as those around him knew him but if he felt insulted or treated unjustly, he could be quick and acute in defending himself and arguing his case. The author can remember an occasion when, whilst he never demanded that people address him other than just plain "Hugh", somebody had treated him with disrespect and addressing him as "Hugh", he turned round and said, "Dr. Schonfield" to you!

The discussion over the series continued as the subsequent episodes appeared and on the 30th April he wrote to John Ranelagh, the Commissioning Editor of Channel Four TV:

> I would have been listening to the discussion programme on *Jesus: The Evidence*, even if you had not recommended me to do so, and I learnt much from it, though not in the sense you had in mind.
>
> From all who took part, except Macoby, I found a great reluctance to consider Jesus in the light of the circumstances in his own country in his time. Nothing was said of the End Time atmosphere, which produced the Essenes with their spate of apocalyptic literature, and which produced the messianic expressions of Jesus, John the Baptist, and others such as a Samaritan Messiah killed by Pilate's forces. It was indeed a period unique in Jewish history and to which Jesus, a descendant of King David, responded. The panel was very ready to talk about Jesus as Son of God, but sought to play down the Messiah, King of the Jews, Son of Man, aspect. They would discuss the Resurrection, but not the birth of Jesus and the large family of Joseph and Mary of which Jesus was the eldest. It was all pussyfooting when it came to honest reality, at least on the Christian side. So the discussion got nowhere. How could it?
>
> But it did contribute something which I had never previously taken into consideration. From the Christian side it evidently went against the grain to think of Jesus as a Jew. The least said about that the better. In the Providence of God He had sent his Son into the world not only to humble himself by taking the form of a man, but even more he had submitted to the degradation of being born a Jew. It would have been so much more comfortable to live with if he had appeared as an Aryan Guru in India, the kind of Christ Annie Besant wanted in choosing Krishnamurti. She had come across those who wanted to speak of Christ, not as Messiah, as Krishna; but this spiritual antisemitism had never impressed itself on me. Evidently it is very deep seated, and calls for challenge if Jews and Christians are ever to become reconciled. It is a much greater problem to have a Jewish Saviour than it was under the Nazis to have a Jewish grandmother. Perhaps you are too young to remember the chant of the Hitler Youth:
>
> *Wir wollen keine Christen sein. Denn Christus war ein Judenschwein.*

So we can see that this was not really so much a question of Hugh defending his own honour but his sheer outrage about the misrepresentation of what he felt were the facts about Jesus and his time. It was this putting of Jesus into his true historical perspective which was combined with the concept of a political messiah which was the guiding principle in Hugh's thinking and work.

However, John Ranelagh did admit in his letter of the 23rd April that the series "gave a rather one-sided account of Jewish conceptions of Messiahship, particularly in the second episode".

The Final Break?

The letter received from Willi Haller written on June the 12th 1984 seems to be almost a complete break:

> Dear Hugh,
>
> I just received your letter, and I am very happy to hear that the response to the message was remarkable at the Cluny meeting and I am glad that it gave Charlyne a lift.
>
> Thinking of our relationship I am filled with a deep sadness. Glancing through your letters over the last six to eight months I find we have almost reached a point of no communication. For you I am "totally ignorant", I "dodge the issue", "the MR [Mondcivitan Republic] is still a good way ahead of where you are now" etc. etc. I am "kicking my destiny" and so forth.
>
> This may all very well be so and it obviously is according to your own judgment, but if I am so much behind of the MR [Mondcivitan Republic] I wonder what kind of effective leadership I could provide moving far behind everyone else. You are addressing the wrong person if you expect leadership from me after what you think of where I stand.
>
> This point being clear I would like to express where I think I stand and where I hope to move in the foreseeable future.
>
> As you may have learned I have given up my job and I have cut down my business activities so that I do no longer generate enough income to support my family. So at least I have taken that hurdle. This step has been an outgrowth of my conviction—which in the end did not leave me a choice—that I have to dedicate my life to the promotion and realisation of the Servant-Nation concept. I have given and I am giving talks on the subject, and as a result a loose group of supporters (or whatever you may call them) has formed which meets once a month trying to grasp what it means and to put it into practice.
>
> Now to be honest I would not consider any one of them nor would any of them consider himself or herself a citizen of the MR but I would say we are on the way to develop a world consciousness. Since we are down to earth people down here and rather practical minded this seems to me a process rather than a snap action so we may learn to look at our nation-states with a growing distance, trying to separate ourselves from taking our unrestricted loyalties to them for granted step by step while at the same time developing new loyalties for the world as a whole. As I expressed time and again, this process hopefully leads to autonomous communities which hopefully eventually link up to an autonomous network of autonomous communities. This is the way I can see the Servant Nation to come into being again, the rebuilding of the House of David by God taking place again.

So all these things were obviously cause for a lot of consternation on Hugh's part. He saw the truth in a certain way and could not understand it when people saw things differently, it seems. There was a certain obstinacy, almost dogmatism here at times.

By the end of the year he had cooled down somewhat and was called as guest of honour on the 1st November at *The Sunday Affair* (which seems to have been a dinner with a speaker – location unknown).

One of our subject's most important works was his translation of the New Testament which had been originally published as the *Authentic New Testament*. In the meantime he had reworked it and it now appeared in November 1985 with Harper and Row as *The Original New Testament: A Radical Translation and Reinterpretation*. At this time *The Essene Odyssey: The Mystery of the True Teacher and the Essene Impact on the Shaping of Human Destiny*, appeared under Element Books Ltd.

However, not everybody was willing to acclaim the author's scholarship and an article by Hyam Maccoby in the *Jewish Chronicle* of January 18th 1985 stated: "Despite Schonfield's learning and ingenuity, his effort, as it staggers on from one conjecture to another, seems to founder into meaninglessness".

An interview with Greg Doudna on the 13th January 1985 in Hugh's London apartment took a more sympathetic stance and is reproduced below because it sheds further light on some of the issues we have already mentioned. This reconstructed conversation was written on January 23, 1985, in Tulsa, Oklahoma, after Greg returned from his trip to England.

Have you continued your research and writing?

Yes, writing books seems to be an addiction with me. My latest one is just coming out, The Essene Odyssey.

Can the Teacher of Righteousness be identified from history?

Probably not, because if he was a figure known to history he would have been identified by now. Even his name isn't known. He went under ciphers for names and I believe he died and is buried in Kashmir, India.

What will your next project be?

I'm making a revision of my translation of the New Testament, The Authentic New Testament, which is the only translation which was not done with theological motives. I translate it as a historian, not as a theologian.

All the other translations?

All of them. Yes. They don't understand that Jesus was messianic, rather than starting a new religion.

It's been some time since The Passover Plot came out. Do you still hold to what you presented in the book then?

Yes. I think it is gradually becoming more accepted and apparent with time.

You were certainly controversial. Do you remember The Plain Truth magazine, which said such a book couldn't be believed even by the author himself, and then after a letter from your attorney published an apology?

The Plain Truth? Yes, I remember. Another group in America even made a movie against the book.

The Final Break?

I was a student at the fundamentalist Christian college[1] which published The Plain Truth. That's past — I'm a Quaker now — but I remember the impact of your books upon me and other fellow students, and our discussions of their ideas —

Good. That's what I need to know. Then they were serving their purpose.

In your books you present Jesus as messiah but not divine, which is objectionable to both Jews and Christians, what has it been like being unacceptable to either? You come from a Jewish background yet —

I am Jewish.

Well, are there any other Jewish groups or people which believe Jesus was the Messiah but without the Christian doctrines of divinity and the rest?

Not apart from individuals. The groups of Jews who believe in Jesus usually accept all the Christian doctrines along with it.

What kind of reaction have your books and ideas received from Jews?

The climate in Judaism is changing. There is more toleration now for unemotional investigation of Jesus. Part of this is due to the creation of the state of Israel, and Jews became knowledgeable tour guides for Christians visiting their sites of history. And with the homeland there is something of a feeling of more security or willingness to re-examine Jesus, and reclaim Jesus' original Jewishness.

Was there ever a point in the first century when Jesus might have been accepted by the whole of the Jews or the Jewish mainstream?

I believe it came close to happening. James, or Jacob, the brother of Jesus at Jerusalem, was very highly esteemed among Jews everywhere, and the book of Acts shows many thousands in Jerusalem who accepted Jesus.

What happened?

Several things, but the main thing was the invasion and destruction of Jerusalem by Rome. The Jewish Christians fled and did not take part in the revolt. After the destruction of Jerusalem rabbinical Judaism developed, which was no longer messianic. There is rabbinical Judaism and there is biblical Judaism. 90% of Judaism today is not biblical Judaism but rabbinical Judaism.

Of course Christianity became Gentile, but did any of the original Judeo-Christians survive in history?

Yes, some small groups have survived to the present day.

They have?! I thought no Nazarenes or Jewish Christians survived beyond the fifth century.

They aren't known as Jews or Christians today but rather survived under Islam. After fleeing Palestine before the fall of Jerusalem, some of these Judeo-Christians settled in areas later conquered by the Moslems. They were required to outwardly accept Islam, which they did, but they retained their knowledge and memory of being believers in Jesus who fled Palestine in the first century. They could accept Islam outwardly because there is some common ground between Judaism and Islam.

---

1   Ambassador College, Texas run by Herbert W. Armstrong. See: Doudna, G. (1989) *Showdown at Big Sandy: Youthful Creativity Confronts Bureaucratic Inertia at an Unconventional Bible College in East Texas*, The Scrollery.

They didn't have to admit more than that Mohammed was a prophet, whereas the Moslems themselves regard Jesus as a prophet, and Islam didn't care what else their conquered peoples believed so long as they acknowledged Mohammed. Some of these peoples have only recently been discovered.

Is there any book you could recommend or refer me to where I could learn more of these descendants of the original Judeo-Christians?

Right here. (Points to his book The Essene Odyssey on the table stand nearby. It is hardbound, not yet available from the publisher, but he lets me have the copy for cost.)

Do you have any thoughts on who the Beloved Disciple of the Gospel of John might have been?

We know quite a bit about him. He was a member of the high priest's family in Jerusalem and it was at his house that Jesus kept the last supper. This house was where the disciples gathered in early Acts. His name was John. In the departure from Jerusalem of the disciples before Jerusalem fell, this John went to Ephesus. He wrote down his memories of Jesus. There was also a disciple of his, also named John, who rewrote and added to what John the Beloved Disciple had written, and that is where the gospel of John comes from. There are graves of two Johns, both of these Johns, in Ephesus today. This second John, the disciple of the Beloved Disciple, was the Elder who wrote the epistles of I. II. and III John. The first John, the Beloved Disciple, meanwhile, had been sent to the isle of Patmos during the Roman persecution of the Christians under the reign of Domitian and wrote much of Revelation. He was sent as prisoner to the island rather than killed because he was an important person.

So the Beloved Disciple could not have been James, the brother of Jesus? The reason I ask this is because of Jesus turning over his mother to the Beloved Disciple, and James is the next oldest brother.

No, James was not the Beloved Disciple. James is well-known by his own name and would have been referred to by his own name. The reason Jesus turned over his mother to the Beloved Disciple John in Jerusalem is because he had a home in Jerusalem where his mother could stay.

You mentioned Revelation being written in the time of Domitian. Do you give any credibility to the early dating theory which says Revelation was written before the fall of Jerusalem?

No. Domitian demanded emperor worship. He demanded everyone who addressed him to call him "My Lord and My God". When Thomas says this to Jesus in the gospel of John, this is the title Domitian demanded for himself.

Is there any evidence that the seventy weeks prophecy of Daniel was used by Jews to mean 490 years and to expect a Messiah in the first century?

Very much so. This figured strongly in the messianic expectations of the general time period, in the first century BC and the first century AD.

Were the sabbatical and Jubilee years known?

Yes. The sabbatical years were known and figure in the story. My book The Jesus Party discusses this. (Pulls the book off a nearby shelf and opens to the page where first century sabbatical years are listed, e. g. 26-27 AD, 33-34, 40-41). The Jubilee year followed every seventh sabbatical year.

Which was the Jubilee year?

It is not known which sabbatical year the Jubilee year followed. It could have been any of the first century sabbatical years.

Do you know anything more about Annas the high priest?

Nothing more than what is known from history.

Are you familiar with the book by William Phipps, Was Jesus Married[2]? He says that he was.

I'm not familiar with the book. Jesus certainly wasn't married. He left his own family, his responsibilities as oldest son, his widowed mother, because of his messianic calling.

Do you have any further light on the three temptations of Jesus?

It happened following his baptism by John the Baptist and realisation that he was to be the messiah. The three temptations represent ideas of what the Messiah ought to be that Jesus rejected.

Has your life's work devoted to the study of Christian origins been worth it? Would you do it again?

It has been my calling. Yes, I think its been worthwhile. All of my life I've been conscious of being prepared in various ways for my work, The tools, the knowledge of languages, documents and manuscripts have seemed to come to me when I needed them. For example, I discovered the Hebrew original of Matthew and translated it...

You have the Hebrew original of Matthew?!

Yes. (He says where it was from)... and it came into the hands of a dealer in rare and old books here in London who would call upon me from time to time to identify manuscripts. He called me about this one, and I saw that it was earlier than the earliest known Greek version and that it had a superior text, and I translated it.

And this has been accepted in the scholarly world?

Its generally been accepted by those who know of it, yes. Let me show you just one example, a minor thing really, of the kind **of** thing this manuscript clears up. Matthew says there are forty-two names in his genealogy of Jesus. Three groups of fourteen. But hardly anyone actually counts the names. There are only forty-one. But the Hebrew manuscript has the missing name, the full forty-two. (Here he takes his copy of the book from the shelf and opens it to a page where he shows me very similar-looking Hebrew or Greek characters.) What happened was in the translation from Hebrew to Greek this particular name's translation into Greek looks the same in Greek as the Greek for "begat." A later copyist thought the manuscript reading "begat begat" must have been a mistake so left out the second set of characters, not realising he was omitting a name which would have been apparent from the Hebrew. Therefore all Bibles today based on the Greek text of Matthew omit the forty-second name, which my translation restores.

2   Phipps, William E.. (1970) *Was Jesus Married*, London: Harper Row.

Interesting. Do you think there are other significant manuscripts or discoveries over there in the Middle East which will emerge of significance comparable to, say, the Dead Sea Scrolls?

Yes, and it is remarkable how much already has been discovered in our tine, when our world is in the state it's in. Perhaps it is not coincidence. The Dead Sea Scrolls, the Nag Hammadi manuscripts, these are major findings. Right now there are reports of the existence of the original gospel written in Hebrew which precedes the four we have today, and which was used by the synoptic gospel writers, which has long been known about but never discovered. It is reported to be in a monastery in Iraq.

This would have a major effect on biblical studies. Unfortunately no one can get to it because it is in the middle of the Iranian-Iraqi war going on, so we'll have to wait until the war there ends.

Have you ever felt there was a barrier or end to the progress which can be made in understanding events of the time of Jesus, that at this distance there are things we can't know and limits to what we can? Have you ever felt stopped at a certain point and felt there was no way of going further?

No, I've never felt like I've gone to where I can go no further. In fact new material and discoveries are coming to us in this time such that knowledge of our past is increasing, not decreasing, with time. We are progressively becoming more informed and knowledgeable about events in ancient times the further chronologically we go from them. The discoveries are revealing Jesus' Messianism at the very time in our world when it needs Messianism today most.

The "Commonwealth of World Citizens" which you founded and to which you allude in your books — is that a practice of what you see as Messianism in our world today?

Yes. Jesus was not starting a new religion but was fulfilling the messianic expectations of Jews of his time. Christians have a false idea that the Jews had an idea of a conquering mighty Messiah and Jesus was not at all like these Messianic expectations so the Jews rejected him. I have shown in my books that the concept of a servant-messiah which Jesus was, was highly developed among the Essenes and sectarians and other Jews of his time. Messianism is the only hope for the world. Nothing else will work.

Not even the Greens?

No. Nothing else will work.

Was Jesus pacifist?

Yes.

So Jesus didn't see himself as part of the Children of Light executing the wrath of God upon the wicked by slaying the Children of Darkness at the day of the Lord in an eschatological holy war like the Essenes thought?

No. The Essenes had developed concepts of the messiah being a man of peace and a servant king. They did not believe the messiah would lead then in a holy war. They believed God would execute judgement, not that the messiah would lead them in doing this themselves.

What was Jesus' view toward the Temple? He calls it his father's house yet he seems to have said something about seeing it destroyed, and the Essenes did not like the Temple.

Jesus took part in the Temple worship and believed in the Temple. As for the statements about destroying the Temple in three days, we don't know that Jesus said that. After the destruction of the Temple and the split with the Jews, the Christians put things into Jesus' mouth. The Essenes weren't against the Temple and Jesus was not an Essene.

The Essenes were not against the Temple—they just wanted to see its worship reformed instead of desecrated?

Right.

Why do you say Jesus was not an Essene?

The Essenes had retreated because they were holy, and they were secretive. Jesus did not believe in being secretive like the Essenes. He said let your light shine rather than putting it under a bushel, and whatever you hear in secret shout from the housetops. Jesus and his disciples were influenced by Essene concepts and teachings, yes, particularly the concept of what the Messiah would be. But Jesus was never an Essene.

These ideas that Jesus was an Essene or studied with them are wrong. Jesus was a Pharisee. He said, "The Pharisees sit in Moses' seat."

That's a strong way to put it — "Jesus was a Pharisee."

I put it in that strong way because people assume he was against the Pharisees. He was part of them.

What then was going on with the animosity the gospels reveal between Jesus and the Pharisees?

There are two things going on here. From Jesus' side, Jesus was against the Pharisees not living up to their own standards. The Pharisees, on the other hand, objected to Jesus associating with the kinds of people a holy person should not associate with — Jesus was not acting like they thought a holy man should. Jesus associated with prostitutes and publicans and people who drank. Jesus was a pub-rounder (laughs).

If Jesus was a Pharisee and practiced the Jerusalem Temple worship, then he did not use the different Qumram calendar for the holy days?

Correct. He used the Jerusalem calendar, not the Qumran calendar.

Which calendar do you think was right — or does it matter?

The different calendar ideas spring from things like when the new moon is observed. If it's a cloudy night then it can become quite arbitrary. I don't think you can say either side was "right."

What did Jesus have in mind for his disciples to do in Jerusalem after he would go through with his crucifixion and resurrection?

He didn't have anything in mind for them, because he believed the Kingdom would be set up immediately. Remember he said to Caiaphas the high priest, "*You* will see the Son of Man coming in clouds of glory." Jesus did not expect any time gap or interim period. Obviously these eschatological expectations did not happen in the first century. With our Western ways of thinking today, its hard to imagine things happening like that today — the signs in the heavens and the rest of what they expected.

Is it relevant for us today?

Jesus fulfilled biblical Messianism for the Jews, and that is relevant. They were wrong about the eschatology and signs in the heaven. That isn't going to happen that way. But Messianism is the hope for the world. Jesus came to be Messiah as one man for Israel. He came to Israel only because one man can't save the world. But the nation of Israel would in turn be the messiah for the world. This is why Jesus told his disciples not to go to the Gentiles — his mission was to Israel only. But Israel in turn would be the means for saving the world. So the world is included in the picture of Messianism.

What about the role of Paul — was he a good guy or a bad guy?

After Paul's conversion he would go to the synagogues in the various cities to preach Jesus. There would be Gentile proselytes in each of the synagogues who would be interested in Paul's message, The word would spread and more Gentiles who weren't proselytes would come to the synagogue to hear Paul, the synagogue being a natural place to reach the public. Paul believed Jesus was Messiah for the nation of Israel and that one had to be part of the nation of Israel to be saved. The question was how were the Gentiles to be incorporated into the nation of Israel which would be God's messianic Servant- Nation to the world? Paul believed the Gentiles had to keep the full law of Moses, too. But Paul argues that by being part of Jesus the Gentiles were part of the nation of Israel since they were part of the Messiah of Israel, and that Jesus had kept the law of Moses for them. Paul argues this to the rest of the Jewish Christians, and he argues this as a Pharisee, using logic of a Pharisee. The other Jewish Christians were not against the idea of Gentiles coming into the movement. They knew that the Messiah would be for all peoples not just Israel. But where they differed was they felt the Gentiles should come to the synagogue and go through the training of a proselyte. They felt that some training and time was required to become part of the new messianic Jewish nation, whereas Paul felt the Gentiles could become part of it instantly without such training. Paul's vision of including the Gentiles was right, and it was shared by the rest of the Jewish Christians, but historically Paul's instant universalism without the training to be prepared for it backfired. This is largely why Christianity developed as a Gentile religion with pagan, non-Jewish character, and why the original Jewish Messianism was cast aside and forgotten.

What about the belief in a resurrection? Could Jesus and the movement around Jesus have existed at all without it?

The Jewish belief in a personal resurrection seems to enter around the time of the troubles with Antiochus Epiphanes, as a way of making martyrdom worthwhile, and this seems to continue in early Christianity, with Paul saying if the dead don't rise then why go through suffering and martyrdom at all...

The idea of expecting a resurrection seems foreign to the way we think today, yet could first century Christianity have existed without it?

Its probably true that first century Christianity could not have existed without a belief in the resurrection.

Then would Messianism today require believing something so foreign to our Western ways of thinking?

Only if you see resurrection in terms of individual identity. But if you see yourself as part of a larger whole of the universe, not as a separate atomic being, then resurrection can have meaning for us today.

So if we individually suffer or even die for doing the right thing, it is redeemed in the long run by the redeemed humane world we helped bring about? And the resurrection of Jesus would become a symbol for this kind of restored earthly creation, just as the deliverance of Israel from Egypt is a symbol for deliverance from oppression and release from sin?

Yes.

What of the recent discoveries related to early Gnostic Christianity, which was so different from the Christianity we know from history, and which did not survive? The Gnostic Christian claims that they were associated with Mary Magdalene in opposition to the Christianity of history centred around Peter....could this be true?

A lot of the differences in the kinds of Christianity discovered have to do with geographical differences, The Gnostic Nag Hammadi manuscripts come from Egypt. It has long been wondered why the New Testament ignores mention of Alexandria, which was a major centre for Jewish learning and culture. Probably the New Testament letter to the Hebrews was written from Alexandria by Apollos, and...

Do you mean Apollos of the book of Acts?

Yes. He was from Alexandria. The gospel of Matthew also probably came from Alexandria. The four gospels were chosen from the four directions of the compass when the New Testament was being put together, so as to represent all areas of Christianity. Mark coming from the west, Luke from the north, John from Ephesus in the east, and Matthew from Alexandria to the south. This is why Matthew has Joseph and Mary spending time in Egypt after Jesus was born, for example.

What was the reaction of your family to you as a Jewish boy taking such an interest in Jesus?

I was always asking questions as a boy. They didn't know what to make of me. They regarded me like Joseph of the Old Testament — a dreamer of dreams. When I was a young boy Jesus wasn't mentioned. Then I heard one day that Jesus was Jewish so I became curious. I borrowed a Bible from our family's landlady who was a Christian, because we didn't have a New Testament in our house. My lifelong interest in Jesus started with that. My parents were upset about it for a few years.

Did your wife appreciate and support your work?

Yes, she was totally with me. I married my childhood sweetheart. She shared with me my calling for my life's work. She died six years ago, after fifty-two years of marriage. After she died, I discovered among her papers poems she had written about me when she was a child — which she had never told me about.

That is touching. And you're still continuing your work?

I'll keep on until my work is finished. My books will be my legacy.

He showed me a collection of artefacts in a nearby bookcase, ranging from prehistoric times to the present. "The history of our world on two shelves", he calls it. "Will the story continue?" I ask.

"I think it will," he answers. He tells me about his close friend H. G. Wells, whose chair he has been sitting in during the course of our conversation. I acquire from him a copy at cost of his The Essene Odyssey, *not yet out in bookstores, and he autographs it for me. Then he gives me as a gift a copy of his book* The Politics of God, *and says, "This will commemorate our visit." Reading the book on the long flight back to the United States from London, I am stunned by the power and force of his conception of the non-coercive, non-geographical nation and government he envisions and founded, the Commonwealth of World Citizens, his vision of the messianic servant-nation in the midst of the world's nation-states, the inspiration of which is drawn for him directly from the figure of Jesus so long ago.*

Not for Want of Trying

The discussion with Willi Haller about the future of the Mondcivitan Republic was still running in the background and Willi wrote to Hugh on the 30th January 1985 in the following vein:

Dear Hugh,

Thank you so much for your letter. It seems as if we are approaching a deeper understanding.

Of course, I am talking about a different kind of community.

As a matter of fact, I am convinced that this is the decisive issue. It is impossible that any individual person can have brought destruction to the Republic (let us give up the scapegoat principle—it is always wrong). It fell apart on its own as its members or at least most of them (including me for many years) did not grasp the implications of what was meant—or did not want to grasp them. The word never became flesh. This is true for both the word "Nation" and as well as "Community".

Any nation consists of communities—of course interdependent communities not independent communities (who could talk about independent communities? Certainly not I).

Alright, an assembly had decided that communities should be formed but they never came into being. The term remained a word and did not grow roots to become flesh. Because a community (in the process of incarnation from word to flesh) develops all aspects of society, economy, education, health care and culture plus administration. And these aspects never became visible otherwise activities or non-activities in London would and could not have wrecked the whole thing.

If a so-called community does not develop these roots you have something like the Rotary Club and membership instead of citizenship. And all your international links are pie in the sky.

I do not blame you nor anyone else. We just did not grasp it. May be the time was not ripe yet. I do not know. But now I know and I am committed to it.

The sequence of the words "Mediation, Service and Example" clearly indicate that we started from the wrong end.

Example, self-commitment, comes first. From that basis we can try to serve and with enough history of example and service we may have the credibility to have the honour to mediate.

But obviously many of us thought that without radically changing their lives and radically committing themselves to our course they might be able to change the course of history by telling other people (the politicians) what to do while sitting in their comfortable armchairs. Sheer hypocrisy—and to believe they might listen and even do what they have been told, it is ridiculous. There are no shortcuts on our long hard road—to use your own words (POG [Politics of God]).

But there were also practical issues to deal with. Stanley Davis OBE (Hon. Secretary), Malta wrote on 29th September 1985 about Hugh's involvement with the Jewish community in Malta and the renovation of the Jewish Cemetery in Kalkara. He talks of correspondence from 1972 so this engagement must have gone back quite a way. By now the cemetery had been cleared of weeds. The Kalkara cemetery is the earliest surviving Jewish burial ground in Malta[1]. An article in the *Times of Malta* describes how it is still being renovated and that it dates back to 1784.

November of 1985 meant travelling again and a US tour covered New York, Boston, Chicago, LA, San Francisco and Toronto. The costs were partly covered by Harper & Row and Element Books. The aim was to present the Authentic New Testament. Joseph Margulies partly sponsored this tour together also. His total investment in the republishing of the books with Element amounted to some $50-60,000. The books concerned were:

> *The Passover Plot*
>
> *The Essene Odyssey*
>
> *Those Incredible Christians*
>
> *The Pentecost Revolution*
>
> *After the Cross*

The contract was such that the sponsor would be repaid as books were sold. There seems to have been some upset between Element Books and Hugh who was beginning to feel his age now. He was not satisfied with the photos they wanted to use for the jacket of *Those Incredible Christians* saying that the book related to the 2nd Century AD and all their pictures were 4th Century. Mark Paterson complained to Michael Mann of Element books on the 16th August 1985 about the way some of this had been handled. Michael wrote to Mark and expressed his frustration with Hugh in no uncertain terms - "Hugh does nothing but send an endless stream of rude letters. Does he ever have a good word for anyone?! If he doesn't stop blaming everyone else shortly I shall feel inclined to stop trying to put all my energy and faith into this project!"

Again we can see that Hugh was not always seen as the easiest person to deal with and he could be very obstinate at times, a character trait which was not improving with age.

Finally Hugh and Mark meet with Joseph Margulies in London Hotel Americana on 21st May 1985 to discuss matters.

As 1986 struck there were matters of state to deal with, Hugh still acting as President of the Mondcivitan Republic. A letter was sent to King Hussein of Jordan with a peace proposal and the idea of the "Abars":

> Peace Proposal To H.R. King Hussein of The Kingdom of Jordan
>
> By The Annunciationary Religious Party of Israel and by The Movement of Intellect of Israel.
>
> By Mediation of The President of The Mondcivitan Republic: - Dr. Hugh J. Schonfield.
>
> The Annunciationary Religious Party of Israel and The Movement of Intellect of Israel are striving, and will strive, for the obtaintion of political power in Israel, and when they will hold it, they will act towards the problem of Israel-Arab relations with a devote and sincere spirit for peace. The two organizations believe that already now peace conversations should be started, and therefore, they state already

---

[1] http://www.jstor.org/discover/10.2307/29778925?uid=3737864&uid=2&uid=4&sid=21104406296283

now the main bases on which they will try to reach peace when they will be in power or in a position in which they may influence political power, namely:

1) In fulfilment of the prompting of God that a new people, a new gentry, will stem up that will cause that the law of God be known and done—Hebrews become Abars, a new nation, by accepting Jesus and Muhammad as messengers and Messiahs (= Christs) of God and by integrating their religion with the teachings of the Holy Bible, the Holy Gospel and the Holy Koran, as it is stated in the Bible and in the Koran (Deut. 52, 21- Surah 5, 70—71).

2) As a consequence, the Abar people consider Christians and Moslems as brothers, having only one and a common religion, and they are disposed to marry into them, and live, act and work with them side by side without barriers nor limitations.

3) The Abar people will enrich and enlarge Hebrew language by means of the bountiful treasure of the Arab language.

4) The Abar people believe that the land that extends from the Egypt river till the Euphrates river was given to the offspring of Abraham:- Ismael and Israel – by God, as it is written in the Bible and in the Koran (Gen. 15, 3 8, Surah 17, 105-106), and that this land was divided into two parts:- one for the Sons of Ismael and one for the Sons of Israel, with the Jordan river as the mark between them, and having each one of them full right and full possibility to live, act and work in the territory belonging to the other part, together with the full right and full possibility to behave and live according to the laws and customs of the part to which each one belongs nationally. Therefore, the two brother countries that exist nowadays in the land of the Sons of Abraham should live, act and work in peaceful cooperation and have a coordinated political, economic and monetary system.

5) The problem of the refugees and/or fugitives that were created by hostile actions between Sons of Ismael and Sons of Israel will be solved by allowing them to go back to the same places from which they went out, or to choose any other place in the land of Israel or in the land of Ismael or anywhere else, and/or within a general, comprehensive and miscellaneous frame of mutual compensations to the Sons of Israel and to the Sons of Ismael for damage and/or loss of life and/or of property and/or of any other thing caused since 1920 by hostile actions and/or by confiscation and/or by any other antagonistic action executed by members and/or by authorities of the other side anywhere in the lands and countries in which Arabs and Hebrews (or Abars) had, or have, political and/or factual power and/or influence.

6) The Abar people will call King Hussein to acknowledge and declare that he is the inheritor, successor and substitute of Ismael, the son of Abraham and uncle of Israel, and if and when King Hussein accede to it, the Abar people will proclaim him as the Protector of Israel. In such circumstances the Abar people will consider that the security and the welfare of the Sons of Israel and of the Sons of Ismael that live, act and work in the common land must be kept by a common force that will act under the direction of King Hussein, and after him, of his legal successors, and in which Abars and Arabs will serve alongside each other with equal rights and duties.

7) When the Abar people will hold power in the State of Israel, they will proclaim the territory of Israel open and free for all mankind, and Jerusalem as the centre and capital of the world, setting up in it and transferring to it all the governing and

leading institutions of mankind. Therefore, there will be no need for Israel to have its own armed forces. Security and order will be enacted by the power and the force of the Protector of Israel:- King Hussein -, and after him, by his legal successors.

8) The Abar people earnestly and respectfully entreats H.M. King Hussein to change the name of his kingdom into "Kingdom of Ismael".

January 1986.

PRESENTED BY THE SECRETARY GENERAL OF THE ANNUNCIATIORY RELIGIOUS PARTY OF ISRAEL AND OF THE MOVEMENT OF INTELLECT OF ISRAEL

Hugh sent a copy of the newly published *The Original New Testament* to his old St. Paul's School for which he received acknowledgement and thanks.

He gave a lecture at the Liberal Jewish Synagogue Finchley on 19th January 1986 where books were to be sent from Element Books for signature. As we mentioned previously, Joseph Margulies was involved in sponsoring this project, including a budget for advertising. Advertisements were placed in the Sunday Times, The Observer, The Guardian, etc.

In fact, sales of books were drying up and Hugh expressed his worry at loss of income in his letter of 1st April 1986 to Mark Paterson.

A letter from Heinz Müller, Willi's neighbour who was involved in the publishing of the books in German, mentions the interest of Dr. Süsman and the fact that he cites Hugh in his newest book *Und die Wüste wird blühen* (the author has not been able to locate this book). There is also talk of a forthcoming TV discussion.

Time is Running Out

A letter from Willi which seems to have been his last to Hugh dated 18th June 1986 strikes a more conciliatory tone:

> Dear Hugh,
>
> I just received your circular letter and I would like to reply to it right away. As you know I am committed to our cause, despite differing opinions on certain issues and I dare say that I am committed more than ever. I am glad to say that I have regular invitations to speak or write on issues which give me the opportunity to speak about the need of a new interpretation and realisation of the People of God concept, a new Servant-Nation—but still progress is slow. For the first time in IFOR [International Fellowship of Reconciliation] (Germany) history we have extensively discussed this issue at the annual meeting here in Germany and we shall pursue the matter further in a special weekend seminar because of the interest it raised. We have recently met Charlyne in Cluny and she told us about the people who visited you on your birthday. I wrote to Christopher Seebach at once and I am waiting for his reply hoping to meet him and the lady (whose name I do not yet know) by the end of July or in August either in Cluny or in Geneva. I would be only too happy to meet people who commit themselves to global citizenship of the MR and I am therefore looking forward to meeting them. My first book (on unemployment and work hour management) has been published but I am still looking for a publisher for my second one (on the need of an alternative society). I am glad to hear that applications are coming in from all over the world and with your previous reports on growing activities in the US it seems as if a solid infrastructure is taking shape. I hope your health is keeping you strong and going. Over here everyone is fine. Matthias has just finished school and will have to start his "alternative service" as a conscientious objector soon. Wule is changing schools. He will go to Rottweil to a "Gymnasium" with a more technically oriented curriculum. He is the engineer of the family. That's all for now. Love Willi.

A letter from Charlyne on the 13th prompted Hugh to reply to her on the 20th May (the author doubts that he would have received Willi's letter by then so the letters must have crossed) where he writes:

> On my birthday I had a visit from Mrs Elly Cantor of Le Projet Faim, and she was joined by a Mr Christopher Seebach of the Aquarian Agency. Both wanted to be better informed about the Mondcivitan Republic. I was told that so much relief work is impeded because of national labels, American or Russian, which create obstacles. They need a neutral world nationality under which to operate, and could see that the Mondcivitan Republic as the impartial Servant-Nation of Mankind could function in this capacity. Mrs Cantor is now taking our literature to her Council.
>
> This could be an important development in making the Mondcivitan Republic more widely known and appreciated, and underlines the need for solid work by our citizens to build up our political structure locally and internationally. As it is, hardly any of our citizens devote themselves to this essential activity. I am expected to arrange and cope with every aspect, which you will agree is grossly unfair.

It is evident that at 85 I cannot expect to be here much longer, or have adequate physical and mental resources. So it is time, if I have set an example with my initiative, that some sense of responsibility and obligation should inspire some of our people to express their gratitude by taking the running of our Republic on their own shoulders.

Because of both my age and developments this has now become much more urgent. I am reduced to begging for what should be offered freely and joyfully, and this shows the measure of my failure. No one is inspired to relieve me of any responsibilities. I am simply put where I have no wish to be, on a pedestal, like a statue.

The Mondcivitan Republic requires a functioning Government with individuals in charge of essential Departments, Citizenship, Public and International Relations projects, etc. We did have this once when I was physically able to cope; but when I had to take a back seat for health reasons everything went to pieces. I had almost to start all over again, because I could not be unfaithful to God's will.

I will not write like this again, and I hope you will pardon the necessity to do it this once. I have also written to Willi Haller. We will see what happens. To be spiritual does not rule out being practical.

My love, Hugh.

The sad fact was that by now there were really no active citizens left. Many had died or lost interest and there was no functioning bureaucracy to give the impression of a functioning Republic. Understandably, Hugh had trouble coming to terms with this and probably had extensive nostalgia for the days when he and his beloved Hélène could stand on the steps of the Temple of Peace in Cardiff, proud to see the Commonwealth of World Citizens, as it was then called, come into existence.

However, as a scholar he never seemed to be other than in demand and his work gained continual appreciation. A letter from the Australian Broadcasting Corporation wanting help with a series of five programmes on the Original New Testament was sent to him on the 11th June 1986. The series had been conceived after the interest shown in the book through an interview which had been recorded with him in the March of that year. There were to be five readings each of three and a half minutes. Below, the script of the first of these talks has been reproduced:

Christianity did not begin as a religion. It began in Israel as a Jewish political movement when the country was dominated by Imperial Rome. The adherents believed that in Jesus of Nazareth, descended from King David, they had found their ultimate ruler and deliverer. This is clearly stated in the Gospel of Luke, in words spoken by the Priest Zechariah:

"Blessed be the Lord God of Israel, For He has visited and ransomed His people,

And raised up for us a means of deliverance Out of the house of His servant David,

As He said by His holy prophets of old; Deliverance from our foes and all who hate us,

To maintain His mercy to our fathers, And to call to mind His holy covenant.

The oath which He swore to our father Abraham, Assuring that fearlessly, freed from foes.

We should worship Him all our days Purely and piously in His presence."

Rome was seen as the Evil Power which must he overthrown before the righteous rule of the Messiah (Christ in Greek) could be established on Earth. Under the name of Babylon, Rome's doom is graphically predicted in the Book of Revelation.

"After this I saw another angel with great authority descend from heaven, and the earth was illumined by his glory, With stentorian voice he cried, 'Great Babylon has fallen, has fallen, and has become the habitation of demons, and the haunt of every foul- spirit, and the haunt of every foul and hateful bird; for all nations have drunk the strong wine of her immorality; the kings of the earth have committed immorality with her, and the merchants of the earth have grown rich through her insatiable desires.

Then I heard another voice from heaven say, 'Leave her, my people, lest you participate in her sins, and partake of her plagues, for her sins have piled up to heaven, and God has remembered her iniquities. Treat her as she has treated you, and doubly so, in accordance with her deeds. In the very goblet she mixed for others, mix double for her. To the extent that she has glorified herself and waxed wanton, by so much render to her anguish and sorrow. For she says to herself, I sit a queen, and am no widow. Sorrow I shall never know.

Therefore in a single day her plagues shall come, death and sorrow, and famine, and by fire she shall be consumed; for mighty is the Lord God who judges her.'"
Here we are in the apocalyptic atmosphere of the first century of our era, which we find reflected both in the events and in the literature of the period. The circumstances can best be understood by the historian rather than the theologian.

1987 saw Hugh on his travels again starting with a trip to Malaysia including Sarawak (one of his closer associates and one-time President of the Mondcivitan Republic was Sir Anthony Brooke who was the last Raja of Sarawak). The trip was a gift from his daughter Joyce who accompanied him who accompanied him. Apparently, he was very impressed by his stay in a Long House on this trip where he was accompanied by Joyce and son-in-law Malcolm.

According to diary entries, there were regular visits to his physician Dr. Page in Golders Green. Daughter Marion lived in St. Albans and Audrey in Reigate. He reminded himself that on 6th January he should write to the Archbishop of Canterbury about Tutu. He had also arranged a meeting with a "Fred" (this may refer to Fred Levison) at Kings Cross Hotel Lounge at 3:30pm. He mentions that his tour was to start on 13th February, returning to London on 27th February. He met up with his grandson Barry on the 15th March and had Charles Pooley (who had been involved in the running of the Mondcivitan School at the Mondcivitan Headquarters and was a retired British Army Major) with his friends to lunch. On the 24th March Joseph Abileah arrived and met him at the Americana and he had a further meeting with him on the 28th March (the reader may remember that Joseph was a leading Mondcivitan who spent his life campaigning in Israel for a Confederation of the Middle East).

It seems as though some of the remnants from the active Mondcivitan days were taking interest in him and there is a note that Pedro Segura and Charles Pooley were to collect him at 2:30 on the 5th April. In that month he would entertain Mark Paterson to lunch, meet a Professor Kararlitzki (the author has not been able to identify who this was) and so on.

In an article in a Malaysian newspaper of 1st March, we find him still talking of being the president of the Mondcivitan Republic with citizens in over 40 countries. According to an article in a Penang newspaper he was there with his daughter and son-in-law on vacation.

Thereafter on to Jerusalem on the 15th April where he held talks on the *Passover Plot* on the 16th and 21st April at the Jerusalem Institute of Biblical Polemics. In the leaflet on the talks we read what we have already mentioned, that his Father was Major William Schonfield who recruited the Jewish Battalions under Allenby in recovering the Holy Land from the Turks and that he was for many years official historian of the Suez Canal Company and contributor to the Encyclopedia Britannica.

In an article in the Jerusalem Post dated 22nd April, when asked how he felt about the fact that the film version of the Passover Plot had been banned by the Israeli film censorship board, he said, "I am not surprised. It was a bad film. It didn't tell the story of my book at all"(the author remembers him making a similar remark to himself). In this article, Hugh discusses the issue of Luke's Gospel relating that "he had uncovered evidence 'never disclosed before' that the evangelist Luke 'borrowed' many incidents, ostensibly about the life of Jesus from the wars of the Roman-Jewish historian Josephus". In this article Hugh is described as "a member of a Liberal synagogue and that he was not uncritical about the Hebrew Bible". It also mentioned that "in the US the Catholic Church tried to keep him from appearing on radio and television".

As always, he prepared his talks carefully in advance and we are fortunate that the script of this interesting lecture given in Jerusalem has survived:

The Origin of the Gospels:

Today I am carrying a great burden of responsibility. I have to make disclosures about the Gospels in the New Testament of a sensational character. These establish that a great deal of what is related about Jesus, especially in the Gospels of Matthew, Luke and John is fictitious, and invented by the authors.

It is well-known that I have spent a lifetime in Christian origins research, and consequently what I am putting forward is not the views of a crank or one who is hostile to a very noble Jew. My conclusions rest on very solid grounds. But I have to speak here very simply, because some of you will be sincere believing Christians, while others will be Jews largely unfamiliar with the Christian Scriptures.

What are known as the Gospels are, in point of time, relatively late documents, and they are in the nature of short biographies offering information of what Jesus had said and done in the character of Messiah (Christ in Greek). This kind of composition was popular in the Graeco-Roman world near the beginning of the Christian Era. There have come down to us lives of the Caesars, and of sages like Apollonius of Tyana.

But writing a life of Jesus had not initially been thought of by his followers because in their belief, after his execution for a crime against the Roman Government, the tomb in which he was placed was found empty. It was held that like the Prophet Elijah he had been taken to Heaven, and would shortly return to Earth to set up his everlasting kingdom. Consequently there was no call for any story of his life to commemorate him. And one of his principal advocates, the Apostle Paul, seeking to win Gentiles to faith in Jesus, but not having known him personally, was concerned rather to suppress information about Jesus the man.

Picture 34: Sir Anthony Brooke

So it was not until a great many years had passed, and Jesus had failed to return to this world, that there was any call in the communities of his followers spread across the Roman Empire, and mostly Gentiles, for more detailed information about him.

By this time two things had happened. The stature of Jesus had grown to that of a divine person among pagan peoples who believed that gods came on earth in human form and that all rulers were divine. And secondly, factual information of the activities of the earthly Jesus were hard to come by because in the Jewish War to gain independence from the Romans in 67-70 CE the whole Land of Israel, and notably Galilee where Jesus had operated, had been devastated by the Roman forces, and the inhabitants largely killed or captured.

At the very time when more information about Jesus was being demanded this had become almost impossible to obtain. There was one source which had reached the Roman world before the war. This was due to the travels of a humble Galilean fisherman, who had been closely associated with Jesus during much of his activities. This man was Simon, nicknamed Kephus (Peter—the Rock), who could relate a number of stories of what Jesus had said and done. But he spoke the Galilean dialect of Aramaic, and required an interpreter, the Gospel writer whom we know as Mark.

According to early Christian tradition Mark later set down an account of Jesus from what he could remember of Peter's speeches, though not in the precise order of sayings and events. This document was published when it was most needed, after the

Jewish War with the Romans. In substance his account is represented by the Gospel of Mark in the New Testament. What is significant about this Gospel is that it contains no Nativity or Resurrection story. Also, what most Christians do not know, this Gospel breaks off abruptly in the middle of a sentence. This could be because of rough usage affecting the end of a MS roll, or because the Church did not like what was stated and removed it. New endings were later substituted, one of which is in the New Testament with which we are familiar, and reflects later orthodox views.

After the Jewish War with the Romans, several Gospels were written for different Christian communities in various parts of the Roman Empire, such as those attributed to Matthew, Luke and John. In these there were clear statements of their late composition. In the Preface to Luke, for instance, the author refers to many who previously had provided an account of the activities of Jesus, and he claims that his own researches provided more positive and reliable information. This statement, as I can now reveal is substantially a falsehood. With the destruction wrought by the Roman War the possibility of obtaining such information no longer existed. But something had happened which lent colour to our author's claim. This was the publication of the Works of the Jewish historian Josephus towards the close of the first century CE.

At that time, of course, there was no such collection of writings as the so-called New Testament. One of the reasons for the failure to discover what I am now disclosing is that when the New Testament was created an artificial arrangement of its elements was devised, namely the Gospels first, then the Acts of the Apostles, then the Letters of Paul, and so on. In fact, however, Luke and the Acts are not distinct works, but a single work in two parts which should not have been separated by the Gospel of John. This two-part work constituted a first attempt to create a "History of Christian Beginnings".

And it was inspired by the publication near the close of the first century CE of Josephus's compositions. One of these was a book in two parts known as *Against Apion*. Both parts are inscribed to a patron of Josephus. So Luke, as we must call him, though he was not the companion of Paul of that name, dedicated his own two part to a presumed patron the Most Excellent Theophilus (God-lover). Luke pretended to have access to circumstances in the life of Jesus by having access to Josephus's records. One of the distinctive aspects of Luke's Gospel is the way in which he continually brings in eminent Roman and Jewish personalities of the time, which give historical colour to what he relates. Where Luke many times differs from the other Gospels both in events and dates, this comes from the influence of Josephus. At the very beginning Jesus is not born in the reign of King Herod, as stated by Matthew. He is born ten years later when Quirinius was Roman Governor of Syria. At that time the Jews were subjected to a census for purpose of taxation. As Josephus relates this census was resisted by Judas of Galilee and his followers. The circumstances enabled Luke to make the parents of Jesus victims of the census, which brings them to David's city of Bethlehem for registration; and so Jesus as a descendant of King David can be born there and thus qualify as the Messiah.

Part of Luke's Nativity Story is borrowed from Josephus's account of the births of the Jewish Biblical heroes Samson and Samuel, and the incident of Jesus as a boy among the doctors of Jerusalem is based on what Josephus relates of his own youth in his autobiography. One story said by Luke to have been told by Jesus himself is the parable of the nobleman who went to seek a kingdom and return. But his people sent a deputation after him, to say: "We do not want this man to reign over us." This is based on what Josephus had related of Archelaus, the heir of Herod the Great, who because of his tyrannical behaviour was hated by the Jewish people. They did indeed send a deputation to Rome to Augustus Caesar to say that they did not want Archelaus as their ruler. The outcome was that Augustus, whom Herod had made his Executor, did not give the Judean throne to Archelaus until he should have proved worthy, and he was quietly deposed. Judea was made directly subject to Roman Government, linked to the Province of Syria.

In another part of Luke's Gospel an account is given of a Roman centurion whose servant was ill. The local Jews sent to Jesus to beg him to come and cure him because this centurion "loves our nation, and had our synagogue built for us himself." Jesus agrees to go, but while he is on the way, the centurion sends a message to him to say, that the centurion himself is unworthy of this favour. Jesus has only to speak a word and the servant will be healed. Luke puts into the centurion's mouth the words: "For I too am a man under authority, and I say to this one come and he comes, and to my servant do this, and he does it."

The incident derives from what Josephus narrates of Petronius the 'good' Roman governor of the Province in the reign of the Emperor Gaius Caligula. The mad emperor had planned to have his statue set up in the Temple at Jerusalem as an object of worship. The Jews sent a deputation to Petronius to intervene on their behalf. But he declared himself unable to do so as he too "was a man under authority" and must obey the emperor's orders. But finally he did yield to the Jewish pleas and agreed not to erect the statue and wrote to the emperor. Gaius was furious and wrote back to Petronius that he must carry out his orders or commit suicide. Somehow this letter was delayed, and another arrived first informing Petronius that Gaius had been murdered. There was great Jewish rejoicing at this relief, and Petronius was held to have been under a direct providence of God, who had saved him for his good action.

It is perhaps worthy of mention that in another place Josephus had written of three persons he knew who were crucified. Two of them died on the cross, but one survived and was restored to health. Did this suggest the two who were crucified with Jesus, but lost their lives while he had recovered?

As I have pointed out the author of Luke-Acts continually goes out of his way to make a parade of his knowledge of prominent persons and events to show how well informed he is. He does this even in relation to the trial of Jesus, for uniquely he mentions that Herod Antipas the ruler of Galilee was at Jerusalem for the Passover, and that Pontius Pilate tried to get him to take the case of Jesus, who as a Galilean was his subject. Thus the timely publication of the works of Josephus near the end of the first century CE provided a fund of information which the author of Luke's Gospel could utilise for his two-part history of Christian Beginnings, and enabled him not very honestly to claim that he had personally carried out an investigation of the circumstances from the beginning, and that therefore his version was more reliable than that of others who had written previously about Jesus. When "Luke" was writing the Land of Israel was in ruins as a result of the War with the Romans, and the newly published works of Josephus in the eighties of the first century CE provided the only readily available access to Jewish events before the war.

As I have already mentioned, even the two-part work Luke-Acts dedicated to a patron was suggested by the two part work *Against Apion* written by Josephus and similarly dedicated to a patron.

The investigation of the New Testament literature calls for the services of the trained and objective historian of the period rather than the theologian. And it is only now that such objective research has sufficiently advanced to begin to make this practicable.

I turn now to the document called the Gospel of John, the one most favoured by Christian theologians. Here quite different circumstances have been at work, and we have some assistance from early Christian tradition. Initially, however, we have to overcome the confusion created by the fact that several persons, all named John, are involved, actually three people.

As regards authorship of the Gospel there has been a natural Christian wish to identify the "Dear Disciple" of the Fourth Gospel with one of the two Galilean fisherman brothers James and John the sons of Zebedee. But the Gospel of John is a highly intellectual work quite beyond the capacity of such an individual.

The "Dear Disciple" John came from a high priestly family in Jerusalem and was a follower of John the Baptist. He then became associated with Jesus in extending the Baptist's proclamation of the coming Kingdom of God on earth. In this John, whose home was in Jerusalem, Jesus had an important contact with Jews in high places, including members of the Sanhedrin, persons like Nicodemus and Joseph of Arimathea. Eventually it was in this man's home at Jerusalem, on the Ophel, that Jesus celebrated the Last Seder. He was at the execution of Jesus by the Romans, and promised Jesus to take his mother Miriam into his own home and be a son to her. His house was to become the first headquarters of the Jewish followers of Jesus as Messiah, the movement headed by the next younger brother of Jesus called Jacob (James).

But I must jump a number of years. Shortly before the siege of Jerusalem the leaders of the followers of Jesus, including his first cousin Simeon, fled to the north to take refuge with the Zadokites there. The John I am speaking of was to settle at Ephesus in Asia Minor. There, according to Christian tradition, when he was a very old man he was asked to dictate his recollection of Jesus. Unfortunately these memoirs fell into the hands of a local Gentile Christian, also called John, who was very ambitious, and is known to us as John the Presbyter. As late as the fourth century of the Christian Era the tombs of both Johns were shown at Ephesus, as related by Eusebius in his Church History.

Three letters of this Gentile John are in the New Testament, and if we compare them with John's Gospel we can realise that the style of writing is substantially the same. The speeches of Jesus in John's Gospel, notably the long speeches to the Jews and to the Apostles, are in the Greek manner, alien to the Hebrew idiom and style Jesus employed, as shewn in the other Gospels. Moreover, this alien Jesus betrays himself by speaking to the Jews of "your Law" (when of course Jesus would have said "our Law") and also using such words as "all who came before me were thieves and robbers." Some bits are left, of course, of the Jewish John's recollections, which gave colour to the fraud.

The resultant divine Jesus has of course appealed to Gentiles, who therefore love the fourth Gospel more than the others. In tracking down the devices of this Gentile John it is to be noted that in the resurrection story in this Gospel the author uniquely makes Jesus appear to the Apostles, showing them his wounds from crucifixion, that he is no ghost. We are given the story of Doubting Thomas, who when he is convinced exclaims "My Lord and my God", according deity to Jesus. Now it so happens that it was made public not long before the Gentile John was writing how the Roman Emperor Domitian had claimed to be divine. His mania was so acute that he insisted that when his officials wrote to him they should always address him as "Our Lord and God Domitian". Hence the words put into the mouth of Thomas.

But we have a further link in this Gospel with the activities of the Roman Government. The successor of Domitian was the Emperor Trajan, and from his reign we have a letter from the Younger Pliny, who was governor of the Roman Province of Bithynia. He reported to Trajan that he had examined some Christians about their doctrine. They told him, as Pliny puts it, "that they met on a certain day before it was light, and sang an antiphonal chant to Christ as to a god."

Such an antiphonal chant was actually made the opening of John's Gospel, where Jesus is the light which drives away darkness. The text is in antiphonal form. A line is chanted by a precentor, and the congregation makes the response line. In my translation of the Gospel (The Original New Testament) I have restored the hymn's antiphonal structure.

There is much more to be done by objective non-theological research to recover the true story of Christian Beginnings, to trace out how a patriotic Jewish Movement of the first century of the Christian Era, which believed that Jesus ben Joseph descended from King David was the awaited Messiah, ultimately became an alien predominantly Gentile religion in which this Jesus was worshipped as Saviour and God incarnate.

We have to face the fact of fraud in the process of transition, a process which started quite early as I have shown. Indeed Paul, the Envoy to the Gentiles, himself had had to complain of letters forged in his name, and he was not the only one to suffer in this way. In the late second century we find Dionysius bishop of Corinth declaring, "As the brethren desired me to write epistles, I did so, and these the apostles of the devil have filled with tares, exchanging some things and adding others, for whom there is a woe reserved. It is not, therefore, matter of wonder, if some have also attempted to adulterate the sacred writings of the Lord, since they have attempted the same in other works which are not to be compared with these." The Book of Revelation in the New Testament was forced to put a curse on anyone who added or took away from the words of the text. As long as anyone is willing to endorse the bogus as an aid to faith there can be no prospect of Malchut Shamaim (the Kingdom of God), peace in our distracted world.

My experience here in Jerusalem with its false identification of places with New Testament personalities and events shows how far mankind has still to go before faith and honesty unite. We clearly need the historian and archaeologist to recover the past as it really was and give us a new understanding of individuals who have contributed so impressively to the human story as Jesus did. It has become a Jewish obligation to promote research which will restore him to his rightful place in Jewish history, and eliminate the pagan inventions for which the Christian Church has been responsible.

Hugh J. Schonfield

April 1987

He flew back to London on the 23rd so it must have been a short and hectic trip, especially at his age. The family had prepared a birthday surprise on the 29th April and Marion collected him at 7pm. There was the note of Barry's wedding on the 4th May and many lunch appointments with his daughters Marion, Audrey and Joyce in his diary entries. He was attending the National Heart Hospital as an outpatient for his heart condition and taking medication prescribed by them.

And My Eyes Shall See Jerusalem Once More

Charlyne had accompanied him on the trip to Jerusalem which had been arranged by Joseph Margulies, and he wrote in a letter of April 29th of his gratitude to her for looking after him. He is beginning to see the end in sight and writes:

> All my life I have been under guidance, and have sought to be faithful at all costs. But I know now that old as I am I shall not see the full fruits, since these cannot come while I live. My responsibility was to carry on despite rejection, knowing there would be times of joy and times of deep suffering. You have had your share of both. I expect much from Willi when he is ready.

This is tainted with a certain feeling of failure and disappointment. We know he was sorry that Willi did not want to do things his way.

He was pretty short of cash after his return from Israel and wrote to Mark Paterson on the same day, hoping that Mark had found a publisher for two books he had written. He said that he had started on a challenging work entitled *Gospel Untruth*.

In his letter to Charlyne of 16th May, in talking about the people he was addressing in Israel, he points out:

> The circumstances do symbolise the position that has to be overcome, where for nearly two thousand years Christianity has substituted a religion in place of a nation and a man-god in place of a messiah. The world cannot come to peace and harmony until the Servant-Nation of Mankind is reborn and carries out its function. But evidently that time is not yet.

So one could ask if Hugh was already beginning to realise that things were not going to happen as he had hoped and predicted. The world of 1987 was a completely different place than 1956. In this letter he goes on to reminisce:

> I was given the function half a century ago of reaffirming this ancient truth and experimentally bringing the Servant-Nation back into operation. What was achieved and symbolized in the Mondcivitan Republic will remain on record. But it has been proved by those who responded to the call that they could not adjust their minds to the concept and devote themselves to the building of such a Servant-Nation, with all that it called for in structure and activity of a unique kind, political and mediatorial. No individual Mondcivitan or group of Mondcivitans has taken up the challenge and gone into action on the basis of our Constitution.

Here it does seem that Hugh had finally come to terms with the fact that the Republic as he envisaged it just was not going to happen – at least not in his lifetime. This was the essence of the battle with Willi who, seeing the writing on the wall, felt that the structural concept had to be radically changed if the Servant-Nation was going to happen in our modern world in any way. On the other hand, Hugh felt he had the blueprint set in stone which had to be fulfilled exactly that way. He goes on to write (on Mondcivitan Republic headed paper carrying the address of his flat):

> I do not complain. But I must face up to reality. And that means that unless some of our citizens now come forward the Mondcivitan Republic will go into cold storage. Everyone will shortly receive a notification. But I have arranged that the record will have an expression as a witness to mankind, when I die.

> There are things on which I now have to concentrate, chiefly the folly by which a religion took the place of a nation, the people of God, concentrating on personal salvation rather than that of humanity. It is our planet which has to be redeemed, so that it can perform its predestined function in God's Universe. A servant-nation, a nation of world citizens, has to pioneer the way forward.

In a way, this last paragraph could be interpreted as opening the way for a different and more fundamental approach but he was aware that during his lifetime he would not be able to call the necessary changes. He had a vision which he put into practice as far as he was able. It would be up to others after him to take up the banner and then perhaps make a practical interpretation in a different way. The whole of the World Citizen movement had fallen much into obscurity by now and old methods of arbitration and diplomacy which had been prevalent back since the monarchies, were giving way to destabilization and fragmentation. The age of so-called terrorism was beginning to dawn.

In July 1987 Hugh had been unwell and had to have a pacemaker fitted. He writes (28th July 1987) to Mark Paterson:

> ".. the pace-maker should last about 17 years, which should be more than ample to see me out, and complete my writing programme".

He obviously had money problems as earnings were down. He mentioned that Joseph Margulies had paid his expenses for the lecture tour in Israel. At this point he also mentions the "startling discovery I have made of the borrowings of Luke from the contemporary histories of Judaism" (see above). He writes, "I need funds *very* badly".

Amazingly, he seemed to make a quick recovery and he wrote to Mark on August the 7th saying in a postscript,

> I am now fit again, though a bit weak in the legs, after my heart operation to insert a pacemaker and getting back to work.

By September he was back to blaming "our citizens" and writes to Charlyne on the 29th:

> "My great grief is that the Mondcivitan Republic has been let down by its citizens and will cease with my death. People still apply to join, but I cannot let them with no support. And yet the world sorely needs The Servant-Nation of Mankind".

By 12th November in a letter to her he writes:

> I have now made the tremendous discovery that much of the Gospel of Luke is a fraud. [See above]. As regards Mondcivitan matters still await a more positive commitment by our citizens. One man cannot build a nation, not even a Servant-Nation."

And that was the point, there were really no active citizens and there had not been for a very long time. Hugh seemed to be unable to face this reality.

He mentions in a letter to Charlyne dated December 3rd that the *New Testament* has been successfully translated into Spanish. He suggests starting French translations of *After the Cross*. He also says:

> There is urgent need for me at my age (86) to hand over the work of the Mondcivitan Republic to younger citizens, and I am seeking guidance to achieve this. I have carefully not used our funds to support myself. So that now there is nearly £10,000 available.

It is not clear what he expected Charlyne to do about it, even with that money available, as he had little contact with anybody else who had been involved by now.

What is of particular note is that it was in this year that Hugh wrote what was to be his last book – *Jesus Man-Mystic-Messiah* which was first published posthumously in 2004 by the Open Gate Press. This book contains a considerable amount of autobiographical information. There is a sense where his identification with what he saw as Jesus' messianic mission had become fused to his own. The book relates, as is stated on the back cover, "the story of Hugh Schonfield's search for the historical Jesus and the Jewish origins of Christianity". In the introduction he writes:

> As I prepare this book for publication, with my eighty-sixth birthday behind me, I am very conscious of the long road I have travelled, and all the books I have written as milestones along it. Many of them relate to an obsession of mine, in time past an unusual one for a Jew, to comprehend the person of Jesus, especially in the character of Jewish Messiah. What Jesus was, and even whether he existed, is again being hotly and publicly debated as I write, and of course I have been caught up in this controversy. Unfortunately, it seems to be extremely difficult for those involved to transfer themselves to the time and country of Jesus and to experience the impact of the contemporary Last Times convictions. Instead they plunge into theology, or consider him as a sage, or as the central figure in a miracle play. Anything but adapt to **his** conscious concerns[1].

And again:

> Moreover, I had the advantage of being, like Jesus, a Jew but not a rabbinist. That is to say, I was—so to speak—on the inside of Jewish ideology, having a native competence to comprehend and share a great many of his convictions and concerns. Also, as it happened, I was from childhood deeply drawn towards the messianic, and by no means hidebound by tradition and religious orthodoxy. For this I should no doubt in large part thank my British background, and on the maternal side some inclination towards freethinking.[2]

Just how important this book was and as evidence that Hugh Schonfield was a scholar without comparison combined with a spiritual example is best described in the words of Robert M. Price's review of the book:

> I recall how my eighth grade Physics professor responded to my teen-age fundamentalist zeal by recommending Hugh J. Schonfield's The Passover Plot. At that time I did not know that this was neither the first nor the last book the indefatigable Schonfield would have written on the subject of Jesus the Nazorean. All I knew then was that here was the voice of doubt. I recall how a fellow fideist warned me, "Don't read that book—it's poison!" That is, the book was inimical to a faith fortified with ignorance. Many years later, teaching a freshman New Testament course at Drew University, I assigned the book. It duly shocked many of the students, though – by this time I recognized how essentially conservative was Schonfield's treatment of the gospels and their historical value.
>
> In the meantime I had read many more works by other scholars on the search for the Jesus of history, and I had come to espouse alternative theories, far to the left of Hugh Schonfield's. And yet it was only after these many years, having read much of the scholarship Schonfield himself appealed to (e.g., the similarly underrated Robert Eisler) that I fully appreciated what vast and deep erudition Schonfield had brought to his task. Among his other books, *According to the Hebrews, Those Incredible Christians,*

---

1 Schonfield, Hugh J. (2004) *Jesus Man-Mystic-Messiah*, The Open Gate Press, London, p.1.
2 Schonfield, Hugh J. (2004) *Jesus Man-Mystic-Messiah*, The Open Gate Press, London, p.4.

The Authentic New Testament, and *The Essene Odyssey* top my list, though I have to admit I love them all. The author was always able to dredge up some eye-popping piece of esoterica no other scholar had considered. I soon learned how little it mattered that the serious student agree with every point, even the main point, of a book. The thing is to find fresh food for thought and to encounter new perspectives not presented in the stale tomes of the orthodox and conventional.

Even in this, his last (and posthumously published) manuscript, Hugh Schonfield manages to stir the pot anew. Out came my underlining pen. Never looked at it *that* way before! And this is so, even though the book is his most basic one on Jesus. He devotes a succinct passage or two to the accuracy of the gospels, the principles to be employed in cutting away mythical accretions, and the great gulf that lies between the original Jewishness of Jesus and his gospel and the Gentile Christian reinterpretation of it. Schonfield's work is rooted firmly in a particular generation of New Testament criticism, that of Rendel Harris, R.H. Strachan, R.H. Charles, and others. On the whole, his estimate of the gospels recalls that of Adolf Harnack: even after you subtract the legendary and Hellenistic distortions, you have enough left to reconstruct a striking historical figure. But when it comes to the teaching and mission of Jesus, Schonfield was much closer to Albert Schweitzer. Both rejected Harnack's view that apocalyptic belief was merely window-dressing for an essentially moral message. Both Schweitzer and Schonfield, apparently independently, came to understand Jesus as a preacher of national renewal and restoration.[3]

All this is evidence that Hugh's mind was just as clear as it had ever been.

On the 2nd January 1988 he once again wrote to Charlyne and stated:

This year in which please God I will reach 87, promises to be one of the busiest in my life, with many things reaching completion. I now have four lectures to give, two in Israel in February followed by a little holiday at Eilat, one lecture in London In March, and another in Canada in April. On top of this I have to work on new discoveries I have made affecting the Christian Story and calling for a new book. Then I have to finalise the affairs of the Mondcivitan Republic.

The last entry in his diary is on the 8th January "Audrey about teatime".

In his letter to Charlyne dated 15th January, he states his concern that she might even not represent his actual position:

This is to answer yours of the 15th, which makes me continue to be concerned that you represent my actual position, not what you believe to be my position. I must make absolutely clear that my function is that of historian, recovering the facts about Jesus and the Early Christians, compared with the fancies of Christianity as a Religion. This has become essential.

Jesus was a Jew, descended from King David, who believed he was the Messiah, the ultimate Jewish monarch. His subsequent pagan followers, for whom a King of the Jews had no significance, made him superhuman and then accorded him Deity as the Second Person of a Trinity.

The Passover Plot had to be the first of my books on this theme, to get the person and activities of Jesus in their correct historical perspective and counter the New

---

3   http://www.robertmprice.mindvendor.com/reviews/schonfield_jesus_mmm.htm, accessed 24th July 2014.

Testament theological imaginations. Religious opinions had to be set completely aside. It was as King of the Jews, rebel against Caesar, that Jesus was crucified.

The Passover Plot discloses how Jesus planned with his eminent Jewish friends in Jerusalem to escape death on the cross by means of a drug administered to him. Gaining from Pilate possession of his body it could be placed in a rich man's tomb above ground and therefore ventilated. Jesus would be taken out at night by Essene (healer) friends, and later he would rejoin his followers in Galilee. The plan worked perfectly, but it had overlooked one matter, the zeal of a Roman Soldier at the cross, who stabbed Jesus to make sure he was dead before handing him over to Joseph of Arimathea and Nicodemus. It is a very dramatic story, and fully explains the empty tomb and why Jesus was expected to rejoin his followers in Galilee. You cannot say "Jesus did not die on the cross". He did not die by crucifixion but by the spear wound the soldier inflicted.

The main point of my book is the plot to which Jesus was a party to save him from death by crucifixion and restore him to his followers in Galilee. I must not speculate about what would have happened if the plot had succeeded, as it turned out the disappearance from the tomb of the body of Jesus—the tomb found open and empty on Sunday morning—would give rise to the resurrection story, and thus in a strange way enabled the followers of Jesus to believe in him even more positively as the Messiah.

Faith had it that he had been taken to heaven, but at the appropriate time would return to set up the Kingdom of God on Earth.

The whole of the Passover Plot is an exciting story, which my book tells—for the first time. And this leads to consequences brought out in the other books.

So here we have the evidence in Hugh's own words – the *Passover Plot* idea is linked to issues brought out in other books. This is particularly true of *The Politics of God* and in fact it is a cornerstone of the Servant-Nation ideology. Hugh wanted Charlyne to translate the *Passover Plot* into French and was convinced that it would cause a sensation in France. This seems to have been his last letter to Charlyne.

On the 24th January 1988 Hugh Joseph Schonfield passed away.

Life Beyond Death

There were many obituaries written in honour of Hugh.

In his will he left 100 pounds each to Willi Haller and Peter Deed and 250 pounds to the Society of Authors.

His ashes were spread in India, Africa and America as Hugh had insisted that his ashes be scattered at the four corners of the earth with part of them near Hélène's. There was a service for the Nigerian ashes held at the Unitarian Brotherhood Church in Lagos on 4th June 1989 and presided over by Rev. Supt. Soyombo-Abowaba (and two others). In this context a short history and sermon were recited. On Hugh and Hélène's memorial in the cemetery the inscription, "They loved Mankind and each other" is to be found.

His sister Marion composed this Memoriam:

IN MEMORY OF DR. HUGH SCHONFIELD—VISIONARY WITH A BLUEPRINT FOR PEACE

From an early age my Father, Hugh Schonfield, felt intuitively that he was destined to have a mission.

His Jewish background followed by a study of Divinity at Glasgow University and later scholarly researches into the early Christian era gave Schonfield an insight into the messianic concept.

During a mystical revelation shortly before the second world war (an experience of which he never spoke publicly until decades later) the certainty was conveyed to him that mankind was indeed part of a Divine Plan and that there was a need for a new "messianism" which would translate the ancient Biblical vision of the Israelites as a "holy nation", by means of which all nations would be blessed, into a contemporary and practical form. The instrument in bringing about the desired peace and harmony between peoples was to be the creation of a holy or Servant-Nation. The citizens of the Servant-Nation would be citizens of the world with no territory to defend or political axe to grind; they would be a living example of nationhood at its best and consequently would be invited to staff the specialised agencies of the U. N., to become the trustees for human rights and the repository of international agreements and conventions. In short the Servant-Nation would be a kind of ombudsman for mankind.

There followed the preparatory years when good people responded to the vision and finally in 1956 the Commonwealth of World Citizens (later to be known as the Mondcivitan Republic) was born at the Temple of Peace in Cardiff, attracting considerable attention from the media.

Hugh Schonfield had very definite beliefs about the form the infant nation should take. This was not to be an amorphous body of well-meaning "world citizens" scattered around the globe, but a tightly structured landless nation with a Government, Ministers, Ambassadors and all the necessary trappings of protocol that would make possible the essential communication with the Governments of nation states. Over the years the Mondcivitan Republic made recommendations to the United Nations and to the great powers with a view to solving problems such as the Cuban crisis, N. Ireland, the Middle East. It was the practice not to intervene unless first-hand knowledge of the circumstances had been obtained and a proposal for settlement arrived at that was equally fair to both sides.

Schonfield's statesmanlike qualities were a great asset.

Mondcivitans also recognised that while conflicts were aroused by differences in race, class and creed yet there existed in mankind a corrective spirit of altruistic humanitarianism and disinterested service whereby division could be converted into harmony.

To be a true citizen of my father's Servant-Nation required an exceptional degree of selflessness, dedication, insight and objectivity that only a comparatively small number understandably achieved and to them, and their loyalty and continued witness we must pay tribute. Sadly the noble concept of a messianic people to bring peace and harmony to earth proved to be ahead of its time; this was naturally a source of disappointment to its founder in his last years when he also feared lest the original vision should become blurred by departures from his blueprint after he was gone.

Despite the troubled times in which he lived my father was an eternal optimist with zest for life and a great sense of fun. He firmly believed that the inherent goodness implanted in man by the Creator would finally triumph, and his convictions and shining example will surely continue to inspire his followers and all who strive for international peace and understanding. Hugh Schonfield the free spirit and original thinker will be sadly missed by all who knew and worked with him.

Marion Singer

In the *Times* of the 26th January 1988 the following obituary was published:

DR HUGH SCHONFIELD
Maverick biblical scholar

Dr Hugh Schonfield, biblical scholar and historian, died on January 24th at the age of 86.

With his iconoclastic views on the Christian story as expounded in the Gospels, Schonfield was a thorn in the side of orthodoxy. No Christian mystery, however sacred, was safe from his controversial historical methods of inquiry.

Thus, in his estimate. Christ had tried to fake his death on the Cross, to leave himself free to "reappear" to his disciples after his death; the successful first century "takeover" of the Church by the Christians of Rome was based on forgeries of letters purporting to come from both St Peter and St Paul, and large chunks of the Gospel according to St Luke were, in fact, plagiarised wholesale from the writings of the Jewish historian, Josephus.

Such doctrinal hand grenades left shrapnel embedded deep in the viscera of believers. Commuted reviewers either savaged or derided Schonfield's works, and in parts of fundamentalist America where he—perhaps not altogether prudently—attempted to expound his "non-religious" interpretation of the Christian story, he was roughly handled by audiences.

Schonfield was born of Jewish parentage on May 17. 1901. But he was not a practising Jew, and his "anti-Christian" standpoint came from no deep-rooted hostility to the religion (he was no kinder about Judaism). It came rather from an impish insistence on dispassionate "historical" scrutiny of things which are, for many, matters of faith.

After going to St. Paul's School and Glasgow University Schonfield worked for several years in publishing at Michael Joseph. Among his early books was a history of Jewish Christianity.

Many aspects of the Middle East's past and present interested him. In 1940 he wrote a book about Italian foreign policy in the region; he was an authority on the Victorian explorer Richard Burton, and wrote a biography of him. Later in life, he published a history of the Suez Canal on the hundredth anniversary of its opening.

During the war he worked for a time with the Near East Department of the Ministry of Information.

After the war he settled down to a career as an author and broadcaster, turning out a stream of works, many in the popular style. In the 1950s, he wrote a series of newspaper articles interpreting the recently discovered Dead Sea Scrolls to a lay public, and they were later published as a book The Bible Was Right.

He also dedicated himself to the cause of world peace, through that non-proselytizing pressure group, the Commonwealth of World Citizens, and through the International Arbitration League. He was once nominated for the Nobel Peace Prize.

Although much of his earlier writing had been of a nature to make the severer sort of scholar look askance, Schonfield's elevation to bête noire status did not come until 1965, with the publication of The Passover Plot. This adumbrated the theory that before the crucifixion, Jesus had arranged to be drugged, and taken down speedily from the Cross by Joseph of Arimathea. This plan, according to Schonfield, misfired when Jesus was pierced by the spear and did actually die from his sufferings.

Outfacing the scepticism of reviewers and the outrage of the faithful The Passover Plot became an immediate best seller, and two million copies were sold here and in the USA. It is supposed to have prompted John Lennon's famous remark that the Beatles were more popular than Jesus Christ.

A great publicist. Schonfield thoroughly enjoyed the controversy he had stirred up. The book's successor, Those Incredible Christians, a story of plot and counter-plot among the early Christians, indicated that he was in a far from repentant mood.

Schonfield continued fertile with ideas, both impish and scholarly, almost until the end. His translation of the New Testament which appeared in 1985, was acknowledged as a landmark, even by those who could not agree with its radical, historical reinterpretation of the Christian story.

Schonfield had a number of books in preparation at the time of his death.

His wife died some years ago. He is survived by three daughters.

A response to this obituary also appeared in the *Times*:

> The admirable obituary (January 26) of the late Dr Hugh Schonfield omitted to say very much about the character of the man—other than mentioning his "impishness" and his love of publicity Hugh was one of the world's carers: for his, and his wife, Hélène's love of people, this correspondent, and no doubt many others who benefitted from their kindness, have reason to be immeasurably grateful. While he was undoubtedly a thorn in the side of Christian orthodoxy, he was far more im-

portantly, a person who lived according to the teaching in the Sermon on the Mount,

It is possibly not common knowledge that Hugh owned to having been baptised.

Picture 35: CND Peace Symbol

(Whether by water or simply by the Spirit of God on a September afternoon in Staines, is not clear.) As a Christian, this correspondent believes that, anointed with the Holy Spirit, Hugh was called by God to be a friend to all who came his way, whatever their colour, race, class or creed—a practical citizen of the world if ever there was one. And if some of his writings were an anathema, even heresy, to orthodox Christians, who can say that he was not also called to make us followers of Jesus THINK?

If our Christian faith cannot stand up to the admittedly scorching inquiry of one such as Hugh Schonfield, then its value might appear to be questionable.

J.M.

In the obituary from *The Independent* from 29th January 1988, there is the interesting statement that "He founded the Peace Publishing Company, in which he had the support of H.G. Wells, whom he greatly admired".

On the 4th February, at the funeral, Marion spoke of her father:

> Hugh loved life. He wrote: "the enrichment I have received being permitted to see and enjoy the world of my fellows with love and in confident faith has been beyond all expectation."

> Hugh's boundless optimism, his confidence that God's divine plan as he saw it for mankind would come to pass, and the conviction he had been called to be instrumental in bringing it about, formed the credo for his book *The Politics of God*. Therein he expounded his faith in the essential goodness of the human race (in spite of so much evidence to the contrary) and his visionary concept of a new and independent breed of people; men and women of every colour and creed whose prior allegiance and service would be given not to nation states but to humanity as a whole; a people whose character would be representative of citizenship of the world.

Thus today Hugh's coffin is draped with the colours of the servant-nation he sought to create—the Mondcivitan Republic or Commonwealth of World Citizens.

Sadly this dream was not to be fully realised in his lifetime. Aware that his remaining days were few, Hugh lately re-issued the call that appears in the epilogue of his books "Godness has decreed for us 'not by power, not by might, but by his spirit'. Who is ready to respond?"

Surely, as he wrote: "... at some future time... the Divine Plan will be fulfilled, because that purpose and design embodies the principles which raise men up to the stature of the children of God. It is for each one of us to choose whether we will make God's will our own today".

Now Hugh's call remains, as a gauntlet thrown into the ring of eternity. He has gone, but by instructing that some of his ashes be dispersed on the lands of Africa, America and India he hoped that something of himself would remain as a link between the four quarters of the world and a symbol of its unity.

Peter Deed, who had been the last Secretary General of the Mondcivitan Republic, recollected his thoughts on Hugh in his obituary:

Hugh J. Schonfield and I

In the middle of 1971 I read a book entitled *The Politics of God*, it became affectionately known as "POG". Having read this book I found an address to write to for further information 27 Delancey Street, London NW1 7RX. So I wrote and was invited to a meeting held there. It was an interesting experience. There were a few citizens in attendance. It was at this meeting I first came into contact with Hugh Schonfield. I found him to be a very humble person with a brilliant mind, a lot of love and vision of the future.

A short while later I attended my second meeting. A good number of topics were including that of needing a new secretary. Having been employed in the hotel industry for 20 years I volunteered to fill the post of secretary. I didn't know what I was letting myself in for, first of all I had to learn how to use a typewriter, this was followed by learning about the files which contained much information of our citizens. Hugh would visit the office frequently with snippets of information, I found him a very easy person to get along with. He always came up with some good suggestions. One of them was that I should visit our citizens in the U.S.A.

So I embarked on my first real mission for the Mondcivitan Republic. I told our citizens what our plans were for me to visit the U.S.A. and I made an appeal for my fare through our monthly newsletter. This was a step of faith and through the appeal the money was donated. Whilst in the U.S.A. I visited a group of World Federalists in San Francisco I also visited a good number of citizens. Hugh Schonfield asked me to convey his greeting and love to those I met, which of course I did. I found our citizens very hospitable and friendly, some of whom I am still in touch with to this very day.

Following my visit to the U.S.A. Hugh decided that instead of being called the General Secretary I should have the title of Secretary General. During my time spent with Hugh I discovered that he had quite a subtle sense of humour. There was one occasion where I complained to him that our citizens were always asking "what is headquarters doing" about a certain situation to which he replied "ask them what the hindquarters were doing", this was followed by him giving a huge burst of laughter. He loved to laugh at his own jokes.

I found my time working for the Mondcivitan Republic of great interest, some of it doing a lot of research and which turned out of great interest whilst at other times it could be boring. One great goal for me was producing and editing the Mondcivitan Republic News Letter. I never failed in finding news items. This was a monthly task. Hugh very often would just drop into the office to see what and how I was doing. Apart from producing the monthly news letter we also held monthly meetings at 27 Delancey Street. These were good for meeting our citizens. Most times there would be Willi Haller who was a great inspiration to us all with his great ideas and suggestions. Also there was Phylis Corke who visited the office once a weeks to help me with the accounts of The Cremer Housing Association Ltd. Of course also there was Steve and Sandy Deed (who later became Steve and Sandy Engelking). Hugh Schonfield was always the Chairman at these meetings. About six years into my employ with the Republic we held a General Assembly Conference at an hotel in Surrey which lasted three days. This went off very well......

…..I continued to see Hugh from time to time. It was very sad when his wife Hélène died. He was a totally undomesticated person so I used to go down to his flat in Hyde Park Square and cook his evening meals for him, this was a great pleasure due to the fact that before I began my work with the Republic I was a hotel chef. Hugh by this time had taken over all the work I had been doing but it was very sad that he didn't have much support. Although his vision of building a Servant-Nation in the early years took off with some acclaim, it never really did reach it's goal so I feel he died a very sad man. I don't think he will be forgotten because he was an eminent scholar and an author of many books that he wrote as a biblical historian.

His work did not end with that last moment of life and there was much unfinished business to deal with.

There was the possibility of a new film version of the Passover Plot being discussed in a letter from Mark Paterson to Charlyne and an exchange of letters in April 1988 with Richard Attenborough about the use of Hugh's book *Richard Burton Explorer* from 1936 for a feature film[1]. Apparently the rumour that he was planning a film had spread[2] but the author has found no evidence that it was ever actually produced.

Hugh's daughter Marion had to deal with all the archive materials and discussed this with Boston University Mugar Memorial Library where the archives are stored. Apparently, Hugh was well acquainted with Howard Gotlieb, director of the Library and the contract with them had been made during Hugh's lifetime in 1970. Hugh's ashes were to be scattered on the Boston University Campus where "he visited with such pleasure and where he was received with great honour and enthusiasm". Marion was also a trustee of the Hugh and Hélène Schonfield World Service Trust as was the author and Peter Deed. There was a flow of correspondence between the three of us also on what to do with the Mondcivitan archives which were finally transferred to Germany where they were scanned and finally deposited with the Bishopsgate Institute in London. Thus the Hugh Schonfield personal archives together with the correspondence with his publishers can be accessed in Boston and the Mondcivitan Republic and International Ar-

---

1 This book has since been republished by the Schonfield Trust.
2 http://adamjones.freeservers.com/burton.htm (accessed 6th July 2014)

bitration League documents can be accessed at the Bishopsgate Institute. This material has been extensively used in the preparation of this biography.

In 1989 (20th January) Fred Levision wrote to Hugh's daughter Audrey:

> .... When I met your father (just before he was in Malaysia) he kindly gave me a copy of the *Pentecost Revolution* which is full of insights and splendidly written. I have to say, of course, that I think he got it wrong about Jesus! Perhaps the writer of the obituary in *The Telegraph* expressed his position well – and it was a heart-warming one - "While claiming to be Jewish, he adored Christ, though with reservations. Christ, he believed, was the Lord's anointed and divinely inspired, but not the Son of God."
>
> Neither Christ nor my father will have rejected him (as the [Hebrew Christian] Alliance unfortunately did) "on the other side".

He is of course relating to the incident where Hugh and Hélène were expelled from the Hebrew-Christian Alliance. Obviously, even after all these years and Hugh and Hélène's deaths, this was still a sore point as great injustice had been done. Hugh and Hélène had been very deeply hurt by what transpired and the dogmatic attitude taken by the Alliance. With hindsight though we can say that it worked in such a way that it led Hugh to take a new path and develop his understanding of the messianic concept of a Servant-Nation which is probably his greatest discovery and contribution to the understanding of Jesus and his times.

In 1989 the Brazilian rights for *Essene Odyssey* were awarded to a Brazilian publisher so now Mark Paterson was working for the Schonfield estate and in 1991 *After the Cross* was published by Element Books. There was a proposal to make a documentary film on the Passover Plot by the American Nation Film Company. It was to have a budget of over 658 thousand US dollars and be completed by January 1992. Joseph Margulies was involved in this project. Joseph was Sales and Marketing Manager of Canada Allied Diesel Company Ltd and had long supported Hugh on various projects as described above. The film company was run by Tad Danielewski who was Polish born and had served in the Polish underground in the Second World War, being interned in a concentration camp. He died in 1993 and that is probably the reason why we find no evidence that this film was ever made. According to IMDb, his last production was in 1983[3].

A number of books were published posthumously like *Proclaiming the Messiah: The Letters of Paul of Tarsus, Envoy to the Nations* by Open Gate Press in 1999 as well as *The Mystery of the Messiah* in the same year and *Jesus: Man-Mystic-Messiah* in 2004, all by the same publisher. Since then the Schonfield World Service Trust has, with the permission of the Schonfield Estate, republished (and continues to do so) a number of books which otherwise would be out of print and also made these available in e-Book format. There is still a lively interest in Schonfield's research and writings even if the books will never again attain the success of *The Passover Plot*. A small international group has, at the time of writing, been making a move to restore the idea of the Servant-Nation and making use of social media. If the possibilities of internet and social media had been available back in the early days of its inception, then things may have turned out differently for the nation which was so dear to Hugh Schonfield's heart.

---

3   http://www.imdb.com/name/nm0199756/

Some Last Thoughts

The reader has to be left to judge whether I have been able to bring this personality to life once again. If this book encourages one to take a look at some of Schonfield's writings and ideas or to think about what role one might have in making the dream of that servant nation which so inspired Hugh Schonfield become a reality, then I will be satisfied.

After all these years of engagement with this body of understanding, I am left wondering whether Hugh Schonfield will just go down in the annals of the forgotten. It would seem that very few have been able to grasp his fundamental message and interpret it for this age just as those that came after Jesus have failed to grasp and implement his teaching and aims.

Perhaps it is the fate of all such men and women that they be misunderstood, misinterpreted and even persecuted. It would seem that we would prefer to worship our heroes rather than listening to what they have to say and then trying to put it into practice.

In a moment of contemplation of this conviction Hugh Schonfield once wrote:

> The service of my life has been devoted to two major activities which are closely related. Through one of them I have delved into the past, and through the other I have projected myself into the future. Both activities have been concerned with a philosophy of life, the detection of a progressive purpose in the story of mankind, which illuminated the way ahead and inspired the particular contribution I have made to the promotion of a united world.
>
> It is no credit to me that I have engaged in these pursuits, since as I must disclose, though the telling is with great reluctance, I have been impelled to do so by promptings I could not disobey. Some who know me have been puzzled, and even irked, by my confidence and assurance in many things I have said and done, especially as what I advocated was frequently in conflict with prevailing opinion and sometimes contrary to my own natural attitude of mind. Very rarely, and never completely, could I bring myself to say what was at the back of my convictions, preferring to seek for convincing arguments in favour of what I contended. If reasoning did not succeed it would be unlikely that a revelation of my experiences would do so. This would certainly be true of the majority, and it would have been of no help in my work to be thought of as peculiar and visionary. I should have gathered around me almost inevitably some who would be chiefly interested in the experiences, which they would relate to their own spiritual systems and concepts, and there would be included those who would claim me as one of high spiritual degree.
>
> While I feel that I ought no longer to be silent about what has so largely been responsible for my outlook and activities, since it explains how my life and thinking has been shaped, I have to make clear my belief that I have been used, as many others have been and will be, because it was necessary, and not because I am of any special consequence. Those who do not know me may be assured that I have a full measure of defects, and I beg them to lay no stress whatever on what would be completely false, an assumption that I have in any way merited my employment. Of what good things may be said of me, one, I suppose, is that I have resolutely refused to allow myself to be regarded as a Master or teacher, to found a cult or benefit materially by such service as I have given to mankind. This to me would so utterly have

dishonoured what inspiration I have had that I would be guilty of treating it as a lie. When I am saying this I do not want it to be inferred that any words of mine have a higher than human wisdom. My ideas are the outcome of my own studies and meditations. But the direction they have taken appears to me to have a certain rightness which has not depended on my skill and scholarship, and which occasionally has been quite unexpected and surprising.

Only at rare moments have I had a startling clarity of perception.

Judaism and Christianity are the primary Messianic faiths. They conceive of man as placed in this world, by God to accomplish a purpose the outcome of which will be an ideal state of human society having knowledge of God and obeying his laws. The purpose is to be fulfilled by means of a definite plan progressively revealed to those entrusted with its furtherance, in order to secure their active co-operation. The plan clarifies the methods to be employed and involves successive stages of development. The whole process is related to human history, and gives a meaning to history: its time-chart covers thousands of years, and allows for setbacks and changes of emphasis arising from human failings, resistance and inertia.

According to this concept every contingency has been foreseen from the beginning; but the plan, since it is God's cannot fail, and his will assures that ultimately it will come to fruition.

With Messianism there is nothing fortuitous in the experiences of man. Whether he is aware of it or not he is evolving under guidance and his destiny is in no doubt. He has. the power to assert himself, to revolt, and temporarily to his own discomfort and suffering to get out of line; but nothing he may at any time do can permanently affect the success of the plan. Equally to his own happiness and well-being man can learn more about the plan and consciously

cooperate in its promotion.

Messianism is thus the expression of a theocratic programme for world government, though the theocracy it envisages is not a Divine dictatorship, but democracy taking its initiatives from communion with the wisdom of God. It asserts that man has a nature which links him with God. It asserts that he has a built-in desire for the things which God wants. Man is brought into relationship with God as to the centre of his own being and of all being, and is connected with God by a spiritual umbilical cord as a channel of communication.

It should have become clear to the reader by now that Hugh Schonfield's underpinning idea was that the biblical call to Israel was to become the servant of mankind and that this call is open to all "whether Jew or Greek" who care to heed the call. He believed to his dying breath that this people would one day have to come to be – even if he would not witness it in his lifetime.

It will be up to us – and perhaps future generations – to heed that call and we will decide whether the ideas from Abraham to Schonfield (so to speak) will be of everlasting value to mankind.

As the words of the Lennon song *Imagine* go:

> *You may say I'm a dreamer*
> *But I'm not the only one*
> *I hope someday you'll join us*

And the world will live as one.

Postscript

When near to the completion of this book, I asked Charlyne Valensin to read it and share her thoughts as she is one of the most learned scholars of the work of Hugh Schonfield and Messianism. This is what she wrote:

Rebuilding the consciousness of a servant-nation according to the way of the spirit, in the light of *A Life for Mankind*

An underground golden thread is running through the life and work of Hugh Schonfield, merging the political with the spiritual according to "the Way of the Spirit", or "the Messianic". This hidden thread transpires throughout his Biography, authored by Stephen Engelking, *A Life for Mankind*, now available. After reading it, one suspects that there is more behind the tremendous wealth of information. Hugh had himself delayed much personal disclosure until he was in his early seventies to avoid some misunderstanding, because of the unusual character of his life. Now, more than two decades after his passing, in the messy planetary situation prevailing in this 21rst century, when spiritual impotence is so high that God can be referred to as an excuse for murder, it is comforting, through Hugh Schonfield's biography, to have a glance at the undaunted spiritual driving-force behind the father of the Commonwealth of World Citizens, Servant-Nation of mankind.

One year before the Second World War started, on September 26th, 1938, Hugh Schonfield was strolling in a garden when he had a startling experience, mentioned in the Prologue of his book, *The Politics of God*. In an altered state of consciousness, he heard these words from the Prophet Zechariah: "Not by Might, not by Power, but by My Spirit", while it was conveyed to his mind that, for the deliverance of humanity, what was called for was a Servant-Nation without a territory of its own, devoted to mediation, service and exemplarity. I was flabbergasted when I first read this. Could a sane person dare write such a thing? Yet I thought: "If that man is not a crank (and how could the author of such a brilliant book be a crank?), it should not be left at that. If he is still alive, I must know more about him at any cost!" I wrote to him, to offer free translation work. As he was then in hospital for heart trouble, thereafter I kept sending him a New Year greeting card every year, until ten years later he suggested that, in case I should travel to England, I might perhaps visit him. I booked my ticket for a flight to London right away.

Hugh Schonfield not only reconciled me with the God of my childhood I had thought outgrown, but gave me hope for the future of mankind and for the solution of conflicts largely based on erroneous religious attitudes, notably in the Middle-East. For most people today, "God" has been superseded by power and technology, while others, claiming loyalty to God, feel entitled to suppress their fellowmen in His name. The true believers are few and demonstrate their faith by their deeds: Hugh Schonfield was one. He used the word God for the sake of convenience only, to express the unutterable. As a historian and a visionary, he knew that, at the very beginning of historical times, God had handed over the world to us with instructions for use, valid today as they were then for those who do not take the Bible literally. The Bible was not a book of religion, but a kind of a spiritual compass to guide the human race on its journey. A small tribal people had been trained for a special "holy" purpose, connected with a higher Plan for the promotion of man's earthly destiny. As religions developed, a dichotomy was created though, and man's eternal abode was transferred to heaven and his terrestrial task neglected. With the destruction of the politico-spiritual structure of the Jewish nation, the biblical concept of a Servant-Nation seemed to have become irrelevant.

Meanwhile, the physical presence of the descendants of that nation, who had almost forgotten the sense of their calling after centuries of wandering in Gentile countries, became a hurdle for all, in Europe in particular. And when they became still more visible through the creation of the nation-state of Israel, their very existence was even more resented by their new neighbours, with the addition of another religious problem. Oddly enough, two peoples claiming Abrahamic descent, and supposed to have been chosen as his descendants to be a blessing for all the peoples of the earth, were contending for the same piece of land, and for Jerusalem especially. So, the Middle-East became a major focal point of world tensions. And unless history and the way the Spirit worked were duly taken into account, there was no hope for the contenders, nor for the world at large.

We are faced with a conundrum, and only Hugh Schonfield's vision of a universal Servant-Nation makes sense and provides a solution. He demonstrated the vital need for that nation in a lecture he gave in the early eighties, in Paris. He had insisted adamantly on having a blackboard brought in order to draw a sketch, as a metaphor of the utmost importance to him. When the Hebrews were wandering in the desert, he explained, they were instructed by God to put up their tents three to the north, three to south, three to the east and three to the west of the Tent where the meeting with God took place. Only the Levites, the priestly tribe (which stood for the holy nation) were not to be located in a place of their own; they were to stay around the Tent of the Meeting to secure a connection between God and the twelve tribes (standing for the whole of mankind). Without the priestly tribe representing the Servant-Nation, devoid of any territorial attachment, the other tribes (mankind as a whole) could not function properly. Only a Nation, not the United Nations, could save the other nations.

And this has somehow been recognized at the international level. At the beginning of WWII, as Hugh Schonfield had frequently pointed out, an ad hoc body, The International Consultative Group of Geneva, had been appointed by the Carnegie Endowment to study the causes of peace failure. Its conclusions were that: "It is now widely recognized that the present plight of civilization is in the last analysis due to our spiritual anarchy and spiritual impotence .It is now clear that no durable international settlement can possibly be arrived at unless the nations accept certain common convictions and common standards as the basis for their own life and of their relations with each other[…] It is the absence of any such basis which has brought civilization to the brink of catastrophe […]The gravity of the present situation is precisely that humanly speaking, we do not see how our disintegrated civilization can come to a new unity."

This was written before the UN was created, before the Cold War, before the EU, before numerous new nation-states emerged out of former colonies ! And the message had gone largely unheeded ! One might have expected that with the ubiquitous Internet the stupendous news could have spread faster. But since the Internet can be used for good or bad purposes, the would-be peoples of gods and sons of gods are already teeming on the net, and the Servant-Nation could be overshadowed by mass media junk. Therefore, the Way of the Spirit meant that one should distrust of numbers. In The Politics of God, Hugh Schonfield wrote indeed: "The way of the Spirit has to mean that the world is to be saved not by the many but by the few. If this is so, it affects fundamentally our whole consideration of the manner and method by which mankind can be brought into harmony and peace."

As his life was nearing its end, he had neverthless resolved to disclose more of his own spiritual life, well knowing that he was offering to put his head "in the lion's mouth by communicating much more fully and openly the circumstances and purpose of [his]calling", for he was called, as he knew from early childhood, "to perform a function for mankind which time in due course would disclose." Now, the reader will find comfort in knowing more about this very uplifting life through Stephen Engelking's *A Man for Mankind*.

To end up our reflection on "the Way of the Spirit" as it worked mysteriously through the life work of one man who, in his own words, had "enjoyed no great fame or popularity" as an individual, nor "been involved in remarkable adventures that are deserving of personal description", we may quote the closing words of *The Politics of God*:

"At present technological invention is far outstripping moral elevation. The soul has to soar as well as the rocket. It falls to the Servant-Nation, as the People of God and the People of Man, to explore and corporately to express the good life for the general benefit. In our day and age, in accordance with the Divine Plan, it is being re-formed and re-animated for this exacting and arduous Messianic purpose. Pray God it will not fail this time!"

"*Not by Might, not by Power, but by My Spirit.*"

Charlyne Valensin.

Appendix

Travels

Hugh Schonfield's extensive travels are partly documented in his passports. In the passport issued on 24th August 1949 we find:

Göteborg 5.9.49
Ostende 6.1.50
Bruxelles Jan 1950
Gare du Paris 10.1.50
Belgique 10.5.59
Villach 7.6.55
Belgie 11.11.1955
Dieppe 29.12.50
France 1x.8.51
Gare du Paris 13.4.51
Le Bourges 31.5.55
Bardonecchia 11.GIU 1953
Belgie 29.4.59
France May 51?
France 26.7.57
Dieppe 30.3.51
Belgique 14.1.51
Belgie 11.3.59
France 6.1.51
Germany dept. 14.1.51
Dieppe 12.11.51
Soviet Union 8.11.52, 10.11.52
Melsbronk 11.1.55
Schiphol 29.1.53
France 9.11.61
Schiphol 14.6.54
Antwerp 13.11.55
Czechoslovakia 7.11.52, 10.11.52, 8.11.52, 10.11.52 Brindisi 18.5.53, 30.5.53
Passau Germany 15.6.55
Dieppe 16.5.1953
Suisse Vallorre 2.6.55
Dieppe 14.6.53
Greece 19.5.53
BRD 15.6.55 Passau, 15.6.55 Kaldenkirchen
Greece 29.5.53
Esbjerg Copenhagen 21.8.53, 4.9.53, 10.9.57, 6.9.57 France?? 2.6.55

Malmö 30.8.53, 4.9.53

Nederland 25.8.57 in, 3.9.57 out

Bologne 7.8.55 exit

Beauvais 29.7.57 out

Shiphol 12.6.54, 22.1.55, 26.1.55, 15.6.55

Belgie 30.1.53

Hook of Holland 16.6.55, Roosedaal 13.11.55

Helsinki 10.9.57

Göteborg 14.9.57

Beauvais 25.7.58

Holland 6.8.58

Belgie 7.9.58

In the passport issued on 10th July 1959, the following entries can be found:

Dieppe France exit 7.9.59

Niederland Shippol in 15.8.59

Schweiz Basel entry 16.8.59

Republic S. Marino 31.8.59

Belgium 29.9.60

France Orly 29.10.59

Lebanon 24.12.62 exit

Malta 23.1.66 arrival

Malta 4.2.68 arrival

Malta 26.2.68 dept.

Jordan 2.1.62 entry

Jordan 7.1.62 exit

France 5.10.64

Malta 10.8.67 exit

Malta 26.7.67 arrival

Malta 1.10.68 arrival

New York 2.9.63 arrival

New York 8.1.67 arrival

New York 18.11.68, 14.4.69

Malta 6.3.69 arrival

Malta 1.4.69 dept.

France 2.10.64, 1.3.65, 4.6.65, 30.4.65, 20.2.65, 31.10.6?France 13.2.6?

Venice 3.10.65

Jordan 1970

Canada Toronto 26.1.69, 21.9.67

Hélène's Passports became rather full too:

Passport issued 24th January 1951:
Belgium 10.5.59
Nederland 22.5.60
Belgium 29.4.59
Brindisi 18.5.53
Paris 9.8.51
France 26.7.57
Dieppe 9.11.51 in. out 12.11.51
Dieppe 16.5.53
Greece 19.5.53
Bardonecchia 17.MAG.1953 in, 11. GIU 53 exit
Greece 29.5.53
Brindisi 30.5.53
Paris 26.2.61
Dieppe 7.9.59
Boulogne 7.8.55
Belgie (Ostende) 10.5.59
Nederland 3.8.58
Beauvais 29.7.57 exit
Calais 30.8.57
Beauvais 25.7.5? in
Dieppe Aug. 59
Turkey 18.4.60
Venice 22.4.61 in, 11.4.61 out
Passport issued 21st January 1957:
Israel 20.3.57 (Visa issued valid until 21.12.57)
Greece 23.3.57
Domodossola 29.3.57
Venezia 25.3.57
France 30.3.57
Paris 31.3.57

Hugh Joseph Schonfield Genealogy

Created on Thursday, 28 February 2013 at 20:21 by Theo Spring.

Mr **Hugh Joseph Schonfield**, son of **Maj. William Schoenfeld** (son of Herr **Hermann Schoenfeld** and Fräulein **Charlotte Hanchen Henschel**) and Miss **Florence May Joseph** (daughter of Mr **Lionel Barnet Joseph** and Miss **Katie L Joseph**). Born on 17 May 1901 in Kensington, London. Died on 24 Jan. 1988 in Camden, 86 years old.

Married **Miss Hélène Muriel Cohn**, daughter of **Mr Hans Cohn** and **Miss Ethel Lyons**, in 1927 in Hampstead when 25 or 26 years old (Miss Hélène Muriel was 22 or 23 years old). **Miss Hélène Muriel Cohn** b. on 2 May 1904 in Hampstead; d. in 1979 in Westminster, 74 or 75 years old.

Notes on Mr Hugh Joseph Schonfield:

1901 17 May B Cert Kensington, London (Q2 1A 165) (Schoenfeld) DOB 17 May 1901

1927 M Cert Hampstead, London (Q3 1A 1794) to Hélène M Cohn (Schonfield)

1988 24 Jan D Cert Camden, London (Jan 14/1944/188) aged 86 (Schonfield)

Lived at 64 Ladbroke Road, Kensington (C 1911).

William Schoenfeld changed the family name to Schonfield (spelled Schonfield (1911)), sometime between 1902 and 1905.

All the Schonfield brothers except Hugh changed their name to Schofield by Deed Poll.

Notes on Miss Hélène Muriel Cohn:

1904 B Cert Hampstead, London (Q2 1A 622)

1927 M Cert Hampstead, London (Q3 1A 1794) to Hugh J Schonfield

1979 D Cert Westminster, London (Q1 15 2762) aged 74

Lived at 39 Goldhurst Terrace, South Hampstead, N W, London (C 1911).

Maj. William Schoenfeld genealogy

Created on Thursday, 28 February 2013 at 19:13 by Theo Spring

Maj. William Schoenfeld,

    son of Herr Hermann Schoenfeld (son of Herr Wolf Schoenfeld and Fraulein Ester Ettig) and Fraulein Charlotte Hanchen Henschel (daughter of Herr Henschel Arndt and Fr. Hannchen David Paul).

Born in 1869 in Dirschau, Germany. Died on 3 Jan. 1946 in Willesden, Middlesex, 76 or 77 years old.

Married Miss Florence May Joseph,

    daughter of Mr Lionel Barnet Joseph (son of Mr Barnet Lyon Joseph and Miss Betsy Jacob) and Miss Katie L Joseph (dau. of Mr Barnet Joseph and Miss Fanny Moses), on 28 Sep. 1898 in Paddington when 28 or 29 years old (Miss Florence May was 25 years old).

Miss Florence May Joseph was born on 23 Nov. 1872 in Frankfurt am Main; died on 8 April 1953 in Hendon, 80 years old.

Issue of Maj. William Schoenfeld and Miss Florence May Joseph:

  i. son Mr Leslie Herman Schonfield b. on 13 Dec. 1899 in Kensington, London; d. in In writing books, he made such a name in Brent, 71 or 72 years old; m. Miss Edna Morris (4 Oct. 1900–1975 in Hendon) in 1924 in Paddington when 24 or 25 years old (Miss Edna was 23 or 24 years old); issue: Mr Jack W L Schonfield (1927 in Willesden) and Miss Barbara F Schofield (1931 in Willesden).

  ii. son Mr Hugh Joseph Schonfield b. on 17 May 1901 in Kensington; d. on 24 Jan. 1988 in Camden, 86 years old; m. Miss Hélène Muriel Cohn (2 May 1904 in Hampstead–1979 in Westminster), dau. of Mr Hans Cohn and Miss Ethel _____, in 1927 in Hampstead when 25 or 26 years old (Miss Hélène Muriel was 22 or 23 years old);

issue (surname Schonfield): Miss Marion I (1929 in Hammersmith–), Miss Joyce W (1932 in Hendon–) and Miss Audrey C (1935 in Hendon–).

  iii. Dau. Joseph: son Miss Lottie Irene Schonfield b. on 15 Nov. 1903 in Kensington; d. on 26 Dec. 1903 in Kensington, a month old.

  iv. son Mr Douglas Lionel W Schonfield b. in 1905 in Dunstable, Luton, Bedfordshire; d. in 1959 in Brighton, Sussex, 53 or 54 years old; m. Miss Nancy Mona Berkeley (16 July 1904–Jan. 1990 in Haywards Heath) in 1936 in Hampstead when 30 or 31 years old (Miss Nancy Mona was 31 or 32 years old);

issue (surname Schofield): Miss Patricia A (1937 in Hampstead–) and Miss Gillian B (1943 in Hendon–).

  v. son Mr Clarence Henshel Schonfield b. on 4 Jan. 1908 in Westcliff on Sea, Rochford, Essex; d. in 1983 in Mendip, Somerset, 74 or 75 years old; m. (1) Miss Elizabeth O Moseley (–dec.) in 1937 in Marylebone when 28 or 29 years old;

issue (surname Schofield): Miss Penelope Ann E (1943 in Maidenhead, Berkshire–); m. (2) Miss Robertina S Bruce in 1950 in Surrey South Western, Surrey when 41 or 42 years old.

vi. son Mr Geoffrey Theodore Schonfield b. in 1910 in Kensington; d. in 1970 in Croydon, 59 or 60 years old; m. Miss Joyce Edith Rex (1901 in Wilton, Wiltshire–dec.), dau. of Mr Alfred Rex (son of Mr Henry John Rex and Miss Mary Ann Candy) and Miss Minnie Clarke (dau. of Mr John Sloman Clarke and Miss Sarah Elizabeth Harvey), in 1941 in Marylebone when 30 or 31 years old (Miss Joyce Edith was 39 or 40 years old);

issue (surname Schofield): Miss Jennifer (1942 in Burton upon Trent, Staffordshire–) and Miss Theo (19 March 1946 in Croydon–).

Notes on Maj. William Schoenfeld:

Commercial Traveller (1891) Army Officer (1898) Iron Merchant (1901) Engineer (1911) London Agents for A Schonfield and Co.

1869 B Cert Russia (? Prussia) (1911) Germany (1901) a Naturalised British Subject

1898 28 Sep M Cert Paddington, London (Q3 1A 200) married as William Schoenfeld to Florence May Joseph

1946 3 Jan D Cert Willesden, Middlesex (Q1 3A 579) aged 76 (William Schonfield)

Lived at 149 North Street, Barony, Kelvin, Glasgow, Lanarkshire (C 1881) (1880-84). Lived at 42 Grant Street, Glasgow (1884-86). Lived at Grant Street, Barony, Kelvin, Lanarkshire (C 1891). Lived at 42 St Charles Square, North Kensington, London (1895 Aron's Naturalisation application). Lived at 52 Ladbroke Grove, Kensington (C 1901). Lived at 64 Ladbroke Road, Kensington (C 1911).

Charlotte, his mother, took British Naturalisation in March 1891, and included all her children

Recorded as Schoenfeld (1881, 1891). William Schoenfeld (or Schonfeld) changed the family name to Schonfield, following his brother Aron in Glasgow (spelled Schoufield (1911)), sometime between 1902 and 1905.

William known as Willie, but may have had the full name David Wolffe

His personal file held by the War Office is No. 511521 (surmise)

Notes on Miss Florence May Joseph:

1872 23 Nov B Cert Germany, a British Subject

1898 28 Sep M Cert Paddington (Q3 1A 200) married as William Schoenfeld to Florence May Joseph

1953 8 Apr D Cert Hendon, Middlesex (Q2 5E 413) aged 80 (Schonfield)

Lived at 21 Lansdowne Road, Kensington (C 1881). Lived at 8 Albion Place, Ramsgate, Kent (C 1891).

Lived at 52 Ladbroke Grove, Kensington (C 1901). Lived at 64 Ladbroke Road, Kensington (C 1911).

William Schoenfeld (or Schonfeld) changed the family name to Schonfield (spelled Schoufield (1911)), sometime between 1902 and 1905.

List of Published Works by Hugh J. Schonfield

An Old Hebrew Text of St. Matthew's Gospel, Translated (translator, with notes and appendices)

Letters to Frederick Tennyson (editor)

The New Hebrew Typography

According to the Hebrews.

The Authentic Photograph of Christ (by Kazimir de Proszynski; editor and author of "historical supplement")

For the Train: Five Poems and a Tale (by Lewis Carroll; arranged poem order, wrote preface)

The Book of British Industries

The History of Jewish Christianity from the First to the Twentieth Century(1936)

Richard Burton, Explorer

Ferdinand De Lesseps

According to the Hebrews

Travels in Tartary and Thibet

Travels and Researches in South Africa

The Suez Canal

Jesus: A Biography

The Treaty of Versailles

Readings from the Apocryphal Gospels

Judaism and World Order

Italy and Suez

This Man Was Right: Woodrow Wilson Speaks Again

The Jew of Tarsus: An Unorthodox Portrait of Paul

Saints Against Caesar: The Rise and Reactions of the First Christian Community

Lost Book of Nativity of John

The Suez Canal in World Affairs

Secrets of the Dead Sea Scrolls: Studies Towards their Solution

The Song of Songs

The Bible Was Right: An Astonishing Examination of the New Testament

A Popular Dictionary of Judaism

A History of Biblical Literature

The Passover Plot: New Light on the History of Jesus

Reader's A-to-Z Bible Companion

Those Incredible Christians

Suez Canal in Peace and War

The Politics of God

The Jesus Party

For Christ's Sake

The Shroud of Turin

The Original New Testament (originally published in 1958 as The Authentic New Testament, updated and re-published under this title in 1985)

The Essene Odyssey

After the Cross

Proclaiming the Messiah

The Mystery of the Messiah

Jesus: Man and Messiah

Translations:

Opgravingen getuigen voor de Bijbel. Het Nieuwe Testament in het licht van de archeologie

Réalités du Nouveau Testament

Jésus, Messie ou Dieu? Ces incroyables chrétiens

En vertu de quelle autorite; le probleme des etats nations et sa solution

La vérité de la Bible

Unerhört, diese Christen. Geburt und Verwandlung der Urkirche

Der lange Weg nach Golgatha, Jesus von Nazareth, Mensch und Messias (Planzeil Golgotha)

Die Politik Gottes

Die Essener. Das Geheimnis des Wahren Lehrers und der Einfluss der Essener auf die menschliche Geschichte

i synomosia tou pascha / η συνωμοσία του πάσχα

Jesus Mesias O Dios

El Nuevo Testamento original

El Complot De Pascua

El Partido De Jesús. Una Revolucionaria Visión De La Historia Del Cristianismo En Sus Origenes

El Enigma De Los Esenios. Los origenes del cristianismo y el misterio del "Verdadero Maestro"

(This list makes no claims to be exhaustive and there is an abundance of other works, collections of essays and a multitude of magazine articles etc.)

INDEX

2001: A Space Odyssey......114
Aaron......101
Abars......174p.
ABC Television......110
Abileah, Joseph......124, 179
Abraham's Vineyard Ltd......61
Acts......55, 165p., 171, 182pp.
Acupuncture......69
Adam Kadmon......79
Adolf Hitler......38, 49, 60p., 66
Advertiser's Weekly......91p.
After the Cross......148, 174, 188, 199
Against Apion......182, 184
Albert Memorial......23
Albright, Dr.......42
Alderman, Mr.......72
Aldingen......145
Alexandria......160, 171
All Jewish......22
All You Need is Love......107
Allard, Baron......89
Allegro, John......89, 101
Allenby, General......42
American Booksellers Association......115
American Express......43
Americans for Fairness to Hugh Schonfield......137
Andersen, Hans......89
Angels of Mons......30, 42
Anglican Church......59, 78
Annunclationary Religious Party of Israel...174
Antioch......55
Antiochus Epiphanes......170
Apocalypse......30, 156
Apollonius of Tyana......180
Apollos......171
Apostle Paul......180
Appelbe, Ambrose......102
Aquarian Agency......177
Arabic......42, 106
Arabs......28, 79, 82, 96, 156, 175
Aramaic......51, 64, 181
Arbitrator, The......98
Archbishop of Canterbury......59, 78, 90, 179
Archelaus......183
Armageddon......30
Armstrong, Herbert......106
Armstrong, Peter......139
Arsac, Mrs.......158
Aspirin......43p.
Association for World Peace......96
Astarte......52

Astrology......20
Attlee, Clement......79
Audrey..45, 50, 65, 69, 89, 115, 141, 179, 186, 190, 199
Augustus......183
Australia......14, 19, 67, 87, 125, 138, 178
Australian Broadcasting Corporation......178
Authentic New Testament 89pp., 115, 160, 164, 174, 190
Babylon......179
Bacterial endocarditis......44
Baden-Baden......96
Baeck, Rabbi Leo......96
Baigent, Michael......151
Balkan War......27
Banstead Wood......65
Bantam Books......106, 110, 118, 159
Bar-Mitzvah......29
Barclay, William......90
Barker-Cryer, Neville......151
Barnes......96, 148
Barnett, R.D.......101
Barrie, Sir James Matthew......23
Barry......126, 179, 186
Battle of Britain......73
Battle of Loos......32
Bayswater......13
BBC......89, 91, 101, 106, 116, 124, 139
BBC Home Service......106
BBC Light Programme......106
Beatlemania......109
Beatles......89, 102, 109, 195
Belgium......28, 89, 212p.
Bell Telephone Company......51
Beloved Disciple......166
Berna, Kurt......124
Bernard Geis......107, 109pp., 115, 121
Berney......115
Berthold, Rudolph......88
Bessie......42pp.
Bethlehem......182
Bevan, Aneurin......79
Bewsher, J.......27
Bible Training Institute......43, 45, 47p.
Bisley......26
Bithynia......185
Black, James......80
Black, Rev. M.......101
Bloody Sunday......27
Boer War......21
Bologna......98

Book of British Industries..............................61
Borwick, Robert...145
Boston..............................31, 130, 174, 198
Boston University................................130, 198
Bottomley Advertising Service Ltd.................50
Bottomley, Holford....................................50, 91
Boy's Own Paper..29
Boyd-Orr, Lord...89
British Empire..19p.
British Society for the Propagation of the
Gospel amongst the Jews...............................42
Broad Walk..23
Brondesbury Park...54
Brooke, Anthony..179
Brown, Douglas..110
Bruce, Rev. M...101
Buchanan Memorial U.F. Church..................47
Buckingham Street...73
Buddhist...59
Buller, Redvers...21
Burkitt, Prof. Crawford..................................64
By What Authority...79
Caesar..180, 183, 191
Caird, George..110
California...........................16, 22, 133p., 136
Californian Gold Rush............................16, 22
Cambridge..64, 82, 113
Cambridge Convention on Foundations of
Peace..75
Campaign for Nuclear Disarmament.............98
Campus, Michael......................................133p.
Canada...98, 190, 212
Canada Allied Diesel Company Ltd.............199
Canal of the Pharaohs..................................136
Candidate..80
Cantaur, Archbishop Geoffrey.......................90
Cantor, Elly..177
Cardinale, Archbishop.................................110
Carroll, Lewis..60
Catholic...................52, 59, 130, 140, 150, 180
Channel Four TV..................................159, 161
Chapman University....................................109
Chapman, Mark.......................................109p.
Charlotte...14
Chesney, Rose.............................60, 87, 147
Chiaburri, Dr..99
Chicago Tribune...................................107, 130
China...98, 107
Chokmah...24
Christ. 20, 42, 57, 59, 64, 102, 157, 161, 165p.,
179p., 182, 185, 195
Christadelphian.....................................30p., 38
Christian..19p., 25, 30p., 33, 38, 42, 45, 47pp.,
52, 55pp., 59, 63pp., 71, 75, 90, 92, 102, 106p.,
110p., 113, 135, 137, 150p., 153, 155, 157,
160p., 165pp., 175, 180, 182pp., 189p., 193pp.,
199
Christian Religion..19
Christianity. 19, 30, 41p., 44, 46pp., 52, 57, 59,
66, 71, 82, 102p., 105, 111, 116, 124, 136,
150p., 153, 157, 160, 165, 170p., 178, 187,
189p., 195
Chums..29
Church 20, 25, 41, 47, 52, 55pp., 59, 65, 70, 73,
78pp., 83, 87, 92, 102, 109, 111p., 130, 135p.,
139, 150p., 155, 159, 180, 182, 184, 186, 193
Circumcision..55
Citizenship..73p.
City of London..30, 34
Civil World Aid..89
Classics..27
Classics, The..................................16, 28, 31p.
Clement of Alexandria.................................160
Cluny..153, 163, 177
CND..98
Cohen Amram, High Priest Ishac.........101, 116
Cohn, Hans..30
Cohn, Helene...50
Coinduit...133
Cold War..79, 82, 97p.
Cole, Maurice..125
Colet Court, Preparatory School....................41
Colet, John..28
Cologne..96, 98
Comets..89
Commonwealth of World Citizens...69, 83, 85,
87pp., 92, 94pp., 99, 101, 106, 148, 168, 172,
178, 193, 195, 197
Communism..83, 110, 150
Confederation.........................14, 123, 156, 179
Conscientious objectors....................30, 38, 69
Conspiracy theories.....................................109
Constituent Assembly....................88p., 92, 142
Constitution...........71, 73p., 78, 92, 94, 102, 187
Conversion...............................42, 46, 48, 57, 170
Coope, John...91
Copenhagen..89, 211
Copywriter..91
Corgi Books.................................106, 110, 152
Cornishman Penzance, The...........................95
Corsica...124
Cottin, Letty..109
County Fire Office Ltd..................................58
Court of International Justice.........................71
Courtneidge, Cicely.......................................62
Covenant of the League of Nations...............98
Cremer Housing Association......................198
Cremer, Sir William Randal..................44, 96p.
Crosby, Caresse..88
Crucifixion...........123, 159, 169, 185, 191, 195

INDEX 223

Cuba...................................102, 149, 156, 193
Cyprus...149
Dakota..109
Dalai Lama..98
Danielewski, Tad.....................................199
Daube, Prof...92
David..........22, 34, 161, 163, 178, 182, 185, 190
Davidson, J.E...49
Davis, Stanley..................................124, 173
Dead Sea Scrolls......82, 89p., 95p., 101, 105p., 113, 160, 168, 195
Death penalty..95
Decapolis..63
Decca Records..102
Deed, Peter.................141, 145, 147, 193, 197p.
Deeson, Tony..79
Delancey Street.............................126, 197p.
Delphi..30, 88
Democracy..93
Denis Archer..61p.
Denmark...89
Derby, Michael R.......................................47
Desposuni...63
Detroit..130
Detroit Free Press...................................130
Detroit News..130
Dimona..134
Dirschau...14
Divine Plan..........................72, 193, 196p.
Dixon, Jeane..121
Dobson...89
Doctor of Sacred Literature.....................90, 92
Domitian...166, 185
Doudna, Greg..164
Du Tillet..50p.
Dublin..27
Duchess of York..65
Duckworth..66
Ecumedia News Service..........................130
Ecumenical Center.................................139
Ede, Herbert...72
Edinburgh Book Festival........................151
Edward VIII..65
Edwards, Harry......................................138
Effigy..25
Egypt. 22, 33, 51, 64, 95, 133p., 156, 160, 171, 175
Egypt22..38
Eilat..133, 190
Element Books......................174, 176, 199
Element Books Ltd.................................164
Elisha Ben Abuyah....................................64
Elmslie, Professor W.A.L......................64, 82
Ena..30
Encyclopedia Britannica..............79, 136, 180

Ephesus....................................166, 171, 184
Epistles of Paul..91
Equity...93
Eschatological...............................109, 168p.
Essene......147, 161, 164, 166, 168p., 172, 174, 190p., 199
Essene Odyssey.....164, 166, 172, 174, 190, 199
Ester née Ettig-Schoenfeldchen....................14
Etchegaray, Cardinal...............................153
Ethel..30
Eton College..121
European Court of Human Rights..............98
Evangelical....................31, 44pp., 110, 136
Evans, Christopher.................................106
Evening News...96
Executive Council.....................................95
Expository Times.................................50, 55
Extension 720..130
Fallows, Mr...97
Feast of Frontiers..............................69, 106
Federalist..98
Fellow Spirit Guest House Centre..............95
Feltham..31
Ferres, Peter...106
Finchley Road..147
Florence..13, 15p.
Flower Walk...23
Folkestone..23p.
Fornication..55p.
Foundation of the Holy Shroud..............124
Four Horsemen of the Apocalypse.............30
France........28, 32, 66p., 70, 82, 95, 191, 211pp.
Frankfurt Book Fair................................117
Franz Ferdinand of Austria........................28
Frederick Müller.......................................98
French..27, 31p., 59, 70, 79, 148, 150, 188, 191
Friedlander, Albert.................................124
Friends...................25, 51, 71p., 75, 87, 96
Frost, David...110
Fundamentalist............106, 137, 165, 189, 194
Fuson, Ben......................................102, 137
Fuson, Ben W..67
Galilea..181, 183p.
Galilee..181pp., 191
Gandhi....................15, 27p., 44, 58, 83
Garibaldi..97
Garstin, E.J. Langford...............................59
General Allenby..30
General Assembly..............................88, 198
Geneva............59, 98, 139, 141, 147, 157, 177
Gentile......25, 51, 55p., 61, 80, 84, 153, 156p., 170, 181, 184p., 190
George V..27
Gerard, Peter...102
Gerizim..101

German...14, 22p., 28, 33, 38, 44, 58pp., 66p., 70, 73, 78, 89, 114, 117pp., 121p., 136, 145, 176p., 198, 211
German Empire....14, 28
Gezer....42
Ghana....98, 144
Gill, James H....137
Glasgow 14, 33, 41, 43, 45pp., 50, 64, 113, 193, 195
Glasgow Bible College....45
Glasgow Bible Training Institute....43, 45
Glasgow University..33, 45pp., 50, 64, 193, 195
Gnostic....19, 102, 171
Gnosticism....102
Gokhale, Professor....89
Golan, Menahem....134
Golden Jubilee as an author....138
Golders Green....60, 143, 179
Golding, Louis....79, 89
Golgotha....117, 124, 131
Gollancz, Sir Victor....28, 78, 96
Gollop, Rev....38p.
Goodruf, Douglas....110
Goose Green Farm....69, 72p.
Gospel of Matthew....38, 64
Gospel Untruth: A Disclosure of Christian Fraud....37, 41
Gotlieb, Howard....198
Graham, Billy....129p.
Graves, Robert....89
Graz University....88
Great Pyramid of Egypt22....38
Greece....88, 211, 213
Greek 16, 32, 63p., 87pp., 160, 167, 179p., 184, 202
Green, Michael....116
Groom, Donald....125
Guildford....138
Gypsies....22
H. G. Wells Society....99
H1N1 virus....43
Hadassah....38
Hadleigh....31
Hadleigh Castle Essex....58
Hahn, Hugo....22
Haifa Symphony Orchestra....124
Halcyon Book Co. Ltd....62
Haley, Bill....89
Haley's Comet....27
Haller, Hansjakob Hugh....118
Haller, Margareth....145
Haller, Willhelm (Willi) 114, 117pp., 121p., 126, 129, 135p., 145, 147, 153, 163, 173, 178, 193, 198
Hammond, Sam....98

Hanby, Donald....101, 141
Hannchen née David....14
Harper & Row....164, 174
Harris, J. Rendel....63p., 190
Harris, Kenneth....101
Hart, Derek....106
Harvey....59
Hebrew....16, 22, 24, 30, 33, 44p., 47, 49pp., 60p., 64p., 89p., 119, 133p., 160, 167p., 171, 175, 180, 184, 189, 199
Hebrew Gospel....38
Hegesippus....59
Heinemann, Gustav....122
Heinz ?....96
Helene....143
Hélène....19, 30, 42, 44, 49pp., 58pp., 65p., 70, 72p., 85, 87, 89, 98, 101, 105pp., 113, 119, 125p., 135, 137p., 141pp., 147, 178, 195, 198p., 212
Hélène'....105
Hengstler....119, 126
Henry Usborne....89
Henschel Arndt....14
Herbert Joseph....46, 79
Herford, Dr. Travers....64
Hermann....14
Herod....182p.
Heston....72
Hibbert Journal....57
High Priesthood....101
Highgate....69, 83, 96, 142
Hindu....59
History of Biblical Literature....102
Hodgkinson's Disease....115
Hogarth Press....58
Holiness....73
Holland....89, 98, 212
Holland Park....22, 27, 29, 106
Hollywood....105, 133p.
Holocaust and Us....147
Holy Blood and the Holy Grail....151
Holy Land....30, 42, 64, 156, 180
Holy People....95
Holy Servant Nation....69
Holy Spirit....157, 196
Home this Afternoon....106
Hope House....102
Hospital....15, 65, 78, 133, 138p., 141p., 186
House of Commons....95
Hungarian Revolution....95
Hutchinson....61p., 70, 110, 118
Hutchinsons....61, 105pp., 115, 121
Huxley, Aldous....60
Hyde Park Square....123, 142, 198
ICC....45

INDEX

Idolatry...25, 55p.
IFOR...177
IHCA...52, 59
Imagine............................85, 109p., 202
Institute of Archaeology......................123
Interfaith Committee Against Blasphemy....136
Interflex...126
International Arbitration League 89, 96p., 195, 199
International authority.........................98
International Cooperation Year..............106
International Court of Justice................79
International Fellowship of Reconciliation..177
International Hebrew Christian Association..52
International Parliamentary Union...........44
International People's College...............102
International, The................................97
Isis...52
Islam....................................150, 165p.
Israel..20, 22, 28, 33p., 57, 80, 82pp., 89, 95p., 101, 107, 117, 123p., 133pp., 138, 147, 150p., 153, 155p., 160, 165, 170p., 175p., 178pp., 183, 187p., 190, 193, 202, 213
Istar..52
Ita, Pro. Eya......................................89
Italy.............................27, 49, 70, 98, 134
Italy and Suez.....................................70
ITN TV..102
Jabotinsky, Vladimir.............................30
Jacob............................61, 139, 165, 184
Jaffe, Marcus....................................110
James..............................139, 165p., 184
Japan.....................78, 84, 89, 147, 155
Jaworsk, Tadeusz...............................137
Jennings, Hargrave..............................54
Jerusalem.....30, 42, 54, 62p., 78, 92, 101, 107, 117, 123, 133pp., 156, 159, 165p., 169, 175, 180, 183pp., 187, 191
Jerusalem Post............................135, 180
Jesus..19p., 30p., 38, 41, 44, 46, 48p., 51, 55p., 59, 61, 64p., 80, 91, 102p., 105p., 109pp., 113pp., 117, 123p., 129p., 133pp., 137, 139p., 150p., 153, 155pp., 159pp., 164pp., 175, 178, 180pp., 189pp., 195, 199, 201
Jesus Christ Superstar.........................105
Jesus Christ XIX Centuries After............61
Jesus Man-Mystic-Messiah..............19, 189
Jesus Scroll, The................................123
Jesus: A Biography...............................83
Jesus: Man-Mystic-Messiah............31, 199
Jesus: The Evidence.........................159pp.
Jew of Tarsus................................79, 83
Jewish......13, 15, 17, 21, 24pp., 28, 30p., 33p., 38p., 41p., 46pp., 51, 56p., 59, 61, 64, 66p., 78pp., 82, 91p., 96, 102, 111, 124, 130p., 133p., 149, 153, 156p., 159pp., 165, 170p., 173p., 176, 178, 180pp., 189pp., 193pp.
Jewish Benedictions and Doxologies.............91
Jewish Chronicle...................38, 82, 164
Jewish Ex-Serviceman's Legion................81
Jewish Ex-Servicemen's Legion...........15, 82
Jewish News, The................................130
Jewish Religious Union..........................15
Jewish Society for Human Service (JSHS) 28, 96
Jews......14, 20, 25, 28, 30p., 38, 42, 44, 49, 51, 54pp., 59, 61, 66, 70, 77pp., 82, 90, 96, 113, 134, 137, 140, 150p., 153, 156, 159, 161, 165p., 168pp., 180, 182pp., 190p.
John Lennon..9
John the Baptist....124, 133, 139, 161, 167, 184
Jones, Rev. G. Randall..........................83
Jordan................63, 78, 101, 105, 174p., 212
Joseph of Arimathea...............184, 191, 195
Joseph, Katie......................................19
Joseph, Lionel B..................................15
Joseph, Lyon.......................................15
Josephus..................22, 29, 180, 182pp., 194
Joyce.......................50, 60, 89, 97p., 186
Joyce, Donovan.................................123
Jubilee........................62, 97, 138, 166p.
Judaism..28, 31, 42, 48p., 51, 82, 96, 102, 105, 150p., 153, 157, 165, 188, 194
Judas..................................124, 129, 182
Judea...183
Judeo-Christian..............................165p.
Judeo-Christianity..............................150
Judith..15
Justice...................71, 78p., 93, 137, 153, 157
Kaddish..160
Kahn, Rabbi Judah..............................131
Kalkara....................................124, 173p.
Kashmir..164
Katz, Israel.......................................135
Kee, Robert......................................110
Kennedy, President John F...................105
Kensington Gardens.............................23
Kensington Park High School.................26
Kew Gardens....................................107
King Edward VII................................22
King Hussein...............................174pp.
King James' Bible...............................44
King's College...............................45, 106
King's College London.........................33
Kingdom of God.59, 75, 153, 156, 160, 184p., 191
Kingdom of Jordan.............................174
Kingsland..33
Kirk Session.......................................47
Kitchener..21
Knap, Prof...98

Knighthood	97
Koran	175
Kumar, Satish	125
Ladbroke Grove	13, 22
Ladbroke Road	29
Lady-Bird	52
Lampell	134
Land Work	30p., 38
Last Times	38, 149, 189
Latin	16, 61, 64
Leach, Alan	96
League of Nations	51, 61, 66, 71, 79, 98
Légaut, Marcel	149pp.
Leigh, Richard	151
Lennon, John	61, 89, 102, 105, 107, 109p., 148, 195, 202
Lennon, Sean	110
Leon Lewis Show	130
Leonard	22
Lester, Richard	109
Letters to Frederick Tennyson	57
Levison, Frederick	44p., 179, 199
Levison, Margaret	110
Levison, Nahum	110
Levison, Sir Leon	44, 49, 52, 59, 62, 65
Levisons, the	65
Levy, Barnet	15
Lewin, Maurice	106
Lewis, C. Day	144
Liberal Jewish Synagogue	149, 176
Lincoln, Henry	151
Lindbergh	51
Linton House Preparatory School	26p.
Listener, The	92
Littlehampton	115
London Free School	126
London Scottish Regiment	15, 21
London Weekend Television	159
Longford, Lord	110
Lost Book of the Nativity of John	55
Lost Ten Tribes of Israel	20
Lubavitch	118
Lucifer	149
Luke	171, 178, 180, 182pp., 188, 194
Luxembourg	38
Lyndhurst, New Jersey	33
Maariv	133
Maccabean	21
MacDonald	79, 129
Macmillan	83, 129p.
Mahometans	59
Malaysia	179p., 199
Malchut Shamaim	185
Malta	114p., 119, 124, 127, 129, 133p., 137p., 145, 173p., 212
Man for Mankind	116, 139
Manchester	96
Mann, Michael	174
Manuscripts	63, 107, 122, 144, 167p., 171
Maple & Company Ltd	54
Margulies, Joseph	157, 174, 176, 187p., 199
Marion	50, 54, 122, 145, 147, 179, 186, 193p., 196, 198
Mary Magdalene	171
Masada	113, 123
Mass media	112
Master-Race theory	70
Mathematics	27, 31p., 150
Matthew	50p., 64, 89, 167, 171, 180, 182
Matthew's Gospel	50
Maugham, Robin	131
Maugham, Somerset	88
McBirnie, Dr.	136p.
McCarthy, J.P.	130
McIntyre, David	44pp.
McIntyre, Jane	44
McLean, Robert	47
Mediation	67, 71, 93, 173p.
Mediterranean	63, 155
Meeting Point	106
Memorandum on the Furtherance of Peace and Social Justice through a World Authority	78
Merida	107
Messiah	19, 31, 38, 41, 48p., 59, 64p., 80, 103, 111, 117p., 134, 137, 151, 156p., 159pp., 165pp., 175, 179p., 182, 184p., 187, 189pp., 199
Messianic	30, 34, 41, 51, 64, 69, 80, 83, 94, 103, 117p., 150, 153p., 157, 161, 164pp., 170, 172, 189, 193p., 199
Messianism	80, 154, 156, 168, 170p., 193
Messina, Roberto	134
Michael Joseph	195
Middle East	9, 101, 105, 107, 123p., 168, 179, 193, 195
Middle-East Confederation	123
Middlesex Volunteers	21
Mind at the End of Its Tether	149
Mineapolis	130
Miriam	184
Mirmande	150
Mohammed	166
Molden-Verlag	119
Monastery of Saint Catherine on Mount Sinai	63
Mondcivitan Community School	126
Mondcivitan Republic	69, 73, 88p., 92pp., 98, 102, 106, 121, 125pp., 141, 145, 147p., 150, 153, 158, 163, 173p., 177pp., 187p., 190, 193, 197p.

INDEX 227

Mondcivitan, The..126
Mondcivitaner Verlag..................................135
Monro, Jack...95
Monroe Doctrine..19
Mont Blanc..34
Montefiore, Dr..51, 57
Montefiore, Rabbi.....................................149
Moody, Dwight Lyman...............................45
Moon and Sixpence...................................101
Morenu..21
Morison, Stanley...60
Moscow..14
Moses...21, 101, 169p.
Moslem..153, 165p., 175
Movement for a Holy Servant Nation............69
Movement of Intellect of Israel...................174
Mrs World..106
Müller, Heinz........114, 117, 119, 121, 124, 126, 129, 131, 135p., 176
Müller, Joachim..98
Munich..96
Murray, Robert..124
Mysticism...22, 79
Naber, Hans...124
Naber, Hans...124
Nablus..101, 116
Nackel..14
Nag Hammadi....................................168, 171
Napoleonic invasion....................................14
Nasser..95
Nathan Solomon Joseph..............................15
National Catholic News Service.................130
National Explorer, The..............................107
National Maritime Museum......................136
Nativity..55, 182
Nazarene...64, 89, 165
Nazarene Gospel..89
Nazareth..............63p., 124, 135, 137, 151, 178
Nazi..77p., 158, 161
NBC..131, 137
Nell, William...124
New American Library.......................101, 107
New Hebrew Typography............................60
New Testament....9, 38, 63, 72, 83, 90pp., 102, 105p., 115, 160, 164, 171, 174, 176, 178, 180, 182, 184p., 188pp., 195
New West End Synagogue...........................15
New York........109p., 118, 121, 130p., 174, 212
New York Post...107
New Yorker, The..109
Newman Society..110
Newman Turner, Frank.................69, 71p., 77
News of the World......................................88
Newsweek..106
Nicodemus..184, 191

Nixon...129
Nobel Peace Prize..........9, 14, 85, 97, 149, 195
Normandy..70, 78
North German Confederation.....................14
Northcliffe Newspapers.........................50, 91
Northcliffian Old Boys' Association............62
Nuclear weapons.......................97p., 107, 149
Nuelba...134
Numerology...20
Observer Magazine....................................133
Observer, The..101
Occult Review...64
Occultist...59, 160
Odusiga, Mr. S.F..102
Old Hebrew Text of Matthew's Gospel.........50
Old Hebrew Text of St. Matthew's Gospel....50
Old Paulines..29
Old Testament.............................63, 66, 171
Ontario..139p.
Ontario Educational Communications
Authority..137pp.
Ontario Television Authority.....................136
Open Gate Press................................189, 199
Operation Dropshot....................................97
Organic farm...69, 77
Original New Testament......164, 176, 178, 185
Ottoman Army..32
Ottoman Empire...27
Oxford University......................................110
Paddington..19, 139
Page, Dr...179
Palestine 15, 30, 33p., 38p., 42, 62pp., 67, 78p., 82, 95, 101, 109, 150p., 165
Palm Sunday..159
Paradise Lost...149
Paralysis..44
Paris.....50, 82, 85, 87, 89, 97p., 113, 129, 151, 189, 211, 213
Parkes, James..79
Parliamentary candidate.............................98
Passover Plot 105pp., 109, 111, 113, 115, 117p., 121, 129pp., 133pp., 148, 164, 174, 180, 189pp., 195, 198p.
Paterson, Mark 105, 109, 133, 135p., 174, 176, 179, 187p., 198p.
Patmos...166
Peace.....14p., 19, 33, 38, 52, 57, 66, 70pp., 74, 77p., 80, 82, 85, 88, 93, 96pp., 101p., 124, 137, 149, 153, 157, 159p., 168, 174p., 185, 187, 193pp.
Peace Army..73
Peace Book Club..70
Peace Pledge Union................................67, 73
Peace Publishing Company.......................196
Peake, Professor.....................................55pp.

Pella..52, 63
Pembridge Villas...19
Penang...180
Penguin...70
Pentecost Revolution....105, 129, 137, 174, 199
People of God..117, 137, 148, 150, 153p., 156, 158, 177, 188
Peter Deed..10
Peter Pan...23
Peters, Esther..98
Petrie, Flinders......................................33, 64
Petronius..183
Pharisees....................................56, 92, 169
Phillips, J.B..90
Pile Peelion..34
Pinhas...101
Pittsburgh...131
Plan of God..155
Planziel Golgotha.......................117, 121, 131
Pliny..185
Plymouth Hebrew Congregation Old Cemetery..119
Podro, Joshua..89
Pogrebin, Letty Cottin..................................115
Poland....................14, 67, 70, 79, 82, 89, 95
Politics of God. 118, 121, 126, 149, 154, 172p., 191, 196p.
Pomerania..14
Pontius Pilate..183
Pooley, Maj. Charles....................126, 145, 179
Popular Dictionary of Judaism.........................102
Princess Elizabeth Hospital for Children.......15
Princess Hospital for Children........................65
Private Eye..159p.
Proclaiming the Messiah...............................199
Prohibition..38, 55pp., 61
Prospect Cottage..................................101, 142
Prussia..14p.
Psalms...63p.
Publisher and Bookseller..............................62
Publisher's Circular...................................62
Publishers' Weekly....................................107
Punch..57, 113
Purim..38
Quaker........................71, 75, 87, 142, 165
Queen..........................14, 21, 41, 89, 179
Queen Anne....................................21, 41, 142
Queen Victoria......................................14, 21
Queen, The...20
Quirinius...182
Qumram...169
Qumran...169
Rabbi......25, 28, 56, 64, 92, 96, 118, 131, 149, 165, 189
Rabbi Leo Baeck..28
Rabbinical Judaism....................................165
Ranelagh, John...161
Rayner, Rabi John......................................143
Readers' A to Z Bible Companion.....................107
Readings from the Apocryphal Gospels.........70
Reform League..
Reform League, The......................................98
Religious Experience Research Unit in Oxford..125
Resurrection. .103, 117, 129, 137, 161, 169pp., 182, 185, 191
Revelation.....102, 117, 157, 166, 179, 185, 193
Richard Burton Explorer.............66, 195, 198
Richmond Park...........................29, 50, 143
Robert Louis Stevenson................................23
Roberts...21
Rock and Roll..89
Rock Around the Clock..................................89
Roman...59p., 80, 117, 133p., 140, 150, 159p., 166, 180pp., 191
Roman Empire...............................154, 181p.
Romanism...154
Rome.......................87p., 165, 178p., 183, 194
Roosevelt..14, 19, 88
Roosevelt, Franklin....................................61
Rotary Club..173
Rotary International..................................78
Rotten Row...23
Royal Family...21
Rubenstein, Harold...................................106
Sabbath..25, 29
Sabbatical..166p.
Sack, Simon Heinrich...................................15
Sacrilegious Movies...................................137
Salt of the Earth.....................................109
Samaritan..101, 161
Samartha, Dr. S. J....................................139
San Francisco.......................16, 174, 197
Sandgate...23
Sanhedrin...184
Sankey, Ira D..45
Satan..149
Schmidt, Wolf...137
Schneerson, Rabbi Menachem....................118
Schneider, Matthew..................................109p.
Schoenfeld, William....................................13
Schoenfeld, Wolf.......................................14
Schonfield, Florence...................................17
Schonfield, Geoffrey...................................70
Schonfield, Gustav.....................................13
Schonfield, William......13p., 17, 39, 42, 80pp., 105, 180
Sciabica, Maria..98
Scotland...14, 21, 80

INDEX

Search Publishing Co.................................59, 61
Search, The..124, 189
Second General Assembly................................88
Second Hague Peace Conference....................19
Secrets of the Dead Sea Scrolls...............96, 105
Seder...184
Seebach, Christopher...................................177
Sermon on the Mount....................55p., 59, 196
Serpentine..23
Servant-Nation...27, 67, 69p., 72, 75, 77, 79p., 83pp., 88pp., 95p., 102, 110, 114, 116, 118, 126, 133, 147p., 153pp., 163, 170, 172, 177, 187p., 191, 193p., 197pp.
Servant-Nation—...118
Service Nation Movement......................69, 77p.
Service-Nation..................67, 69, 71, 73, 79, 94
Shaftesbury Theatre.....................................121
Shonfield, Rosalie...110
Short History of Jewish Christianity..............47
Sibylline Oracles..80
Signet Books..98
Silesia..14p.
Simeon...184
Simpson, Wallis..65
Sinai...63, 95
Sinaitic Palimpsest...63
Singapore...138
Singer, Joseph..122
Six Day War...107
Smike..97
Smith, Dr. Morton..160
Smoking...105
Society for the Constitution of a Holy Nation 71, 73, 78
Society of Friends.....................................71, 87
Son of David..22
Son of Man.............................51, 159, 161, 169
Song of Songs.......................................101, 140
Sorensen, Lord...106
Sorensen, Rev. R.C......................................102
South Africa..27, 89
Southend and Westcliff Hebrew Congregation 39
Southend and Westcliff Zionist Association...15
Southend-on-Sea..31
Soviet Union....44, 61, 78, 82, 84, 95, 97p., 211
Spall, Noreen...134
Spanish Flu...38, 43
Speech which moved the World....................59
St. John's Church...25
St. John's University at Delhi........................92
St. John's University, Ambur, India...............90
St. John's Wood...149
St. Paul................................17, 55, 80, 149
St. Paul's Preparatory School........................27
St. Paul's School 17, 28, 32p., 46, 113, 176, 195
St. Petersburg..14
Stalin...44, 78, 88
Starr, Dr. Lilian..149
Steiner, Helen..130
Stevenson, Bertram F....................................60
Suez...32, 70, 79, 87, 95p., 101, 116, 118, 136, 180, 195
Suez Canal. .9, 32, 79, 87, 95p., 101, 116, 118, 136, 180, 195
Suez Canal in Peace and War......................116
Suez Canal in World Affairs.............87, 96, 116
Suez Crisis...95
Sunday Dispatch..64
Süsman, Dr..176
Sutherland, Bill..125
Sutton-in-Ashfield..101
Swabia...114
Sweden..89
Switzerland..87, 118
Synagogue 15, 22, 24, 29, 41, 48, 91, 131, 149, 159, 170, 176, 180, 183
Synoptic gospel..168
Syria...51, 107, 182p.
Syriac...51, 63
T & T Clark.....................................50, 55, 64
Tabernacle...156
Tablet...59
Tanzania..125
Taurus..20
Taxbiex..115
Teacher of Righteousness............................164
Tel-Aviv...133
Telegraph, The..199
Temple......................133, 155p., 168p., 183
Temple of Peace in Cardiff............66, 178, 193
Temple..168
Ten Eventful Years..79
Tennyson...57, 60
Territorial Force Reserve...............................15
Test Ban Treaty...149
Texas State Library.....................................139
The Bible Was Right.......................96, 98, 195
The Farmer..69
The Jesus Trial...................................137, 139p.
The Mystery of the Messiah........................199
The One True Sanctuary.............................101
The Passover Plot..121
The Plain Truth...................................106, 164p.
The Search..58p.
The Sign..131
The Sunday Affair.......................................163
The Treaty of Versailles: The Essential Text and Amendments...70
Theodore Roosevelt................................14, 19

Thessalonians..................................149
Third General Assembly......................90
Thorndike, Sybill.............................102
Those Incredible Christians 107, 109pp., 115p., 118p., 174, 189, 195
Tibet..98
Time Magazine................................106
Times Diary, The.............................118
Times of Malta................................174
Times, The......................................90
Times, The...............95, 118, 136, 174, 194p.
Tintern...........................101, 115, 142
Tirole Gardens.................................89
Tolstoy...15
Tolstoy'..15
Topolski, Felix................................140
Toronto....................139p., 174, 212
Treaty of Versailles......................38, 59
Tulsa, Oklahoma.............................164
Turner, Frank Newman.................69, 71
Twentieth Century Fox...................113
Unerhöht diese Christen, Geburt und Verwandlung der Urkirche...........119
United Kingdom...........14, 27, 52, 82, 89, 95
Université Holistique......................149
University of Glasgow..............45, 47, 113
University of London.....................106
USA....14, 19, 27, 33, 38, 45, 49, 52, 61, 77p., 82p., 87, 89, 95p., 98, 101p., 105pp., 110, 115p., 129p., 139, 157, 195, 197
Utopia...148
Valensin, Charlyne..145, 147, 150p., 153, 158, 163, 177, 187p., 190p., 198
Vallentine Mitchell.....................96, 116
Vatican............................133, 135, 150p.
Vedanta Movement..........................75
Velensin, Charlyne..........................157
Verlag Gustav Lübbe........................131
Vermes, Dr.....................................159
Victorian...................................20, 195
Vienna............................96, 98, 142
Vietnam............................84, 102, 106
Villa Salvatore..............115, 119, 138p.
Wall Street Crash............................54
Waltham....................................42, 44
War on Want..................................96
War Resisters International..............125
Warwick..98
Waterloo Bridge..............................72
Webb, Ron...................................126
Wells, H.G........24, 99, 102, 140, 149, 172, 196
Wellsian, The..................................99

Werblovsky, Prof............................123
What Are We?.................................22
White House..................................110
White Lion Street Free School........126
White, George.................................21
Wieslaw, Prof. Ismail........................89
Williams, Canon Lukyn....................64
Wilson, Canon.................................55
Wilson, Woodrow................27, 33, 38
WJR Radio....................................130
Wolf..14, 134
Women....14p., 23, 38, 52, 67, 74, 88, 96, 102, 110pp., 141, 196, 201
Women Against War........................88
Women Citizens' Association..........96
Woodhead Plant Ltd........................34
Woolf, Leonard......................29, 57p.
Woolf, Virginia.................................57
Worcestershire..............................143
Workmen's Committee on behalf of the Northern States in the American Civil War,..97
World Association of World Federalists..........98
World Citizen Movement................188
World Citizen, The..........67, 72, 75, 77pp.
World citizens..............67, 69, 71, 73, 77, 193
World Citizenship 67, 73, 83, 88, 102, 126, 144, 148p.
World Commonwealth.....................75
World Commonwealth University.....88
World Council of Churches......83, 139, 151
World Federalists.....................98, 197
World government..............72, 94, 98
World Parliamentary Conference.....89
World Service Trust.....77, 106, 141, 144, 198p.
World War I...............15, 27p., 30pp., 41, 82
World War II.......69, 74, 78p., 85, 94, 193, 199
World War III..........................87, 97
Wurmbrand, Rev............................124
Yadin, Yigael.................................123
Yerby, Frank..................................129
Yeshua...................................133, 137
Yosselof...96
Zadokites......................................184
Zaky, Adrien..................................147
Zebedee..184
Zechariah......................................178
Zionism..39
Zionist.............................15, 30p., 38
Zionist Federation...........................38
Zodiacal signs...........................20, 54
Zürich......................................114, 129

www.ingramcontent.com/pod-product-compliance
Lightning Source LLC
Chambersburg PA
CBHW060520080526
44586CB00012B/556